MW01053127

MEANINGFUL LIVING

ספר תפארת רויזא
The Bruckstein Edition

MEANINGFUL LIVING

A Path to Finding Fulfillment in Daily Life

Rabbi Moshe Meir Weiss

 The Judaica Press, Inc.

© Copyright 2001 by Rabbi Moshe Meir Weiss

ALL RIGHTS RESERVED.
NO PART OF THIS PUBLICATION MAY BE TRANSLATED, REPRODUCED,
STORED IN A RETRIEVAL SYSTEM OR TRANSMITTED, IN ANY FORM OR
BY ANY MEANS, ELECTRONIC, MECHANICAL, PHOTOCOPYING, RECORDING,
OR OTHERWISE, WITHOUT PERMISSION IN WRITING FROM THE PUBLISHER.

ISBN 1-880582-80-5

Cover design & typography: Zisi Berkowitz and B. Goldman

For Library of Congress information, please contact the publisher.

THE JUDAICA PRESS, INC.
718-972-6200   800-972-6201
info@judaicapress.com
www.judaicapress.com

Manufactured in the United States of America

RABBI MOSES FEINSTEIN

455 F. D. R. DRIVE

New York, N. Y. 10002

———

ORegon 7-1222

משה פיינשטיין

ר"ם תפארת ירושלים

בנוא יארק

בע"ה

כו' שבט תשד"מ

לכבוד קהל אגודת ישראל בסטעטן איילנד, ה' עליהם יחיו.

בשמחה שמעתי איך שבית הכנסת אגודת ישראל בסטעטן-
איילנד, זכה לקבל לרב ומרא דאתרא את תלמידי היקר
והחביב הרה"ג ר' משה מאיר ווייס שליט"א – הריני בטוח
שאנשי הקהלה יהנו מאוד מרבנותו של הרה"ג הנ"ל מחמת
מדותיו והנהגותיו הישרים ומחמת ידיעותיו הגדולות
בש"ס ובהלכה, שיועילו לו ליעץ ולעזור אנשי קהלתו בכל
אפשרות שיהיה לו.

ובאתי בזה לברך לתלמידי הרה"ג ר' משה מאיר ווייס
שליט"א וגם לכל הנהלת וגבאי בית הכנסת וגם לכל חברי
ביהכנ"ס הנ"ל שינהם רבנותו בהצלחה גדולה לתפארת ה' ולתורתו
ויזכה ללכת בראש אנשי קהלתו לקבל פני משיח צדקנו בקרוב.

בידידות משה פיינשטיין

HaRav Moshe Feinstein, זצ"ל, wrote this letter on 26 Shevat 5744, in praise of the
author, Rav Moshe Meir Weiss, upon his assumption of the position of Rav of Agudas
Yisroel of Staten Island.

אברהם פאם
RABBI ABRAHAM PAM
582 EAST SEVENTH STREET
BROOKLYN, NEW YORK 11218

ב"ה יום ראשון חי"ת

הנה יבי"ב הרה"ג המהולל מאד מאיר וויס שליט"א, חתן ספר החולין
לבסוף, רצוני לתת ברכת הברכות, עם קביעי ריו/כ/כם לחבק בעול שלי דית והרומה,
בדרי חיזוק והתאזרות הלדות והמולות כ: ג ג בולבד את
חזקה אל חבר באמוני שיון ולג/ו/ האמת יד בדר בלוד אמוקן,
אושאמני להתאמינים כו יקבו אמונו חשבה אל קבובה ג וירב, כי בכר
ובצא באמחבר לתבלא דברשתינו הבולבות ודברני האמר שיושינם ול מל
ונבושים לוד.
וגוני אברכם ש חבב/ סערו נו דמל/שת חן ומוב לפשל מאומון
חולבת, אמוק ברריאות הבף והומות הוף ושאמת לדר,
אברכם ידרק הכרב פ/ס/ם

RABBI MOSHE FEINSTEIN זצ"ל
Founder

RABBI REUVEN FEINSTEIN
Rosh HaYeshiva

RABBI GERSHON WEISS
Menahel-Ruchni

ישיבה ר'סטעטן איילנד
yeshiva of staten island
The Andrew N. & Rose Miller Yeshiva
1870 Drumgoole Rd. E. / Staten Island, N.Y. 10309
(718) 356-4323

RABBI YISRAEL H. EIDELMAN
Executive Vice-President

RESIDENT DIVISION OF

EXECUTIVE OFFICES: 141-7 EAST BROADWAY / NYC 10002 / (212) 964-28[

It is with great pleasure that I write this haskama for HaRav Moshe Meir Weiss נ"י, a distinguished talmid of our yeshiva.

In the Yeshiva HaRav Weiss was זוכה to be משמש my father the Rosh HaYeshiva, the Gadol HaDor HaRav HaGaon Rav Moshe Feinstein זצ"ל, from whom he gained many insights. These insights, coupled with his growth during his years as a talmid, enabled HaRav Weiss to develop the ideas and principles that he personifies, and that he teaches to his many talmidim.

HaRav Weiss's abilities in the oral medium of lectures, shiurim, and tapes are legendary. His famed ability to articulate is extraordinary. He now desires to utilize the written word to inspire and elevate as well. There is no doubt in my mind that HaRav Weiss will be equally successful in this endeavor.

May Hashem grant him and his wife Miriam Libby שתחי' continued hatzlacha in disseminating Torah to all of Klal Yisroel.

13 Menachem Av 5758
HaRav Reuven Feinstein

In memory of

Mrs. Rose Bruckstein

Reciting Tehillim filled her days
Outstandingly beautiful was her shalom bayis
Speaking sheker was something she assiduously avoided
Ever the modest person, she maintained a low profile

Bnei Torah she raised despite many hardships
Russian immigrants in her neighborhood she introduced to Yiddishkeit
Usually completed Tehillim every day or two
Cheering widows, shut-ins, and the ill occupied her time
Kibbud av v'aim was a mitzvah she observed meticulously
Surviving the Holocaust, she remained true to Hashem and His Torah
The bris and yeshiva education of a Russian child she arranged and paid
Excelled in preparing for, and honoring, the Shabbos
Instead of buying a diamond ring, she bought a Sefer Torah
Never will this wonderful aishes chayil be forgotten

Her husband, children,
grandchildren, great-grandchildren,
and all who knew her and miss her

.תנ.צ.ב.ה

האשה הצנועה
מרת
רויזא ברוקשטיין
בת ר' אליעזר ליפא ע"ה

ר דפה צדקה וחסד בהצנע כל ימיה
ו להחיות לב נדכאים וחולות דרכיה
י וצאי חלציה לומדי תורה ותומכיה
ז כו ללמוד מיראתה וטוהר נשמתה
א ת כיבוד אב ואם קיימה בכל דקדוקיה

ב אהבה חיתה עם בעלה בנועם מדותיה
ת הלים גמרה כל יומים בכוונותיה

א ת שבת קודש כבדה בכל כוחותיה
ל עולי רוסיא עזרה מתוך רחמיה
י פה וטוב היה לה ספר תורה מכל כספיה
ע ברה ימי הזעם באמונה באלוקיה
ז כרה יהיה ברוך עם כל קדושי עמה
ר אשונה היתה לדבר מצוה בכל כוחותיה

ל שונה דברה אמת כל ימי חייה
י ראת ד' ואהבת חסד נטעה בלב בניה
פ יה פתחה בחכמה כל ימיה
א שת חיל היתה לבעלה ותפארת לבניה

נפטרה ביום כ"ב אדר ב' ה'תש"ס
ת.נ.צ.ב.ה.

נר זכרון

לעילוי נשמת האשה החשובה
מרת רייזל ע״ה **בת ה״ר אלטר יעקב דוד** ז״ל
נפטרה ט״ו אלול תשנ״ה
אשת חיל עטרת בעלה ה״ר אליעזר זאכטער תחי׳ לאוי״ט

לעילוי נשמת האשה החשובה
מרת רחל ע״ה **בת ה״ר יהודה** ז״ל
נפטרה ו׳ שבט תשנ״ח
אשת חיל עטרת בעלה ה״ר משה זיטצער הלוי תחי׳ לאוי״ט

In loving memory of our beloved
mothers, grandmothers and great-grandmothers
Rose Zachter, ע״ה
and **Ruth Sitzer,** ע״ה

לע״נ **משה בן יהודה לייב Sitzer** ע״ה

Phyllis and Mel Zachter
Cindy, Elie and Ephraim Becker
Yaakov and Yehuda Zachter

DEDICATED BY

Cipora and Max Brandsdorfer

In loving memory of

Alexander Figula

ישראל בן מאיר מרדכי ז״ל

- *A valiant survivor of the Holocaust*
- *From the original settlers of modern Meiron*
- *Raised a beautiful Torah mishpacha in America*
- *Lived to see three generations of Torah nachas*

ת.נ.צ.ב.ה.

———•———

In loving memory of

Meir and Molly Brandsdorfer

שלמה מאיר בן יהושע ז״ל
מלכה בת מרדכי ז״ל

- *From the original Bobover families in America*
- *From a great line of Sanzer chasidim*
- *They survived the horrors of Aushwitz and Siberia
  to persevere in their commitment to Yiddishkeit
  and raise a family dedicated to Hashem and His Torah*

ת.נ.צ.ב.ה.

*May the merit of the study of this sefer
help to bring a refuah shleimah for*

ישראל דוד בן מאטיל חיה Weiss שליט״א

and

אלטע פרימעט פעסיל בת מרים Weiss שליט״א

and

lehavdil bein chaim l'chaim

לע״נ

דבורה בת יוסף צבי ז״ל

In loving memory of our fathers

ר' אברהם אלטר בן משה Vegh ז"ל

ר' יהודה אריה בן אהרן הלוי Yager ז"ל

ת.נ.צ.ב.ה.

Who instilled in us the meaning
of being an "erlicher yid"

Dedicated by Robby and Roz Vegh
Staten Island, N.Y.

Meaningful Living

Table of Contents

Acknowledgements xvii
Introduction xxii

Improving Our Lives

Becoming a Kinder Person 3
The Yetzer Hara and the Fly 6
Beware the Enemy Within 12
How to Pray with Kavanah 15
Shemoneh Esrei Meditations 20
Cleaning Up Our Speech 25
Yisro's Inspiration Can Be Ours 31
Bikur Cholim—Comforting the Sick 34
Avoiding Conflict 45
Sleep Secrets 48
Fleeing From Sin 55
Living Eternally Through Our Deeds 62
What Goes Around Comes Around 65
Surrounding Ourselves with Positive Influences 69
Discovering Guidance in the Strangest Places 72
Reaping Summer's Benefits 76

Improving Our Relationships

Child Raising Turbulence: What Happened All of a Sudden? . 83
Raising Wonderful Children 98
Maintaining a Healthy Marriage 102
Tips for a Happy Home 107
Respecting Other People 111
Avoiding the Envy of Others 121

Timeless Timely Lessons

Elul: Wrapping the Year Up Right 131
Elul: Preparation is Crucial 135
Elul: Avoiding Discouragement 139
Rosh Hashanah: Emulating Hashem's Compassion 144
Rosh Hashanah: Heeding the Shofar's Blast 152
Yom Kippur: Tipping the Scales. 156
Sukkos: Stop Kvetching! 162
Sukkos: "Drinking In" the Sukkah 166
Simchas Torah: Approaching Torah with Joy 170
Simchas Torah: Discovering the Many Facets of Torah 174
BHA"B: Fasting for a Reason 179
Chanukah: Spreading the Light of Torah 183
Purim: Giving the Day to Children 189
Purim: Keeping the Mitzvah Responsibly 192
Purim: An Interview with the Yetzer Hara 195
Pesach: Remembering Those in Need 201
Pesach: Educating the Next Generation 206
Pesach: Opportunities for Inspiration 212
Sefirah: Paradigm Shifts from Pirkei Avos 218
Sefirah: Learning Day and Night 223
Sefirah: Our Customs Guide Us 228
Shavuos: Becoming Ambassadors of Peace 231
Shavuos: Committing Ourselves to Torah 235
Tisha B'Av: Avoiding the Perils of Habit 240

In Memoriam

The Legacy of Rav Avigdor Miller, zt"l 247

Glossary 267
Bibliography 277

Acknowledgements

"Thank you" is one of the finest expressions in the English language. It sweetens marriages, strengthens friendships, and brightens people's days. It also offers us an easy way to sanctify Hashem's Name—as we encounter toll collectors, bank tellers, shopkeepers, and others—and is a fulfillment of both "*V'ahavta l'rei-acha kamocha*—Love your fellow man like yourself," [*Vayikra* 19:18] as well as "*Y'hi ch'vod chavercha chaviv alecha k'shelach*—Let the honor of your friend be as precious to you as your own," [*Pirkei Avos* 2:15]. It therefore gives me great pleasure to begin this sefer with a series of heartfelt and profound "thank you's."

Of course, I begin with immense thanks to Hashem Yisborach for giving me the ability to teach and expound upon his glorious Torah! The activity of thanking Hashem is indeed precious, and it grants life to those who engage in it meaningfully. We are taught that the angel in charge of the dead is called "dumah," which is spelled in Hebrew with the letters "daled"-"vav"-"mem"-"hei." When rearranged, these letters also spell "modeh," to give thanks. Perhaps this is an allusion to the fact that by properly thanking Hashem we can ward off the angel of death.

This is the sentiment we voice in Modim D'rabbanan (the prayer of thanksgiving we recite during the repetition of the Shemoneh Esrei) when we pray, "*Kein t'chayeinu us'kaimeinu...al she-anachnu modim lach*—So too give us life and sustain us...since we give thanks to You." I thank Hashem for helping me find favor in the eyes of my students and for the ability to mine His Torah for practical lessons to enhance the spiritual lives of my readers. I pray to Hashem that He continue to grant me the health and knowledge to disseminate His beautiful Torah for many years to come!

This sefer would have been absolutely impossible without the extraordinary assistance of my close friend, Shelley Zeitlin. He took the dictation of the first draft of these writings and edited them into works of beauty. Sheldon, I want to express publicly my deep gratitude to you, and may Hashem fulfill all your desires for good.

Speaking about dictation, this sefer owes a debt of gratitude to AT&T Wireless! Most of the dictation for this work was done over the cell phone while driving in the car (of course, we know now that we should exercise caution by using a hands-free device whenever driving!). This sefer is thus truly a product of "*Uv'lechtcha vaderech*—learning while traveling," as well as a manifestation of how Hashem gives us modern technology so that we can harness it for the use of Torah and mitzvos.

Writing a sefer is only the first step in successfully bringing it to the public. Editing, designing, printing, distributing, and advertising are complicated, expensive, and grueling tasks. Many would-be authors have been defeated by these daunting challenges. In this regard, I have the good fortune of having R' Aryeh Mezei, shlit"a, on my side. As my publisher, he has rolled out the red carpet for my Torah writings. I can't even begin to express my thanks to him and his staff for making the difficult process of putting out a sefer not only possible for me but enjoyable as well! Aryeh, you have proven yourself to be a true friend. I wish you success in all your endeavors, and may you succeed in bringing to the Jewish world the light of Hashem's Torah through the publication of many more seforim!

Once my manuscript was given to Judaica Press, the process of refinement began in earnest. R' Nachum Shapiro, shlit"a, pushed aside a host of other duties to lovingly convert my writings into a cohesive work of art. Nachum, thank you for the countless hours of diligence, hard work, and expertise that you put into my writings! Thanks also to Bonnie Goldman for expert art direction and editing, Zisi Berkowitz for her formatting and design work, Chana Leah Hirschhorn for proofreading, and R' Daniel Shore, shlit"a, for searching and finding the sources for many of the quotes in this sefer.

I would also like to express my heartfelt appreciation to the wonderful Tomchei Torah (Torah supporters) who have made dedications in this sefer. Thank you for your wonderful generosity and friendship! May Hashem bless you and your families that you should always be able to give and never need to take from others, and may you be rewarded with good health and happiness for many years to come!

As I did in my first sefer, *Passionate Judaism*, I would like to express my deep appreciation to the institutions and wonderful people that give me a reason to teach and discover Torah novellae. They are: the Agudas Yisroel of Staten Island, where I have had the privilege and pleasure to serve as Rav for the last eighteen years; Dial-a-Shiur, the international Torah phone service, headed by R' Eli Teitelbaum, shlit"a; my weekly cassette subscribers who have been listening to my shiurim—some for over a decade and a half, and who provide me with much of my ability to support my family; *The Jewish Press*, which has honored me with a weekly column and given me the ability to spread Torah to hundreds of thousands of Jews throughout the world; the *Country Yossi* radio program and magazine, headed by my good friend, Yossi Toiv; and my Boro Park Daf Yomi group, now entering its eleventh year with the help of Hashem! Also warm thanks to my good friend, Robby Nueman, for orchestrating my shiurim in Kew Garden Hills, Queens. I would like to take this opportunity to wish all my wonderful mispallelim and talmidim both spiritual and material success for many years to come.

Of course, all that I have is in large part due to the wonderful upbringing I received from my dear parents, Mr. Herman Weiss, zt"l, and, tibadel maichaim l'chayim, my wonderful mother, Mrs. Agi Weiss-Goldman, shlit"a. They gave me a loving home and instilled in me a desire to "make a difference" with my life by spreading Hashem's Torah to the masses. My parents provided me with an excellent education in Torah and middos by sending me to the Yeshiva of Staten Island. It was there that I had the great zechus of being "in the mechitza" (environment) of the gadol hador, R' Moshe Feinstein, zt"l, zy"a. I was also fortunate to be molded by the masterful "hands" of R' Reuven Feinstein, shlit"a, R' Gershon Weiss, shlit"a, and R' Chaim Mintz, shlit"a. May Hashem bless them with everything wonderful! My mother, after the sad passing of my father, remarried a wonderful man, R' Yaakov

Goldman, shlit''a. Together they serve as wonderful role models for me and my family. They are always there for us with love and devotion. Mommy and Saba (what we affectionately and respectfully call R' Goldman), may Hashem bless you with long years of good health, happiness, and much nachas from each other and all your descendants! With love and appreciation, I remember my wonderful in-laws, Mr. Aaron and Devora Gelbtuch, zt''l. May their neshamos have an aliya and may they continue to have nachas in shomayim from their entire mishpacha.

Hashem has blessed me, b'li ayin hara, with a true aishes chayil. My wife, Miriam Libby, tichy''a, has always been at my side helping me succeed at my Torah activities! It is she who helps me distribute thousands of tapes. She orchestrates many of my shiurim and helps me with my duties as Rav of the Agudah. She waits up for me when I come home after midnight from my late night Daf Yomi. Miriam Libby, I wish you good health and happiness, and may we together merit to raise our children to be happy y'rei shamayim and see nachas from many generations, *ad bias goel tzedek bimhaira b'yameinu*—until the coming of Moshiach, may he come speedily in our days.

Introduction

One of life's biggest challenges is infusing our mitzvos with meaning and passion. It is all too easy to fall into the trap of performing Hashem's commandments in a mechanical and habitual fashion. This was actually one of our primary short-comings at the time of the fall of the first Bais Hamikdash, as it says in *Yeshaya* [29:13] "*Vayomer Hashem yaan ki nigash haam hazeh b'fiv ubisfosav kabdaini v'libo rachak mimenee vatehi yirasam osee mitzvas anashim m'lumada*—Hashem said: Because the nation came close to me with their mouths and honored me with their lips, but their hearts were far from me and their mitzvos were done out of habit and routine."

The first step in performing mitzvos with feeling is to know their meaning, as it says in *Pirkei Avos*, "*Lo am ha'aretz chassid*—An ignorant person cannot be devout" [*Pirkei Avos* 2:5]. For example, when moving the hands by the blessing of

"Borei m'orei ha'eish" during Havdalah, it is easier to have kavanah if we know that the significance of clenching and unclenching our hand is that, on Shabbos, our hands have to be "closed" as we refrain from creative activity, but during Havdalah our hands can "open" once again to engage in such activity. Therefore, one of the aims of this sefer is to explore the reasons for many of the mitzvos that we do every day.

Every morning in Birchas Hashachar we pray, "*V'dabkeinu b'mitvosecha*—help us cleave to your mitzvos." While the simple meaning of this prayer is that we should always be involved with mitzvos and have many opportunities to serve Hashem, I believe there is another intent to this request. We are asking Hashem to help us attain the proper mindset to embrace mitzvos lovingly and not perform them hurriedly, as if we wish to rid ourselves of them.

The phrasing in Ahavah Rabbah (the second blessing of the morning Krias Shema) reinforces this explanation. There, we petition Hashem, "*V'dabeik libeinu b'mitzvosecha*—Let *our hearts* cleave to Your mitzvos," which indicates that this is a petition related to the heart. Thus, for example, we are commanded to distance ourselves more than four amos (cubits) from the door of the shul when we pray, so as not to give the impression that our prayers are a burden from which we want to escape as soon as possible.

In his sefer *Darash Moshe*, R' Moshe Feinstein, zt"l, quotes the selichos liturgy in which we say, "*V'ruach kodsh'cha al tikach mimenu*—Don't take Your Holy Spirit away from us." How, he asks, does Dovid Hamelech's prayer, which referred to his own ruach hakodesh (prophetic knowledge), apply to us? In fact, who are we to suggest that we have ruach hakodesh in the first place, when the Gemara questions whether even the brilliant Rabban Gamliel possessed it?! R' Moshe answers that the ruach hakodesh to which we refer here is not the prophetic kind, but the spirit and zest that should accompany our performance of mitzvos. We are asking Hashem to preserve this passion in us.

R' Yehudah Zev Segal, zt"l, of Manchester, England, was once seen taking his daily walk using a different route than he usually took. A student commented that this was the Rosh Yeshiva's way of combating the ever-present danger of falling into habitual behavior. This is why men put on tefillin next to their heart, to drive home the message that the actions of the hand should always be invested with feeling.

Similarly, we pray in Aleinu, "*V'yodata hayom v'hasheivosa el livovecha,*" that we should be able to internalize and perform lovingly and meaningfully that which we initially appreciate only on an intellectual level. We praise this same virtue in Birchas Krias Shema: "*Ashrei ish sheyishma l'mitzvosecha v'sorascha ud'varcha yasim al leebo*—Fortunate is the man who listens to Your mitzvos and sets Your Torah and Your words upon his heart."

The *Mishnah Brurah* [siman 62:2] states that those people who say Krias Shema slowly, and carefully pronounce the words, will have the fires of Gehinnom cooled down for them. He explains that this is a reward, measure for measure. Since someone cooled down his "heat," his natural tendency to speed through Krias Shema, Hashem will cool down the fires of Gehinnom for him.

We can extend this promise to other mitzvos as well. If we curb our natural tendency to perform mitzvos hastily, then Hashem will certainly reward us. Therefore, my main goal in this sefer is to encourage the reader to a more meaningful way of living by discussing the most common mitzvos and the ideas that underlie them.

The Jewish calendar is replete with special days that offer us a myriad of lessons. *Meaningful Living* seeks to explore some of these thoughts and insights, so that we can celebrate them more significantly. Tefillah is especially vulnerable to the pitfalls of habit. Since our prayers are repetitive in nature, we often fall prey to distraction. Indeed, the mishnah in *Pirkei Avos* [2:13] warns us, "*Al ta'as tefiloscha keva*—Don't make your prayers like a fixed routine." The fact that we say our prayers in Hebrew, which requires (at least for non-Israelis) the extra step of translation, only compounds the challenge of maintaining concentration. This book also offers some guidance to help us meet that challenge.

In the preface to his sefer, *Trumas Hakri*, the *Ketzos HaChoshen* teaches that Hashem does not flatly reject the prayers that we utter without proper kavanah. Rather, they remain in limbo until we say a prayer properly. This prayer then acts like a huge tow truck and pulls all our weak prayers up to Heaven with it. So, when we revitalize our prayer habits, we are not only investing in the future but rescuing our past tefillos as well.

Every generation has its challenges. While thankfully we don't have to contend with the temptation of idolatry, and, fortunately, we don't have to deal with inquisitions and pogroms, we too have our tests. In the last decade, we have seen a growing number of adolescents rebelling and losing their way. In this sefer, I offer a number of ideas for preventing the spread of this frightening epidemic.

The brilliant mystic, R' Chaim Vital, zt"l, said that our true character is revealed in the way we treat our spouses. One of life's greatest accomplishments is a happy and successful marriage. Sometimes a simple tip can make a world of a difference. For example, the Torah informs us that a man's wife is an "*eizer k'negdo*—a helper opposite him." She complements him and completes him where he is lacking, and the reverse is also true—a woman is complemented and completed by her husband. In fact, for a marriage to work, it is not necessarily advantageous that a husband and wife possess the exact same character traits. For instance, if your spouse is disorganized, instead of getting frustrated and angry all the time at the mess, spend some time showing your partner how to be organized. After all, growth is what marriage is all about.

If you find my advice on marriage and raising children useful, I urge you to look at my other sefer, *Passionate Judaism*, which contains additional thoughts on these vital subjects.

Many of my thoughts and Torah concepts have come from listening to and reading the teachings of the tremendous Gaon, R' Avigdor Miller, zt"l. I have included in this sefer a tribute to this spiritual giant (a man who exemplified the concept of "Meaningful Living"), which I hope you will find inspiring. If my words encourage you to listen to his tapes or study his magnificent seforim, that alone would make this entire sefer worthwhile.

Most of the essays in this sefer end with a blessing. The opportunity to give another Jew a blessing is an exceptional pursuit. The Torah teaches us, "*Va'avarcha m'varchecha*—I will bless those who bless you" [*Bereishis* 12:3]. Therefore, whenever we wish well to another Jew, we automatically receive a blessing from Hashem. Not a bad deal! I hope you find this sefer both inspiring and enjoyable, and may Hashem bless you with good health, happiness, and everything wonderful.

ברוך שהחייני וקימנו והגיענו לזמן הזה
Tammuz 5761
Moshe Meir Weiss

Improving
Our Lives

Becoming a
Kinder Person

In the entirety of Scripture, there aren't many people who have been given as many accolades by Hashem as Noach. The Torah waxes reverently about Noach's character. It extols him as a tzadik, as being tamim, unblemished, and as one who "walked with G-d." Furthermore, the Torah calls him an "ish"—what we would call "a *mentsch*."

And yet, above and beyond all of these qualities, there is one praise of Noach that preceded all of the aforementioned traits. The parshah starts off, "*Eila toldos Noach, Noach*—These are the "offspring" of Noach: that he was Noach." This is explained by the *Baalei Tosefos* to mean that he was an "ish neicha," a gentle and kind person. Hashem holds the trait of kindness in such high regard that He gives it precedence over all of Noach's other virtues.

This is a lesson of profound importance. In Yiddish, we · refer to a kind person as an "*eidele mentsch.*" This is a wonderful quality to look for when you are dating, searching for your mate for life. Consequently, it is an important characteristic to cultivate in oneself. However, with today's frenetic pace of life, this is no easy task. The competitiveness of the workplace and the myriad conflicting obligations that prey upon us daily are not the ideal breeding grounds for developing kindness. Many people coming into marriages are already tense and have low frustration tolerance—even before the first child is born and the real pressures begin to mount.

Unfortunately, the rigors and pressures of the many tests that our children encounter in school put them into a pressure-cooker at an awfully young age. Educators, unfortunately, walk a tightrope in our society, for without the incentives of tests, the level of accomplishment in schools would probably drop. There must, however, be a happy medium—our children shouldn't become ulcer-prone at a young age because of an overdose of book reports, school projects, and multiple tests on the same day.

On Shemini Atzeres, during Mussaf, when the chazan petitions for rain, he mentions that the angel in charge of rain is called "Af-Bri." The Sages explain this strange word-composition, which means "anger-health" in English, as referring to two types of rainfall. Rain can arrive as an angry tempestuous storm or as a healthy, life-giving shower. The commentaries tell us that rain, which in Hebrew is called "geshem," actually refers to all gashmius, all of our materialistic livelihood. Thus, the name of the angel might be alluding to the fact that if there is anger in the home, one will see angry and unfortunate results—the "af attribute"—from the guardian angel of sustenance. On the other hand, if there is a healthy, calm relationship in the home and everyone works diligently to create a calm and pleasant environment, then the "bri attribute" of the angel will come to the fore, with the blessing of a healthy parnasah for the family. This is exactly what the Gemara teaches us in *Bava Metzia* [59a]: "*Okiru nesheichu k'dei d'tisashru*—Honor your wives in order to become wealthy."

Shlomo Hamelech, the wisest of all men, taught us, "*Ma'aneh rach meishiv cheima*—The soft answer dispels wrath" [*Mishlei* 15:1]. We are taught that the grandest crown that one can acquire—above the crown of royalty, priesthood, and even Torah—is the crown of a good name. The way to acquire such a crown is to speak and deal gently with others, and work hard to exert a calming influence on the people around us.

May Hashem give us the ambition and talent to attain the trait of kindness, and in that zechus may we all merit life's many blessings.

The Yetzer Hara
and the Fly

If I were to ask you to compare the yetzer hara to a living creature, you might answer with responses like: a black widow spider, a menacing cheetah, or possibly a deadly cobra. Now keep in mind that in *Masechtas Bava Basra* the Gemara tells us that the *"yetzer hara, hu hasoton, hu Malach Hamavess*—The yetzer hara is the same as the satan and the angel of death." He is described as being all three of these rolled into one—a package deal. However, the Gemara also makes an interesting analogy between the yetzer hara and a certain creature that would probably never have entered your mind.

To which horrible being does the Gemara compare this evil force? In *Masechtas Brachos* [61a] the Gemara tells us, *"Yetzer hara domeh l'zvuv*—The yetzer hara is similar to a fly."

That's it?! A fly?! What similarity is there between the yetzer hara and a harmless housefly?

Actually, there is a lot we can learn from this analogy. Especially if you just returned from a picnic lunch or vacation, you might still have a vivid remembrance of those pesky little flying insects, and you might begin to appreciate the similarities.

First, there's a striking similarity in character. Like a fly, the yetzer hara has a distinguishing trait: It never gives up. It keeps coming back. If a person were to start a fight with someone and was then beaten by his victim, would the person continue to come back for more? Not likely. But the fly is persistent. No matter how many times you shoo it away with your hand, it keeps buzzing right back at you. The yetzer hara manifests the same behavior. No matter how many times you beat it, it keeps coming back for another try!

As the Gemara teaches us, "*Yitzro shel odom misgaber olov b'chol yom*—A person's evil inclination prevails upon him every day" [*Kiddushin* 30a]. If we manage to fight off the yetzer hara today, he will be back tomorrow with stronger force. That is why *Pirkei Avos* [2:4] tells us, "*Al ta'amin b'atzmecha ad yom moscha*—Do not trust yourself until the day you die." Do not think that you have overcome the yetzer hara for good, not even on the last day of your life.

We should keep in mind that the greater a person becomes, and the bigger a tzadik one is, the stronger his yetzer hara becomes. The higher we rise, the more we have to overcome. This is in order to preserve our bechirah, our free will, and to make sure we continue to be worthy of reward for our actions.

It is recounted that at the end of each year the Vilna Gaon would count the time he wasted over the year by not learning Torah. He was an incredible tzadik, of course, and those moments added up to a very small amount of time. Yet when someone approached him and exclaimed how lucky he would be if only he had the Gaon's yetzer instead of his own, the Vilna Gaon was shocked. He couldn't understand what the other person could possibly mean, for the Gaon's yetzer hara was equal to his tzidkus, his righteousness. Measure for measure, ounce for ounce, our yetzer hara is as strong as we are.

This is why all the baalei mussar and the Chofetz Chaim in the *Mishnah Brurah* emphasize how important it is to learn mussar. No matter how many seforim we may have learned, we must keep working on ourselves continually.

Therefore, we must ask ourselves, "When was the last time I worked on my middos?" If the answer is months ago, or even weeks ago, we'd better get a move on it, because the yetzer hara, like the fly, keeps trying to prevail over us every day.

If we think about it, we can see why the yetzer hara is not compared to something a little more dangerous like a cobra or a hornet. If we look closely, we will find that the yetzer hara is actually not strong at all. Indeed, the Gemara teaches us that initially the strength of the evil inclination is as weak and flimsy as a spider's web. Only if we give in to the yetzer hara does its strength grow. We have to remember this sound rule: "*V'im ein HaKadosh Boruch Hu m'sai'ei'a lo, eino yochil lo*—If the Holy One, Blessed be He, does not help a person, he cannot win." However, we must also remember that its opposite is also true. With just a little siyata d'Shmaya, help from Hashem, we can fight the yetzer hara and win.

Let us now go further with our comparison. A fly does not appear dangerous. So too, the yetzer hara appears in disguise. He does not stand in front of us and declare, "Sin is here!" The Medrash tell us that when Yaakov Avinu fought with Eisav's angel, the angel didn't look evil. In fact, he was dressed as a talmid chochom, a scholar! Indeed, many people fall into the deadly sins of machlokes and loshon hara thinking that they are doing something for the sake of heaven. Just look at Korach, who convinced himself that he was championing the cause of Bnei Yisroel, but was swallowed alive because he succumbed to the lures of jealousy and pride!

The yetzer hara, a professional expert in deceit, has the ability to turn things around and make them appear as the opposite of what they really are. Thus, for instance, he will try to tell us that Torah is out of our reach, that it can only be found in the heavens, or that it is on the other side of a river that can't be crossed. But the Torah testifies "this is not so!" *"Ki lo bashamayim hee, v'lo me'eiver layam...ki karov ailecha hadavar m'od*—Torah is not in the heavens, nor is it on the other side of the sea.... It is indeed quite close to you" [*Devarim* 30:12]. The Torah tells us not to listen to the yetzer hara. Really each and every person has the inherent ability to rise to great heights and become a talmid chochom. But the yetzer hara turns the facts around on us.

Now is the time to start doing teshuvah. If, for example, we are not up to par in respecting our parents or spouses, now is the time to correct the situation. We might scrutinize our kibbud av v'eim and come to the realization that we do fight a lot with our parents. At that point, the yetzer hara will step in and remind us that we are popular with our friends. That will start us thinking that perhaps the deficiency is not in us, but in our parents. Similarly, a husband may begin to consider that the marital harmony in his home is not what it should be. His wife is always upset with him, and she is always sulking. Once again, the yetzer hara will step in and make him think, "I am popular with my friends and colleagues!

This situation *must* be my wife's fault."

The yetzer hara turns it all around. Instead of leaving us to realize our own shortcomings, the yetzer hara makes us believe the problem rests with others. That is the meaning in the Gemara, "*Kamma gavnin l'yetzer hara*—the yetzer hara has many colors." His crafty talents can make things look different than they really are.

Flies are drawn toward sweet substances. If candy or sugar is left out, it will certainly attract flies, which adore sweets. The yetzer hara loves sweets, too. If a person goes around looking for "sweetness," saying, "What am I going to do now? How can I have a good time?" the yetzer hara is attracted to him. If a person is devoid of ruchnius, of spirituality, the yetzer hara hangs around him like a fly.

The Gemara [*Masechtas Tamid* 32], tells us a golden rule: "*Mah ya'avid inish v'yichyeh, yomis es atzmo*—Whoever wishes to live (a real life) should kill himself (i.e., restrain himself from overindulging in the physical pleasures of life). *Mah ya'avid inish v'yomis, y'chayeh es atzmo*—Whoever wants to (spiritually) kill himself should 'live it up.'"

Another place flies can be found is in a place of tumah, impurity. Flies are attracted to garbage. If a person hangs around devorim tmei'im, impure things and places, he will become a product of this environment. If a person brings tumah into his living room, he will not receive protection just because there are massive seforim shranks on the other side of the room. The yetzer hara is attracted to the tumah.

Chazal tell us, "*Kol Yisroel yeish lahem cheilek l'Olam Habah*—Everyone in Klal Yisroel has a portion in the World to Come" [Beginning of *Pirkei Avos*]. Why does it say "*l'Olam Habah*" and not "*b'Olam Habah?*" The *Imrei Binah* explains that if it had said "*b'Olam Habah*" we would think that everyone is born with a portion reserved for them, and if we are good we will get our plot. "L'Olam Habah" tells us that we have to work *towards* it, to create our own share. "*Poel adam y'shaleim lo*—The work of a person will be his payment." What we do creates what we'll get. When we do good, we create our Olam Habah. When we do bad, we create our Gehinnom. We may ask ourselves, what difference does it make whether we begin with a share waiting for us in the World to Come or we must create it ourselves? In fact, it makes a dramatic difference.

Whenever we may pause to think about the end of our life, when we will have to give a din v'chesbon, a tally and accounting of our actions, the yetzer hara helps us rationalize that we will get by. When Hashem will ask us why we didn't work harder at our mitzvos, the yetzer hara will tell us that we can respond with a clear conscience that we were extremely busy and needed time to relax. Then Hashem will lead us into a tiny room. We may ask, "Is this all? Is this my share?" And Hashem will answer, "This is what you put away for yourself." Had there been a ready-made portion, we would have that now. But since we had to create the portion for ourselves, if we didn't work much, we clearly will not have much.

Do we hide behind excuses? Don't we realize that we can't expect a great future, *l'netzach netzachim*, forever and ever, unless we prepare it for ourselves?

Beware the Enemy Within

We have a powerful enemy that can destroy us if we are
not vigilant. This enemy is the yetzer hara, our evil inclination. We read in dismay how the wily snake (symbolic of the
evil inclination) brought down Adam and Chava, the exqui-
site creations of Hashem's own handiwork. Not only did the
yetzer hara succeed in getting Adam to mess up on his first
day of existence, he succeeded in getting Adam to transgress
the only command that he was given. He also succeeded in
driving a wedge between the first and most perfectly
matched couple, a wedge that would last for one hundred and
thirty years.

No sooner have we finished reading about this tragic
downfall than we are confronted with another horrifying
debacle. We watch as the yetzer hara torments Kayin with the

misery of jealousy. And, even after Hashem warns Kayin to beware, he succumbs to the wiles of his yetzer and commits the heinous crime of murder, against his own flesh and blood, his brother, Hevel.

It is not coincidental that we find these two stories at the beginning of the Torah. Hashem is teaching us the facts of life. Every day the yetzer hara tempts us, and tries to get us to sin in a whole variety of ways. From tempting us, for example, to not get up in time for davening, to telling us to touch the tap instead of washing liberally, to seducing us into snapping at a spouse or rushing through our prayers, he is at work from the moment we get up until we close our eyes at night. And then he tempts us to forget about Kriyas Shema!

R' Itzele Blazer teaches us how dangerous the yetzer hara is. He cites the Medrash [*Bereishis Rabbah* 34:1] that, while the righteous control their heart, the wicked are controlled by their heart. This means the wicked are swayed by their base desires in every which way. If this is so, R' Itzele Blazer wonders, why does the Gemara in *Nedarim* say that the wicked are always full of regrets? Why should the wicked regret their sins if their heart *always* controls them? Rather, they should be in a constant state of drinking and merriment, and never be mindful about the consequences. He answers, based on the *Chovos Halevovos*, that the yetzer hara doesn't merely want to get us to sin. No, he wants to destroy us completely, taking away from us both this world and the next. He therefore tempts us to sin, since that will ultimately cause us to lose Olam Habah. Then, to top it all off, he allows us to feel deep regret, which robs us of enjoyment in this world as well. How we must shudder in dread from the awareness of this enemy that exists within us every day!

The *Pele Yoetz* teaches us that when one has mastered a

certain area, and is not tempted to sin in that specific region of life, he is considered a "tzadik," a righteous person, in that matter. Similarly, the person who has repeated a certain transgression so often that he doesn't hesitate to commit it is considered a "rashah," a wicked person, in that area. The "beinoni," or intermediate person, is the one who is bombarded by both his good and evil inclinations and faces the inner battle of deciding which way to go. Thus, for example, one who talks in shul without even a moment's hesitation or regret is unfortunately wicked in this area. One whose conscience tugs at him in this regard is a beinoni. Similarly, one who turns to gaze without hesitation at an immodestly clad woman has totally fallen prey to the power of his yetzer hara.

As an example of the domination of the evil one, I remember one Thursday morning during Sukkos when, in many areas, it was raining right before breakfast time. How many of us were tempted to shun the sukkah because of a few stray drops? How easy it was for the yetzer hara to keep us away from this glorious mitzvah!

Forewarned is forearmed. Let's be vigilant of this enemy lurking within us and be strengthened and reassured by the awareness that those who try to combat the yetzer hara receive Divine Help to succeed. Indeed, this is what we thank Hashem for in the blessing, "*Ozer Yisroel b'gevurah*—Who girds Israel with might." Hashem gives us the strength we need to combat this enemy. May it be the will of Hashem that we succeed in this daily test of life, and in that merit may we earn the many rewards of those who valiantly serve Hashem.

How to Pray
with Kavanah

The Hebrew word for prayer is tefillah. The root of tefillah is "pileil," which means to think and consider. In parshas Vayigash [48:11], Yaakov Avinu said to Yosef, "*Ra'oh panecha lo pillalti*—I never thought to see your face again." This is also the same root word as that of tefillin. We must conclude that prayer and donning of tefillin can only be properly achieved through thought and concentration.

We know that the Gemara [*Taanis* 4a] teaches us that the avodah shebaleiv, the "service of the heart," is prayer. The word "shebaleiv" literally means, "That is in the heart." Using a fascinating analysis, let us look at the "heart" of the word "leiv," i.e., the inside letters of this Hebrew word. This word is made up of two letters, the "lamed" (which if spelled out is spelled "lamed"-"mem"-"daled"), and the

"beis" (which if spelled out is spelled "beis"-"yud"-"tof").
Thus, the inner letters, the letters inside the word leiv, are
"mem" [מ]-"daled" [ד] (omitting the "lamed"), and "yud"
[י]-"tof" [ת] (omitting the "beis"), which when rearranged
spell the Hebrew word "**tomid**." The **tomid**, of course, is
the daily offering for which our prayers, in the absence of
the Beis Hamikdash, substitute. Once again, the message is
clear: If we perform true service *in the heart*, our prayers will
then truly correspond to the daily offerings that they are
supposed to represent.

To drive home the supreme importance of concentrating when we pray, R' Yonasan Eybeschutz, of blessed memory, writes the following scary warning: It is due to the
many prayers of Jews who pray without kavanah that we
lose many of the righteous people of the generation.
Perhaps the linkage between prayer and the great ones of
our people is that our gedolim are the "heart" of our nation
and, if our prayers lack heart, Hashem punishes us measure
for measure, and takes away the heart of our people. This
surely is a strong incentive for us to work on putting more
heart into our davening.

The *Meiri*, in *Masechtas Brachos* [27a], writes that, in his
time, when on Shabbos and Yom Tov large masses of people
would come to the only synagogue in town, some sages
would daven privately in their homes first and come to shul
later. This was because they knew they wouldn't be able to
concentrate in the midst of all the mayhem. They felt strongly that "prayer without kavanah is no prayer at all." (Please
understand, of course, that it is not appropriate for us nowadays to adopt this policy for ourselves.)

The Mabit, in his sefer *Beis Elokim*, writes that this is why
we pray, "*Shema Koleinu*—Listen to our voices," pleading with

Hashem that, "Even if our prayers consist of only *voice* and no thought, please listen to them anyway." He adds that this fits especially well in the nusach sefard, which concludes the blessing with the words, "*Ki Atah shomei'a tefillas kol peh amcha yisroel b'rachamim*—For You are the Almighty, Who listens to the prayers of all *the mouths* of Your nation Yisroel, with mercy." Again, this re-emphasizes the plea that even if it is only the prayer of the mouth, and sadly not the prayer of the mind, Hashem should please listen and accept our prayers anyway, through His great mercy. Of course, it is our job to not pay Hashem mere lip service, but to offer Him real, meaningful, and thoughtful prayer.

R' Elya Lopian makes it clear that there are two important parts to proper kavanah. First, one has to focus on the fact that he is talking to Hashem. Second, he must understand what he is saying. Our sages give us some helpful tips to aid us in concentrating better and not being distracted while davening. The Gemara in *Brachos* recommends that one should pray in a place that has windows. Thus, if we find our minds wandering from thoughts of Hashem, by looking out the window and seeing the sky we will be able to redirect our thoughts to Hashem. So too, the Gemara [*Brachos* 6b] advises us to have a "makom kavua," a fixed place where we pray all the time. This, too, is to help facilitate better concentration, for we are less likely to become distracted when we are in familiar surroundings.

The familiar sight of worshippers "shuckling" back and forth is also due in part to the pursuit of better kavanah. Besides the benefit of getting all our limbs into the action of praising Hashem, thus fulfilling the verse, "*Kol atzmosai tomarna Hashem, mi chamocha*—All my bones say, 'Who is like You, O' Hashem?' " [*Tehillim* 35:10]. Many commentaries tell us that the purpose for the custom of shuckling is to facilitate better concentration. It is interesting to note, though, that this practice is controversial and not universally accepted. The *Derech Chaim*, among others, says that, in truth, shuckling prevents proper kavanah. The *Pri Megadim*, however, offers a logical compromise: One should see for himself which way works better and act accordingly.

I have personally found the following piece of advice very helpful in chasing away the cobwebs of weariness and worldly distractions while praying. The *Sefer Yereim*, the *Yaaros Devash*, and R' Yaakov Emden all offer this valuable and practical advice. They suggest that, before every Shemoneh Esrei, we should try to mentally add something personal to as many of the brachos as we can. This addition will jog our minds out of their routine and encourage us to focus on the subject at hand.

Thus, for example, when saying the second brachah, about techiyas hameisim, we should train ourselves to have in mind friends and loved ones already in the next world, and affirm our belief in Hashem that they will be resurrected. When saying the fourth blessing of daas, knowledge, we should plan to ask for a different aspect of knowledge each time. We might ask to understand our children better, to have an easier time with our Torah study, or to grant us understanding in how to please our spouses better. When we get to the blessing of s'lach lonu, the blessing of forgiveness, one day we might focus on the sin of snapping at our mate, another day we might beg for forgiveness for lashon hara, or for not spending enough time with our parents.

In the blessing of refa'einu, when we ask Hashem for the continued blessing of good health, we might focus on alternating aspects of health, asking Hashem that we should be spared from cancer, diabetes, heart disease, kidney problems, asthma, and the like. If we adopt this personalized method of prayer, we will surely find that we will begin paying much more attention to how we speak to Hashem.

In the merit of our working on praying more meaningfully and effectively, may we be zocheh that Hashem fulfill all our requests in the best way possible.

Shemoneh Esrei
Meditations

The middle brachos of Shemoneh Esrei are dedicated to the supplications pertaining to our needs. A proper and deeper understanding of these blessings can greatly enhance the quality of our lives.

The first of the middle blessings is the request for understanding, intellect, and wisdom. When we ask Hashem, *"Chaneinu me'itcha dei'a,"* the *Mishnah Brurah* [siman 115:1] teaches us that we should have in mind that Hashem should give us a virtuous and just mind, to know how to choose what is good and to be naturally disgusted with what is bad. We ask Hashem to help us naturally be drawn to good and be repelled by what is evil.

Note that, when asking for knowledge, we stress *"chaneinu me'itcha,"* bestow it on us *from You.* Although admittedly one could learn some wisdom from the goyim (as the Gemara says, "*Chochmah b'goyim, ta'amin*—If one says there is wisdom amongst the nations, believe him"), we ask Hashem, "Please let our knowledge come from You, through the Torah and its Sages."

The *Siddur Shaar HaRachamim* cites from *Yeshaya* [27:11] the verse, "*Ki lo am binos hu, al kein lo yerachamen'hu osei'hu*— For they are a people without sense, therefore their Creator will not show them pity." The Gemara [*Brachos* 33a] paraphrases this by saying, "*Kol mi sh'ein bo deah, asur l'racheim alav*—It is forbidden to have compassion upon someone who doesn't have understanding." While a full understanding of this statement is beyond the scope of our discussion here, this is the reason we start off our petitions in the Shemoneh Esrei with a personal request for seichel, for our supplications are based on a plea for compassion, and as we just stated, one needs a modicum of good sense in order to deserve compassion.

Interestingly, although every other one of the middle blessings starts with a request, this, the first, does not! The first brachah, "Atta Chonein," does not start with a petition but with a praise, namely that Hashem graces us with knowledge. Why the departure from the request formula for just this one brachah?

The *Talmud Yerushalmi* gives an interesting reason. It informs us that although we do not make personal requests on Shabbos, the prayer for intellect was so important that it was originally included in the Shabbos prayers. However, in order to conform to the regulation of not petitioning on Shabbos, the blessing starts off with praise instead of a plea. Over time, this blessing was dropped from our Shabbos liturgy, but the original formula remained intact.

The *Iyyun Tefilla* gives another answer. He points out that on Motzoei Shabbos, the havdalah prayer, "Atta Chonantanu," is inserted within the text of "Atta Chonein." Since it is inappropriate to begin personal petitions before Havdalah, the beginning of "Atta Chonein" had to be constructed as praise since it precedes the havdalah prayer insert.

The *Siddur HaMeforesh* suggests that, while we readily understand that our health, livelihood, and harmony are in the Hashem's hands, we might mistakenly think that *we* are responsible for our intellect and knowledge. Therefore, to dispel this notion, we start off the blessing of seichel with the emphatic statement that only Hashem imparts to us our knowledge.

I'd like to offer an additional understanding of the way this blessing begins. Throughout the middle blessings, we make the explicit assertion that our prayers affect everything we have. The exception to this is intellect. The gift of knowledge could not possibly be totally dependent on our prayers since, without understanding, we wouldn't be able to articulate a prayer for it in the first place. And therefore we declare our realization that when it comes to intellect, we have it only by the grace of Hashem who bestows it upon us even before we pray. Thus, the phrase "atta chonein," for "chonein" is related to the word "chinam," which means free. The acquisition of knowledge has to be given to us freely by Hashem, for it must exist in order for us to know how to pray for everything else.

The second of the middle blessings is the request for aid in doing teshuvah, repentance. It is interesting that in requesting help with repentance, we start off with a plea to help us return to Torah. I believe this is because the Gemara tells us, in *Masechtas Kiddushin* [30b], "*Borasi yetzer hara, uvarasi lo Torah tavlin*." Hashem says, "I created the yetzer hara and I created the Torah as an antidote for it." Thus, the best way to embark on a campaign of teshuvah is to intensify our Torah study, thereby foiling the evil inclination's attempts to cause us to sin and block us from repentance. The *Nefesh HaChaim* adds that Torah is compared to a mikvah. Just like the waters of a mikvah purify the entire body, so too the Torah has the strength to purge sin from one's entire soul.

Let's take a closer look at the first verse of this blessing. "*Hashiveinu Avinu l'Sorasecha*—Return us, our Father, to Your Torah." We do not ask Hashem to introduce us to the Torah or help us with our Torah study, but rather to return us to His Torah. Perhaps this is because there are no neophytes to Torah study, for we all learned the entirety of Torah in our mother's wombs. Therefore, our request is only to return us to the Torah that we've already learned (at least) once before. This is a fundamental belief that one should focus on, since it precludes one from saying (or feeling) that it is too late in life to start studying Torah. Nor can one say he or she is not cut out for it; that it's not their "cup of tea," for each and every one of us has already finished Shas and much more. So we just ask "*Hashiveinu Avinu—Return* us to Your Torah!"

The next verse of this brachah also contains a glaring question. "*V'karveinu Malkeinu l'avodasecha*—Bring us near, O King, to Your service," namely, to mitzvos. Why do we use the phrase, "Bring us near?" Wouldn't it be more appropriate to say "*Azreinu*—Help us," with your mitzvos, or "*Sa'adeinu*—Support us," in our efforts. Why the emphasis on "*korveinu*," bringing us closer? The *Avnei Eliyahu* explains that the intent is that we should merit going to Eretz Yisroel and thus be closer to the Makom HaShechina, the resting place of the Divine Splendor [*Siddur HaGra*, bracha 7].

Perhaps we might suggest another answer. We know that in our contemporary Orthodox society, we do all the mitzvos that we possibly can, and we try to do them in the best ways possible. However, what is often lacking is the inner focus of doing Hashem's will. Too often our mitzvah observance is unfortunately habitual, robot-like and devoid of any linkage to the One Above. Often, we might just follow the routine of behavior that we've practiced since kindergarten, without any thought of Hashem. As proof of this, we should ask ourselves how many spoons of cholent we've eaten in our lives. After calculating that astronomical number, let's figure out how many of these were accompanied with the thought that we were celebrating Hashem's special Shabbos day. Need I say more?

We therefore plead to Hashem, "*V'karveinu Malkeinu l'avodasecha*—Bring us near to Your service." Help us feel close to you and think of You when we do the mitzvos. Let us upgrade our observance to that of meaningful connectivity with the Almighty rather than just "*Mitzvas anoshim m'lumada*—Mitzvos done by rote*," the mere habits and routines of one's youth.

Let us conclude with the wish that in the merit of our working on our prayers, Hashem will fulfill our requests and bless us with health, happiness and everything wonderful.

Cleaning Up
Our Speech

In *Masechtas Sanhedrin* [99b], it says, "*Amar R' Elazar: Kol Adam l'amal nivrah, she-ne'emar 'Adam l'amal yulad.'*" R' Elazar tells us that every person, whether man or woman, is born to work, to toil, and he cites a posuk to prove it. Everyone was born to work in this life. That's what Olam Hazeh, this world, is all about. Only in Olam Habah, the next world, can a person sit back and relax, enjoying his rewards.

But R' Elazar goes on to say, "*Eini yodeiya im l'amal peh nivrah im l'amal m'lacha nivrah.*" He tells us that he is not sure whether a person was born to toil with his mouth, or with his hands and body.

What does the Tana mean that he is not sure? The average person works with his or her hands. To earn a living, most of us must use some elbow grease, so to speak. The *Ya'aros*

D'vash tells us that R' Elazar is not talking about earning a living. He is discussing spiritual, not material, fulfillment. There are mitzvos we do with our mouths, such as delivering Divrei Torah, davening, and speaking kindly to others. There are also mitzvos we do with our hands and bodies, such as sukkah, lulav, matzah, l'vayas hameis, and so on.

R' Elazar was asking which type of mitzvah is more purposeful and works best to bring us to inner fulfillment—the mitzvos of the peh (mouth) or the mitzvos of the yad (hand)? We might think, he tells us, that since a person learns in order to act, "*lilmod al m'nas la'asos*," our goal is to perform, so the mitzvos of the *yad*, the ones involving action, must be the most important. Furthermore, we would reason, mitzvos of the hand take more effort and work than the workings of the mouth so it would stand to reason that the category of the "hand" is the greater fulfillment.

However, R' Elazar concludes, "*K'she'omer 'ki akaf olov pihu,' hevei omer l'amal peh nivrah.*" R' Elazar quotes the posuk in *Mishlei*, "To put a saddle on the mouth," thus proving that it is in the area of controlling our speech that our greatest challenge lies. He therefore concludes that a person is put on this world primarily to toil with his mouth and that this is the most important arena for personal fulfillment.

After all, what is the basic difference between Adam, man, and the animals? In the final analysis, an animal works hard just like a person to acquire food and shelter. But when Hashem created Adam, Hashem put a *nefesh chaya*, a living soul in him [*Bereishis* 2:7]. Targum translates this as "*ruach m'mal'lah*—a speaking spirit," the power of speech. The vehicle of the neshama, the human soul, is the mouth. In this area, humans are unique. Only human beings have the power of speech.

Pirkei Avos [5:1] tells us, "*B'asara maamaros nivrah ha'olam*—with ten utterances the world was created." The world was created through speech, and we, too, have the power to make or break lives with the power of speech. As the posuk in *Mishlei* tells us, "*Maves v'chaim b'yad lashon*—Life and death are in the hands of our speech" [18:21].

We can also see this from the *arurim*, the curses that would come upon Bnei Yisroel if, chas v'shalom, they went off the proper path. Grouped together with forbidden relations and idolatry is the curse, "*Arur makeh rayeihu basoser*—Cursed is the person who smites his friend secretly" [*Devarim* 27:24]. Rashi tells us that this refers to the sin of lashon hara (gossip). Lashon hara is put on the same level as avodah zarah (idolatry) and gilui arayos (immorality).

If we look back through history to one of the most horrifying punishments Hashem ever brought upon humans, we recall Korach and his supporters. The earth opened up and swallowed them. They descended straight to Gehinnom. What had Korach done? He had caused strife. He had spoken against leaders of the nation. He had sinned through his power of speech.

We can also look at Dor Hamidbar, the generation that left Egypt and died in the desert. A whole generation died because of the episode with the spies, because they spoke lashon hara about Eretz Yisrael. Yaakov Avinu lost thirty-three years of his life because of the words of complaint he uttered to Pharaoh. Rashi tells us the Beis Hamikdash was destroyed because of lashon hara, and the Gemara in *Taanis* tells us that rains are withheld, causing hunger, hardship, and all kinds of other tzaros, all because of those who speak lashon hara.

We find another example of the deadliness of sinful speech in *Masechtas Sanhedrin*. After the Gemara discusses the transgressions that require misas beis din, capital punishment, it proceeds to enumerate specific sins that are even worse than those. One loses not only his or her life in this world for these, but also one's eternity. And one of those terrible aveiros is *hamalbin p'nei chaveiro b'rabim*—embarrassing a person in public [*Bava Metzia* 59a]. If you commit murder, you can still get Olam Habah. If you commit idolatry, you can still get Olam Habah. But people who habitually embarrass others lose their Olam Habah.

Another example of the devastating spiritual consequences of undisciplined speech involves speaking during Chazaratz Hashatz, the repetition of the Shemoneh Esrei. The *Shulchan Aruch* [*Orach Chaim* 124 seif 7] tells us just how bad it is: "*Hu choteh, v'gadol avono mi-n'so*." Not only is that person a sinner, but his transgression is "too great to bear!" The *Mishnah Brurah* [seif katan 27] quotes the *Elyah Rabbah* who says in the name of the *Kol Bo* that many shuls were destroyed because of this deed. The *Tosfos Yom Tov* tells us that pogroms were caused by this sin. We may ask ourselves, "Why is a little talking in shul so terrible? We keep kosher, we are shomrei Shabbos, and we give our children good Torah educations! What is so terrible about a little talking?" But we must not underestimate the importance of this matter. By talking when we shouldn't or saying things that we shouldn't, we are effectively destroying our *kedushas hapeh*, the holy quality of our speech. We are failing at one of our primary purposes in life.

Now let's look at the positive aspects of *amailas hapeh*, the work of the mouth. Listen to Chazal describe the makings of a tzadik: A person who answers "amen" ninety times, says four *kedusha*'s, ten *yehei shemei rabah*'s, and recites one hundred brachos every day is called a tzadik. Just by using his mouth properly, a person can earn the lofty title "tzadik"!

The Ramban wrote a well-known letter, called the *Iggeres HaRamban*, to his family, telling them how to succeed in life. One of the first things he writes is, *"tisnaheg tamid l'daber kol d'vorecha b'nachas l'chol adam u'v'chol eis."* That is, always speak gently and kindly, no matter whom you are speaking to, and no matter what time or what kind of day it has been!

I once heard from R' Avigdor Miller, zt"l, that the letters in the word *"ka'as,"* anger, are the same as those in *"eches,"* poison. That is exactly what anger is: poison. And by not speaking in anger, by not flying off the handle, we can enrich our lives and the lives of others. We must try not to blow up at our spouses, our children, or our colleagues. Change in this area can profoundly improve our family lives. We should drop arguments that resurrect past differences. When we come home after a hard day, we should make sure not to "start in" on everybody. We can tell our parents how much we appreciate the chinuch they gave us, and tell them that we are attempting to raise our children in the same way. Striving to improve in these areas will not only help towards our fulfillment in Olam Hazeh, but it will bring reward in Olam Habah as well.

It is incumbent upon all of us to learn how to use our mouths more wisely. We have to know what to say, how to say it, and when to say it. And let us not forget, *"Lo yomush sefer torah mipicha*—the Torah should never depart from your mouth" [*Yehoshua* 1:8]. Learning Torah is not a function of the mind alone. The Gemara in *Eiruvin* [53b] tells us that Bruriah, the famous wife of R' Meir, came upon a man studying Torah silently and kicked him. Whether or not the kick was truly a physical one is irrelevant. She was admonishing the man, citing what it says in Shmuel, *"Arucha b'kol u-shemura,"* which means if you use your whole body to learn

Torah, then it is preserved; if not, then it is not kept. Using our bodies to learn means mouthing the words as we study.

A revealing Gemara in *Brachos* [8b] advises us, "*Kol hamashlim parshiyosov ma'arichin yomov u-sh'nosov*—Whoever is "maavir sedrah" (reviews the weekly parsha) twice in the mikrah (original Hebrew) and once in targum (translation), lengthens his days and years. Similarly, in *Shabbos* [119b] it says, Whoever answers "*Amen. Yehei shemei rabah…*" with all his might causes a bad decree against him to be ripped up. One who recites the Shema properly, "*mitztan'nin lo Gehinnom*—the fires of Gehinnom are cooled for him" [*Brachos* 15a]. Even if he needs Gehinnom, it is lessened.

We have to train ourselves to daven properly. It's hard—there's no doubt about it. After all, it's the same drill all the time, three times a day. We sometimes look at it as something to get over with. But we must appreciate that prayer is our connection to Hashem. If we pray correctly, Hashem will help us and give us what we need. And if we praise Hashem and thank Hashem for all He does for us, then we will certainly find favor in His eyes.

It all begins and it all ends with the mouth. This is our path to personal fulfillment. As R' Elazar tells us, "*L'amal peh nivrah*—Our job is to perfect our speech." We certainly have our work cut out for us. In the merit of our efforts, may we be zocheh to achieve success.

Yisro's Inspiration Can Be Ours

Yisro, the father in-law of Moshe and once the high priest of Ohn, fully embraced Judaism after having studied all of the world's religions. Since we all must try to strengthen our belief in Hashem, it would be useful for us to discover and analyze what it was that convinced Yisro to believe in Hashem and to reject all other religions.

The answer to this question is expressly stated in the posuk [*Shemos* 18:11] which quotes Yisro as saying, "*Atah yadatee ki Hashem Hu HaElokim; ki badavar asher zadu aleihem*—Now I know that Hashem is the true G-d, for that which [the Egyptians had] perpetrated [against the Jews] befell them."

After intense analysis of the ten plagues and the splitting

of the Red Sea, Yisro perceived a common thread among them. The common denominator is the attribute of Hashem's justice called middah k'neged middah. This means that Hashem rewards and punishes "measure for measure." Thus, for example, Yisro observed that the Egyptians threw Jewish babies into the Nile, filling it with Jewish blood, and causing the fish to eat Jewish children. In turn, Hashem struck the Egyptian's beloved Nile by turning it into blood, and killing the fish in the process. Similarly, the Egyptians did not allow the Jews to bathe, causing them to be infected with lice. As a consequence, Hashem afflicted the Egyptians with lice. They darkened Jews' lives with servitude, and therefore were punished with a period of impenetrable darkness. They beat the Jews; Hashem beat them with hail. They screamed at the Jews; Hashem punished them with the incessant noise of frogs and again by the tumultuous thunder that accompanied the hail. Ultimately, because of all the babies they sent to a horrific watery grave, they drowned and went to watery deaths themselves.

Since Yisro was far more than a casual observer, he noted even deeper levels of "measure for measure." For example, he realized that Pharaoh diabolically wanted to wipe his hands clean of any direct complicity in the enslavement and massacre of Jews. Therefore, he relied on Jewish taskmasters to oppress their Jewish brethren, and forced Jews to kill other Jews. He asked the Jewish midwives to abort the Jewish babies, and forced Jewish parents to throw their own babies into the water. The Nazis, y'mach shmam v'zichram, used similar tactics, employing Jewish kapos to beat their brethren. They established the "Judenrat," a council of Jewish leaders, to decide which Jews would be "relocated" to the death camps.

Thus, at the Yam Suf Hashem instructed Moshe, "*Hashem yilacheim lachem, v'atem tacharishun*—Hashem will do battle for you and you will be silent" [*Shemos* 14:14], thus forbidding the Jews to raise a hand against the Egyptians. Instead, fittingly, the Egyptians killed themselves by plunging directly to their deaths in the sea.

Yisro's observations went still deeper. He noted that the Egyptians demonstrated a total lack of gratitude to Yosef's descendants, who had preserved their grain and thus saved all the Egyptians from starvation. Measure for measure, Hashem bombarded the Egyptians with plague after plague that were directed against, and completely obliterated, the food supplies in Egypt. The plague of blood destroyed their irrigation, and during the plague of lice all the earth turned into lice, ruining all their farmland. The plague of *arov* (wild beasts) began to wipe out the crops, which were almost totally destroyed during the plaque of hail. Locusts ate the remaining vestiges. And, when it seemed that there was nothing imaginable left to do that could further disrupt the ability of Mitzrayim to produce food, the plague of darkness came and interrupted the entire process of photosynthesis.

Thus, what swayed Yisro to the monotheistic belief in Hashem above all other deities was his accurate, astute observation of the absolute consistency in each and every punishment delivered to the Egyptians. This precluded the possibility of even a remote element of chance, proving the existence of the Jewish G-d beyond a doubt. May we follow in the footsteps of Yisro, studying carefully the events of the Exodus, and through them become stronger in our belief in Hashem.

Bikur Cholim—
Comforting the Sick

The mishnah in *Pirkei Avos* [1:4] tells us that the world exists due to three things: Torah, avodah, and gemilus chassadim. Torah is the learning and studying of the Oral and Written Law. Avodah is prayer. Gemilus chassadim is kindness.

If we are properly motivated, we can readily attend to our responsibilities of Torah and avodah. We can make sure to daven everyday and set aside time to learn Torah. But what about chesed? We would all probably say that we are ready to help anyone in need. All they have to do is ask! Thus, we take care of fufilling our obligation to do chesed in an extremely haphazard manner. We should treat chesed as we do Torah and avodah. We must set aside time for it on a daily basis.

A practical area of chesed is the mitzvah of bikur cholim,

visiting the sick. The *Aruch HaShulchan* in Yoreh Deah [siman 335, seif 4] tells us that it is "*mehamitzvos hayoser gedolos*," one of the most important mitzvos. Indeed, though there are 613 mitzvahs, there are some that are greater than others, ones that the Ribbono Shel Olam Himself personally demonstrated to us. Bikur cholim is one such mitzvah.

The posuk in *Bereishis* [18:1] tells us, "*Vayeira eilov Hashem*—Hashem appeared to Avraham." But the text does not elaborate; it does not inform us that Hashem told Avraham anything at all, just that He appeared to him. Rashi elucidates that His purpose was for bikur cholim. It was the third day after Avraham Avinu had had his bris milah, when the pain is usually the most intense, so Hashem was visiting Avraham as a chesed, and so that we would learn from Him how we ourselves should behave.

A lot of us will say we just don't have the time to visit the sick. We have families, houses, and full-time jobs. How can we possibly find the time? But is there anyone busier than the Creator of the universe, Who continually wills the entire universe into existence, every second of every day? If Hashem found it important to visit a sick person, we must also find the time.

The Rewards of Bikur Cholim

There are many reasons to do this mitzvah. The Gemara in *Nedarim* [40] discusses the rewards for performing the mitzvah of bikur cholim. Perhaps we can all use the wonderful incentives the Gemara gives us to help us along. Rav tells us that whoever goes to visit the sick, "*Nitzol meidino shel Gehinnom*—will be saved from the punishment of Gehinnom." Now, we can all readily admit that we are not exactly perfect. We know we have failings and weaknesses, whether in lashon hara, kashrus, anger, or any other negative traits. We all have marks against us. And when we come before Hashem on our final day of judgment, we will not get away "scot-free." But, with this mitzvah on our side, Hashem will pay us back middah k'neged middah, measure for measure [*Shabbos* 105b]. Just as we put out the fires of sickness and fever by visiting a sick friend, so too Hashem will put out the fires of Gehinnom for us [*Maharsha*].

The reward for this mitzvah is not only in Olam Habah, however. As we say in our early morning brachos, this is one of the deeds for which we reap rewards in Olam Hazeh as well. Indeed, there are four rewards for the mitzvah of bikur cholim that Hashem promises we will reap in this world. The posuk in *Tehillim* [41:3] states that Hashem will "*Yishmireihu, v'chayeihu, v'ushor ba'aretz, v'al titnehu b'nefesh oy'vav.*" "Yishmireihu" means that Hashem will guard him. From what does a person most need protection? From the yetzer hara. When we visit a sick person, we alleviate their pain. Hashem will alleviate and quench our fires—our evil inclinations. We can see quite tangibly how visiting the sick quells our yetzer hara. Hearing someone who is quite sick reveal that he would do anything to spend just one more Shabbos with his family makes us stop and think of our own mortality. Indeed, when we see another human being on I.V., or other machinery, we take it to heart and grow fearful. When we witness a sick person up close, we can become appreciative of our lives and fearful of punishment. In *Tehillim* [41:4] says, "*Ashrei maskil el dol*—Fortunate is the one who visits the sick with wisdom." One who visits the sick learns an invaluable lesson and gains a strong weapon against the yetzer hara.

"Vichayeihu" means that Hashem will give the person

life. What kind of life? A life free of yesurim, suffering. Just as we alleviate the suffering of the choleh, Hashem will alleviate our suffering.

"V'ushar b'aretz" means that the person will be upright in the land. The Gemara describes this reward as "shehakol miskabdin bo." He will be so venerated that people will feel honored just to be associated with him. When we visit the sick, we are giving them honor and respect. We are showing them that they are worth the time and effort we are taking. Measure for measure, Hashem will grant us the respect of our neighbors.

The last reward we receive, "v'al titneihu b'nefesh oy'vav," is something we all value highly—namely, true friends. When Hashem sees that we exhibit true friendship by taking time out from our busy schedules to perform the often depressing and frustrating mitzvah of visiting the sick, he rewards us in kind by giving us true friends whom we can always count on.

R' Akiva Eiger, zt"l, (who was of course very busy with the study of Torah) used to visit people in the hospital every day. He would inquire about their health; he would discuss their cases with their doctors; he would research new medical procedures. And on days when he could not get to the hospital himself, he would hire two people to go there for him and tell them that R' Akiva Eiger was checking up on them.

Bikur cholim is an astonishingly uplifting experience. The Torah tells us that Hashem remains by the bed of a sick person. Therefore, the Gemara tells us, we should not go visit someone when we are shabbily dressed. We should make sure our appearance is presentable, for when we go to visit the sick, we stand in Hashem's presence. Of course, we all know Hashem is everywhere, but the Shechinah is more concentrated in the area of someone who is sick. This is why it is better to pray for a choleh at his or her bedside—because the Shechinah is right there. And when you daven at the bedside, it can be in any language, whereas when you daven elsewhere it is ideally supposed to be in lashon hakodesh, in Hebrew.

Wishing Someone a Refuah Shelaimah

When we tell the sick to have a "refuah shelaimah," what are we wishing them? That they should feel better. But who are we to tell them to feel better? In fact, the *Shulchan Aruch* in *Yoreh Deah* [siman 335, seif 6] tells us that the proper wording is really, "*HaMakom yerachem alecha b'soch shaar cholei Yisroel.*" However, this wording sounds too much like the wording used to be *menachem aveilim*, to comfort mourners. We certainly don't want to inadvertently scare the sick person. So nowadays we use a different formula, namely, "have a refuah shelaimah." This term, however, is missing an important ingredient. For not only do *we* wish that the ill person get better, we are really expressing the wish and prayer that *Hashem* cure the person quickly and completely.

We see an illustration of this from the following story. R' Tzvi Kluger once went to visit the Belzer Rebbe, zt"l, when he was sick. As he was leaving, he wished him a refuah shelaimah. The Belzer Rebbe stopped him and said that it is more proper to say, "The *Eibishter* should send a refuah shelaimah." He was emphasizing that we should really mention Hashem's name when we wish someone a refuah shelaimah. So let's get in the habit of saying, "May Hashem bless you with a refuah shelaimah b'soch shaar cholei Yisroel (among the other sick Jewish people)."

The reason that the *Shulchan Aruch* uses the wording,

"*B'soch shaar cholei Yisroel*," is because, if we put the sick person together with all the other sick people in Klal Yisroel, there is a greater chance for refuah because the many are answered more quickly than an individual.

On Shabbos, however, we say something different. The correct formula is, "*Shabbos hi m'lizok urefuah krova lavo*—though Shabbos prevents us from crying out, may healing come quickly." Since Shabbos is a day of rest from crying and complaining, we ask that, in the merit of our maintaining a happy mind-set in honor of the Shabbos, the refuah should come. The commentators tell us that the reason we don't simply wish someone to have a refuah shelaimah on Shabbos is that, if the healing doesn't begin right away, then the statement would be considered *hachana*, preparation, for after Shabbos. Shabbos itself, however, has an intrinsic ability to heal us. The root word of *refuah* is *rapei*, to heal. The numerical value of *rapei* is equal to that of Shabbos, thus indicating that Shabbos has tremendous healing powers.

Smart Bikur Cholim

According to the *Kitzur Shulchan Aruch* [siman 193, seif 3], the mitzvah of bikur cholim is actually a three-part commandment. The first part of the mitzvah is to investigate. The word "bikur" means to examine, to discover the needs of the afflicted person. Indeed, no two sick people have precisely the same needs. The Gemara in *Nedarim* [40a] tells us that R' Akiva used to go to a sick person's house and sweep the floors and sprinkle air freshener. In this respect, bikur cholim is a perfect mitzvah for women, who often know best what needs to be done when someone becomes incapacitated.

The Slobodka Rosh Yeshivah, R' Isaac Sher, zt"l, once

met a man in the street carrying a plate of food for a choleh. The man, feeling it improper to meet the Rav with his hands full of food, tried to hide it. When R' Sher asked him what it was and heard the explanation, he informed the man that he should proudly carry this meal, as it is comparable to carrying a lulav and esrog.

R' Gottlieb of Yerushalayim once went to visit a sick man and asked him if he needed a loan. The man broke down and said that many people had come to visit him to make him feel better, but this offer was just what he needed, for it addressed his most prevalent worry. Now he would no longer have to worry where the mortgage payments would come from. We must investigate what the person needs, whether it is a home-cooked meal, money, a baby-sitter, or simple companionship. We must use our seichel, our common sense, when it comes to this mitzvah.

There is a halacha that you should not visit a person who has a bowel disorder. This is so the person will not be embarrassed by having to excuse himself each time he must leave to use the restroom. From this we learn an important lesson. In general, you should not visit a person if you will make him or her uncomfortable. The purpose of bikur cholim is to cheer the person up. If by visiting them you will make them uncomfortable, don't go. If a woman does not like to be seen without makeup, or she is embarrassed by her appearance, or she doesn't want people to see her in that horrible hospital gown, then do not visit her. Your visit will only cause more distress and will not improve the patient's spirits. That is certainly no mitzvah.

There are stories of gedolim who brought chess sets to people in the hospital and played a game with them. They talked sports. When my daughter was in the hospital once, one wonderful couple brought my daughter a bubble machine so that she would do her breathing exercises. This is "smart" bikur cholim. Find out what the person or family *really* needs.

Offering Companionship

The second requirement of this mitzvah is companionship. However, we must offer proper companionship. Some people go to visit a sick person merely out of a feeling of obligation. Although they perform the mitzvah, they do so without emotion, without compassion. They sit for ten minutes and then leave, without giving much to the person, without really being there. It is many times appallingly obvious that they came merely out of duty, because they felt they had to. We must let a sick person know that we care, that we hurt for him or her. A person can tell whether someone is visiting out of friendship or out of guilt or obligation. When you go to visit someone, tell him how much he is missed at work. Tell her how the house is not up to its normal standard. Don't tell them everything is fine. This might sound like a wonderful thing to do, but it makes a person feel un-needed, like everyone can get along without them.

Praying for Recovery

The third part of bikur cholim is davening for the recovery of the person. All the time you took out to visit the hospital—the time you spent with the person, the wonderful food you brought—will leave the mitzvah incomplete unless you pray for his or her recovery. And if you daven at their bedside, that is even better, as we mentioned above.

In addition, the *Rama* in the *Shulchan Aruch* [*Yoreh Deah* 335, seif 10], citing the Gemara, tells us that if someone we know is sick, we should not hesitate to go to a chochom and ask him to pray for that person. Whether a Rebbe, a Rosh Yeshivah, or a well-known tzadik, we should seek someone out and ask him to daven on behalf of our friend.

Many people are not sure whether or not to visit a person in a coma. The halacha is that you should go—and there are three reasons. The first is that the person is defenseless. He or she is at the mercy of the hospital staff. The nurses are caring people, of course, but they certainly give more attention to some patients than to others. Those who are constantly receiving visitors will receive the best treatment, for the nurses and other staff will want to make a good impression. Another reason is that, by actually *seeing* a person in that condition, you will pray for him or her more sincerely. And the third reason is that you will be able to pray for the person in the presence of the Shechinah, which is always at the bedside of a sick person.

A Mitzvah Without Limit

The mitzvah of bikur cholim does not have a prescribed amount. The Gemara [*Nedarim* 39b] tells us it is possible to do it a hundred times a day. This is not an exaggeration by any means. If someone ever had to take care of an elderly parent or grandparent, they can understand how it would be possible to help someone a hundred times a day. A person should also try to be sensitive about when to leave. Do not overstay your welcome; try to recognize when the patient wants to be left alone.

The halacha [*Yoreh Deah* siman 335, seif 9] states that it is a mitzvah to visit a non-Jewish sick person also, in order to prevent hatred. So the next time you visit someone in the hospital and there is someone in the next bed, turn to them and tell them you hope they feel better too. This is not just a mitzvah of bikur cholim; it's a kiddush Hashem as well!

R' Aryeh Levin used to go to the nurses' station and ask them which patients had not received many visitors. He would spend most of his time with those lonely patients. It is a terrific idea to find out if there is someone from out-of-town in a hospital. This person is likely not to have many visitors. R' Zelig Pliskin recommends that if we see a person does not have many people coming to see him, we should visit and encourage others to do the same.

The *Igros Moshe* and the *Pachad Yitzchok* both state that if you simply cannot get to the hospital, a phone call is considered fulfilling the mitzvah as well.

I once had occasion to call a friend who had been sick for a couple of weeks. He was glad to hear from me and told me that I was one of the first to call him. We should not be fooled into thinking that "everyone else is visiting or calling." It's best to be aggressive in this mitzvah and not wait.

When we hear a siren wailing, our thought should be, "I hope Hashem sends a refuah shelaimah." We should not view sirens as an annoyance and nuisance, but as an opportunity to pray for another human being in distress.

When my daughter was sick and in the hospital for six weeks, my wife and I were there alternately around the clock. One Erev Shabbos, ten minutes before licht bentchen, a family came in to deliver a full thermos of hot soup. They waited until the last minute before bringing it, because they wanted me to enjoy the food hot! Indeed, that soup gave me strength to deal with my beloved daughter and the doctors all

Shabbos. It is important to offer help to the support system of the patient. Helping their family is also part of the mitzvah. The Vizhnitzer Rebbe said that is why in the Shemoneh Esrei we say, "*Rofeh cholim u'matir asurim*—Who heals the sick and releases the bound," together. When Hashem heals the sick, He is setting the family free from the burden as well.

If we are faithful in this mitzvah, we will be rewarded greatly. "*Hashem tzilcha al yad yeminecha*—Hashem is like a shadow on your right hand" [*Tehillim* 121:5]. What is the attribute of a shadow? It imitates whatever it is a shadow of. So too, if we carry out this mitzvah properly, Hashem will reward us middah k'neged middah. As the posuk testifies, "*Ashray maskil el dal b'yom raah y'malteihu Hashem*—Fortunate is he who deals wisely with the needy; in his time of trouble Hashem will save him!" In the merit of this glorious mitzvah may we always be blessed with good health and everything wonderful.

Avoiding Conflict

The Gemara in *Gittin* relates that once there was an exceptional Torah scholar by the name of Genivah. When he entered the yeshivah, an odd thing happened. The head of the academy silently motioned to his disciples that they should not stand up for him. This would seem to have been a breech of Torah law, since we are instructed [*Vayikra* 19:34], "*V'hodarta p'nei zakein,*" to revere a Torah Sage. As we have mentioned elsewhere, "*zakein*" is an acronym for "*zeh kana chachmah,*" one who has acquired much Torah knowledge. Later on, the Rosh Yeshivah explained that, since Genivah was a quarrelsome person, he didn't deserve the respect that standing up for him would have shown.

However, there is one obvious question: Doesn't everyone have some fault? After all, we are taught, "*Ki Adam ein tzadik ba-aretz asher ya-aseh tov v'lo yechetah*—There is no righteous person in this world who does only good without any sinning" [*Koheles* 7:20]. Therefore, we would think that they should have shown reverence to Genivah for his Torah sagacity, notwithstanding his fault of being argumentative.

The explanation, however, is one that is a major fundamental of Torah living. The Rambam teaches us, "*Kol HaTorah nitnah la-asos shalom b'olam—all* of the 613 mitzvos were given with the aim of creating peace and harmony in the world." As the verse states, "*Deracheha darchei noam, v'chol nesivoseha shalom*—The Torah's ways are ways of sweetness and all its paths are paths of peace" [*Mishlei* 3:17]. We show Torah respect only to those who have absorbed their Torah, making it part of their being and practicing its teachings. The *Chovos Halevavos* [*Shaar Avodas Elokim*, 84] refers to one who just studies without practicing as a "*Chamor nosei seforim*—A donkey bearing books." Or, in a more contemporary vein, we might refer to such a person as "a glorified seforim shrank (bookshelf)."

Thus, the head of the academy indicated that since Genivah was not a man of peace, it was a sign that he had not absorbed properly enough the Torah he had learned. For if he had absorbed the Torah, it would inevitably have transformed him into an ambassador of tranquility. Thus, he was not yet deserving of Torah respect.

We are taught, "*Talmidei chachomim marbim shalom b'olam*—Torah scholars increase peace in the world" [*Brachos* 64a]. So to qualify as a true "ben Torah," one has to be a champion for peace. Whether it is in the home with one's spouse, dealing with one's parents and in-laws, or any other inter-personal relationships, a Torah personality practices the pursuit of peace at all times. He acts to squelch any beginnings of feud in the synagogue. He is never the one making a tumult by stirring the pot of rumors and controversy amongst others. He is always on the lookout for compromise and reconciliation and never involved in finger-pointing and meddlesome gossip.

With this in mind, it behooves us to impress upon our children that to learn in yeshivah and then fight with their friends at recess, or act with disdain for their English teachers, is an absolute contradiction to that which they are supposed to accomplish through their Torah study. Stressing these ideas will help to ensure that, when our children grow up, they will be prepared to be gentle and compassionate husbands and wives. If they are raised with a passion for shalom, it will serve to protect them from the tremendous misery of marital strife and divorce.

When we notice a quarrel or feud, we should point out (if it is already out in the open) that this is definitely *not* the Torah way and that we should always stay far away from such behavior. The character trait of shalom is the greatest inner strength that one can acquire, for we see that the verse equates might with peace. As it says in *Tehillim* [29:11], "*Hashem oz l'amo yitein, Hashem yevorech es amo vashalom*— Hashem will give strength to His nation; Hashem will bless Yisroel with peace."

May we always merit, for ourselves and our loved ones, peace of mind, peace with the family, peace for Klal Yisroel, and the ultimate peace of the coming of Moshiach speedily in our days.

Sleep Secrets

In *Yad Hachazakah* [*Hilchos Deos* 4:4], the Rambam tells us that the average person should sleep eight hours each night. For many of us in modern America, this is unfortunately a pipe dream. However, this statement of the Rambam brings to our attention an incredible reality—approximately one third of our lives should be spent sleeping. There is almost nothing else we can point to and say we do as consistently throughout our lives. Obviously, then, it would be fitting for us to learn the Torah approach to sleeping, so that after 120 years, when we appear before Hashem for our final judgment, we will be able to say, "At least give me credit for this third of my life." Let's see how we can all acquire at least thirty-three percent of our Olam Habah!

The Sanzer Rav, the *Divrei Chaim*, zt"l, used to eat whole morror at each Pesach seder. One year, the Rav's personal physician advised him not to do so, as his heart was not strong enough. In light of the physician's warning, thousands of people watched with anticipation at the seder. With morror before him on the seder plate, the *Divrei Chaim* started to make a brachah. All assumed that he was going to bite into the morror, despite the danger to his life. But the brachah the Rav made was "*Asher kiddishonu b'mitzvosov v'tzivonu lishmor es hanefesh*—Who has sanctified us through mitzvos, and commanded us with the mitzvah of guarding our lives." (This bracha is not made nowadays.) Then he put the morror down. He said, "*Rabosai*—this year I'm fulfilling a bigger mitzvah of morror than ever before. Until now it was only *mi-d'rabbonan* (a rabbinical decree)—but this year it is a *d'oraysah* (a commandment from the Torah) of '*V'nishmartem m'od l'nafshose-ichem*,'—to vigilantly guard our lives" [*Devarim* 4:15].

Let us try to regard our sleep in such a lofty manner as well! In addition to teaching us that sleep is important to our health and our bodies, the Rambam is teaching us something else: We know that our livelihood is fixed from the beginning of the year. How much we are going to earn is already written in the Heavenly books from Rosh Hashanah. Overdoing it will not glean us any added extra benefits. On the other hand, we also cannot say, "All right, if the amount I'm going to make has already been decided, I'll take a long vacation and buy a lottery ticket." It just doesn't work that way. We must make the proper hishtadlus (effort), with the emphasis on the word "proper." When R' Moshe Feinstein, zt"l, came to America in 1937, there was a big nisayon (test) for people at that time. They couldn't get jobs unless they worked on Shabbos. In his droshos (speeches), he would say, "We must understand that if we work on Shabbos, we will not make an extra penny, because what we will earn has already been determined on Rosh Hashanah. We have to make the proper hishtadlus, but working on Shabbos, chas v'shalom, is not considered proper hishtadlus. That won't bring us an extra cent."

Accordingly, if the Rambam tells us that the proper thing to do is sleep eight hours each night, behaving like a workaholic to bring in extra money is not considered proper hishtadlus, as it is detrimental to a person's health. It won't bring us more money, even though we might think it will.

Sleep is a tremendous gift, but it can also be a terrible yetzer hara. There is a fascinating midrash in the beginning of the Torah. Before creating woman from man, Hashem first anesthetized Man. "*Vayapel Hashem tardemah al Ha'adam*—Hashem caused a deep sleep to descend upon Adam" [*Bereishis* 4:21]. R' Yehoshua says in the name of R' Levi that this is the first time the term "vayapel" (a descent, or fall) is mentioned in the Torah. It is noteworthy that the Torah's first mention of a downfall is connected to sleep. R' Yehoshua thus concludes that the beginning of a man's downfall is through sleep.

When a person is asleep, he is neither learning Torah nor earning a livelihood for his family. Note that the word "tardemah" contains the letters of both "mes" (death) and "reid" (downfall). Similarly, the other word for sleep, "tenumah" also contains the word mes. We also know from the Gemara [*Brachos* 17b] that sleep is considered to be one sixtieth of death. So clearly we must be wary of sleep. The mishnah in *Pirkei Avos* [3:9] warns us that oversleeping and missing Shacharis is one of the things that propels a person from this world.

Shulchan Aruch can be a powerful mussar sefer if it is learned properly. In *Shulchan Aruch* [*Orach Chaim* siman 4, seif 18], we learn that one who gets up from sleep must wash his hands. We wash because the hands move during sleep, and touch certain parts of the body that are normally covered.

However, we also wash our hands because they are "tomeh," or spiritually impure. When we wash our hands for "tumah," there is a special way to do it: we wash three times alternately [*Orach Chaim*, siman 4, seif 4]. Why, upon arising, is one considered to be "tameh?" It is because when we go to sleep and our neshama rises to Hashem, our body consists solely of "gashmius," of physicality, and that is considered to be "tameh." The purpose of life is the "ruchnius,"—the spirituality—the tefillos, the chesed, the tzedakah, and all the other good things we do. At night when our body is in a state of sleep, there is only material, without the spirituality. (This, by the way, is why we don't follow the custom of some Non-Jews who have "wakes" for the dead, laying the deceased in an open casket and passing by it to say "good-bye." We don't want to look at a person without a neshama.)

It is an important point to know that when we go to sleep our neshama ascends. Another term for sleep is "sheinah," consisting of—"nash," (switching around the letters "nun" and "shin") which means going, and "kah," which is one of the names of G-d—thus, a person's soul goes to G-d. The *Chayei Adam* brings down from the *Zohar* that every night a person's neshama goes up to be judged. It is easy to understand, then, why the *Mishnah Brurah* [*Orach Chaim*, siman 239, seif katan 9] teaches us that before going to sleep, we should each make a cheshbon hanefesh, a spiritual accounting, of that day's activities, and realize that we are going before the *Kisei Hakovod*, Hashem's holy throne. In this way, we can resolve to rectify what we have done, and Hashem will judge us favorably and gladly return our souls for another day.

Before retiring for the night, the Chofetz Chaim says that we should especially go over the common sins we may have committed, like lying. Did we lie to our boss, our spouse, or our employee? Did we speak lashon hara or indulge in *leitzonus* (scoffing)? Were we lax in observing kashrus? Did we waste valuable time that could have been devoted to learning Torah? Were we insensitive to our spouse, or our siblings? It is also important, says the Chofetz Chaim, to forgive those who may have offended us. We should never bring a complaint about anyone to bed with us. We must learn to forgive. We are going before the Ribbono Shel Olom to be judged; what better way to prepare than to forgive others?

Now, if this is true with everyone, it is especially true with husband and wife. People who came from Europe would advise their children, "Tateleh, mameleh, when you get married, never go to sleep angry at your spouse—even if it means not going to sleep until late at night."

If we want shalom to reign in our homes, and if we want the Shechinah guarding over us, there must be shalom between husbands and wives.

These are the proper steps to prepare for sleep. When a Jew goes to sleep, we do not just "zap out." Since we are going to face the Ribbono Shel Olom, we want to be prepared. Every time we sleep it's like a "mini-Yom Kippur." If we discover a personal shortcoming, we should say "Vidui" and make a commitment to change.

The Shelah Hakadosh brings down from the Rama that before going to sleep we should kiss the mezuzah, which is a sign of Hashem's protection. Nighttime is a time of danger. In the daytime, when a person has his neshama within him, this "ruchnius," this spirituality, protects him. At night, though, we lack this protection, and we must seek protection in other ways. It is also a good suggestion to give tzedakah before going to sleep, as it says, "I with righteousness see your face." In other words, my soul goes to greet Hashem only after giving tzedakah.

The Ribbono Shel Olom could have created us so that we wouldn't need to sleep for eight hours, but He didn't. He wants us to sleep, but we have to use sleep positively. We know that if we eat on Erev Yom Kippur, and then fast on Yom Kippur, it's as if we fasted for two days, because we have prepared for the mitzvah the way Hashem wants us to prepare. Similarly, we can use our sleep to prepare for performing the next day's mitzvahs, and thereby transform sleep into a mitzvah. Our intention as we go to sleep could be, for example: "I'm going to sleep to have the energy to learn Torah tomorrow." "I'm taking a nap so that I can better perform the mitzvah of hachnasas orchim, welcoming guests." By using sleep this way we have converted one third of our lives into time spent preparing for mitzvos. A Yiddishe mother realizes that she is sometimes short-tempered due to lack of sleep. She should say, "I'm going to sleep so that I will be better rested to take care of my family, so that I can promote shalom bayis and fulfill all the mitzvos." This is using sleep positively.

Sleep on Shabbos is special, for it contributes to our delight from Shabbos. When we nap on Shabbos, we fulfill the "menuchah," the resting aspect of Shabbos that is inherent in it from the time of Creation.

It is immensely important to recite the brachah of "Hamapil" before falling asleep. Some people worry about there being a "hefsek," an interruption, and thus are afraid to make the brachah. They worry about the events of the day, and fear that they may not fall asleep immediately. A woman may be concerned that her husband will come home and want to talk to her after she has made the brachah.

Nevertheless, we all must try our best to always recite this brachah. Says the *Divrei Chaim*, "Going to sleep without Birchas Hamapil is like eating without making a brachah." R' Meyer from Premishlan said that if a pregnant woman says Hamapil, it will guard against miscarriage. We say birchas hamapil to thank Hashem for the great gift of sleep, which reenergizes us. If troubling thoughts disturb us, this brachah can help us. Great care should be taken to say birchas Hamapil prior to going to sleep. It should be learned by heart and said as close as possible to the moment of actual sleep.

Finally, I recommend that once or twice a year we should get up to say Tikun Chatzos, the special prayers for the middle of the night in which we mourn the fact that we no longer have the Beis Hamikdash, the holy Temple in Jeruslem. It doesn't even have to be the entire Tikun. As the *Kitzur Shulchan Aruch* says, "Better a little with kavanah than a lot without!" Perhaps when we come home late after a simcha, it would be a good opportunity to say this special tefillah. It will exert a tremendous influence on your children if they witness you saying this special tefillah.

May the Ribbono Shel Olom grant us good sleep and good health, so that we will be able to serve Him properly and with vigor.

Fleeing From Sin

"**H**ayam ra'ah vayanos—The sea saw and fled" [*Tehillim* 114:3]. This verse refers to krias Yam Suf, the miracle of the splitting of the Red Sea, one of the most momentous events of all time and something that we herald every day in our prayers. But what does it mean? Fled from what? Fled from whom? A little-known medrash asks exactly this question. There, the answer is given: It fled from one who fled. Or, more precisely, it fled *because* of one who fled.

To whom is this referring? The medrash answers: It refers to Yosef, when he was being tempted by Potifar's wife, whose name was Zeluchia. She was, we are told, a fabulously beautiful woman. However, the Medrash tells us that Yosef's temptation was of a spiritual nature.

There is actually a difference of opinion in the Midrash whether the woman Yosef later married, Osnas, was really the daughter of Dina and Shechem (the opinion with which most of us are familiar), or whether she was actually the daughter of Potifar and Zeluchia. According to the latter opinion, Yosef Hatzadik felt an attraction to Potifar's family because he knew his bashert, his destined bride, was in the family! And it was quite possible, within this context, that Zeluchia might be his bashert. He didn't know that his bashert was really her daughter. Thus, there was a spiritual attraction pulling him toward Zeluchia.

So what did Yosef do when, one day, he found himself alone with her and she tempted him, trying to seduce him? He fled, leaving his torn-off clothing, and he went outside. Then the medrash tells us rather cryptically, "The sea saw and fled, it saved Yisroel and buried the Mitzriyim. *Nos mipnei hanos*—It fled because of the one who fled."

We see that the saving of Klal Yisroel from the hands of the Egyptians was not in the merit of Moshe, or Aharon, or Miriam, or even the millions of Jews who went through the *kur habarzel*, the "iron furnace" of Mitzrayim. Rather, it was only because Yosef fled from sin that Klal Yisroel was saved at the Yam Suf.

Let's look at this a little more closely. There is a famous question by the Ramban. Yosef's behavior, in leaving his cloak in the possession of Potifar's wife, makes no sense. Why did he leave such damaging evidence in her hands? After all, the Ramban points out, which of the two of them was stronger? Don't forget that Yosef was one of the twelve shvatim, one of the *shivtei kah*, and he had super-human strength! When Yehudah threatened Yosef, "If you don't watch out, I'll wipe out all of Mitzrayim," he still sensed a power emanating from Yosef that terrified him. Are we to believe, then, that Yosef was physically incapable of getting his clothing back from Potifar's wife? Why would he leave the most incriminating possible evidence in her hands?

The answer, according to the Ramban, was that hakoras hatov (gratitude) overcame Yosef. How could he wrench something out of Potifar's wife's hand? He was so indebted to his master for giving him a new life, and for giving him the responsibility of running his house, that it would have been wrong for him to fight with his master's wife, even under these circumstances. So, because of hakoras hatov he risked everything, putting himself in jeopardy.

Others take a different approach. They say, quite logically and quite simply, that Yosef didn't have a moment to spare because he heard Potifar, the master of the house, coming into the room. He was therefore caught in a dilemma and he ran out as quickly as possible. The question remains, however: If he left his clothing there, what did he accomplish in getting out as quickly as possible? With the evidence in her hands, he was as good as caught. Perhaps he hoped that she wouldn't accuse him.

But R' Chaim Shmulevitz, zt"l, offers a fascinating interpretation. He says that Yosef saw that he was in a situation where he was clearly being tempted; it was a situation where sin abounded. There was literally sin in the room! At any moment he might succumb to his yetzer hara, his evil inclination. It is precisely because of this moment and incident that he's called Yosef Hatzadik. He said, "Sin is here! I can't afford to spend even another minute in this room and, whatever the consequences, I must leave immediately." So, R' Chaim Shmulevitz says, Yosef knew that by leaving his clothing there he was going to get himself into a lot of trouble. But he also knew that if he stayed there any longer, he might not be able to overcome his yetzer hara, so he chose to distance himself from the aveira (sin) as quickly as possible. He didn't waste a second, so that he would be sure not to succumb to his yetzer hara.

This, R' Chaim Shmulevitz says, is the test of distancing ourselves from sin—"*Harchokas ha'adam min ha'aveira.*" Having a life infused with holiness means sometimes denying ourselves even permitted things if we suspect they're going to make us vulnerable to sin. We must search out and address our weak spots.

One might think that the concept of separation from that which is permitted so that one should not be tempted to sin is a *middas chassidus*, that it is only for extraordinarily pious individuals, and not relevant to the average person. But the Gemara in *Bava Basra* [57b] tells us otherwise. It asserts that if someone has a choice and goes in the direction of sin anyway, in spite of the fact that he shuts his eyes and resists temptation, he is considered a rasha because he made himself vulnerable to sin. This Gemara underscores the importance of not placing ourselves in circumstances of vulnerability to sin.

The Gemara in *Avodah Zarah* [17] emphasizes this point. It tells us that R' Chanina and R' Yochanan were once traveling on a road when they reached a fork. One road led to a place of avodah zarah (idolatry); the other road led to a place of *z'nus* (immorality). One suggested to the other that they choose the path that led past the place of idolatry, since G-d had already removed the yetzer hara for idolatry from the world. The other countered that, on the contrary, they should choose the other path and test their yetzer hara, in order to earn more reward for overcoming the temptation to sin. The Gemara concludes that the first opinion was correct, because you can never be sure that you will be victorious over your yetzer hara. Perhaps your yetzer hara will defeat you.

The Gemara in *Sanhedrin* [107] states clearly that a person should never bring himself/herself to be tested. The Ribbono Shel Olam can test us by putting us into various situations; we are assured of ample opportunities for us to prove ourselves. We must not seek out situations to test ourselves, lest the yetzer hara overcome us. Finally, our davening also reflects this thought. Every day we pray in Birchas Hashachar, "*V'al tivi'eynu lo lidei nisayon, v'lo lidei vizayon*—Do not bring us to tests or disgrace."

Now let's return to our discussion about Yosef fleeing from Potiphar's wife. If you think of it, had he not left his clothing in the hands of Potiphar's wife, Yosef Hatzadik would never have become viceroy of Mitzrayim. After all, his act of fleeing from sin set in motion the chain of events that led to his eventual rise to greatness. His subsequent imprisonment is what led to Yosef's interpreting the dreams of Pharaoh's two ministers while in prison and ultimately to interpreting the dreams of Pharaoh himself.

While all that is true, nevertheless, the Ramban says in his famous *Iggeres* that, for a Torah discussion to be meaningful, we must derive from it something that will positively affect our lives. Simply put, we learn in order to *do*. As we say in Aleinu, "*V'yodata hayom v'hasheivosa el livovecha*—You should know today and you should bring it into your heart" [*Devarim* 4:39]. This second step, bringing it to our hearts, internalizing intellectual concepts, is the difficult part. We can only achieve this by asking ourselves how we can apply these lessons to our own lives?

Following are some examples of how we can "flee from sin":

1. We should not travel too close to the start of Shabbos. Who knows when there could be a sudden traffic jam? Who

can foresee if a sudden downpour will flood the roads and cause accidents? Here is a perfect example of "*harchakas haadam min ha-aveira.*" By leaving enough time for travel erev Shabbos, we are doing our best to arrive in plenty of time, even if unexpected problems arise. Whenever I hear that on erev Shabbos there will be snow and especially if there will be freezing rain, I raise the alarm in my congregation that those who need to travel should leave early. All it takes is one accident on the highway in such weather to cause a person to be late for Shabbos!

2. In the aforementioned Gemara, the two Amoraim were talking about passing a street with a beis zonos; there wasn't even a risk of seeing actual sin, only passing the place of it! Similarly, we must consider the possible effects of unsupervised media which as we know can be terribly decadent and immoral, in our homes. Is allowing these influences into our homes being "marchik min haaveira?" Some of the magazines nowadays are quite literally a "beis zonah," a house full of immorality!

3. When we go to socialize, if there is a person who indulges in what he or she calls "healthy gossip" and we know it is definitely (or even possibly) lashon hara, we must remember to distance ourselves from sin by distancing ourselves from such company. Another wise way to prevent sin is to refrain from sitting next to people who constantly lure you into talking during davening!

4. It is interesting to note that the Gemara does not give us a specific a formula for shalom bayis. Why is there no detailed advice regarding such an important topic? Actually, a Rav might give completely different advice to different couples, for what is appropriate for one couple may be totally inappropriate for another. To know what to stay away from,

we have to know ourselves and understand our weak spots. If there are areas in our marriages which often generate arguments and disagreements we would be wise to learn what they are and avoid them even before trouble starts to brew!

In the final analysis, we must ask ourselves what our own mindset is. Do we think, "What does the *Shulchan Aruch* say? Is it mutar (permitted) or is it assur (forbidden)?" If that is the approach we take, we must be mindful that there is something called a "novul birshus haTorah," which is someone who manages to be disgusting even within the limits of the Law. We must do some serious introspection in order to understand our own unique yetzer haras. By knowing ourselves, and the nature of our weaknesses, we can more diligently be *marchik min haaveira* and more successfully prevent ourselves from actually sinning.

May we succeed in this crucial area of life and merit the help of Hashem in this and all our endeavors.

Living Eternally
Through Our Deeds

Parshas Noach opens with the following statement: "*Eila toldos Noach; Noach ish tzadik, tomim*...—These are the offspring of Noach; Noach was a mentsch, righteous, and unblemished..." The question leaps out at us! When the Torah starts with "these are the offspring," we expect the follow-up to be his three children, Sheim, Cham, and Yafes. Why instead does the Torah follow with a volley of accolades about Noach himself?

Rashi [*Bereishis* 6:9] answers this question with a novel idea, saying that the Torah is teaching us that the primary offspring of a righteous person are his or her good deeds. R' Moshe Feinstein, zt"l, in his monumental work *Dorash Moshe*, wonders why the Torah chooses "offspring" as a metaphor for man's relationship with his good deeds. Why aren't they described as his accomplishments, achievements or merits? Isn't "offspring" a biological description?

He goes on to explain that the Torah is revealing to us two incredibly important attitudes and approaches that we should have towards the good deeds we do. Firstly, he says that the Torah wants us to feel for our *ma'asim tovim*, our good deeds, the same love that we feel for our children. We should not undertake to perform such mitzvos as visiting the sick, comforting the mourner, and attending a funeral, merely out of a sense of duty and commitment, but rather we should do all these things from a feeling of true love.

Secondly, R' Moshe enlightens us that, just as a dedicated parent is always trying to improve their children, to make them better, kinder, more compassionate and more beautiful, so too we should constantly try to upgrade the quality of our mitzvos. We should always strive to learn how to fulfill them in better, finer, and more beautiful ways. Whether it is concentrating more deeply on our prayers, bentching licht with more kavanah, reciting kiddush more sweetly, making sure to have a lovely tallis, or sharpening our chesed skills, the comparison of good deeds to offspring is there to teach us how the pursuit of refinement of our mitzvos parallels closely our dedication to the bettering of our children.

I would like to add some other suggestions as to why the Torah refers to good deeds as our offspring. It is obvious that the development of our offspring comes about through the *joint* cooperation of husband and wife. The Torah is teaching us that, similarly, the right way to do good deeds is with husband and wife working together. It is not a "good" deed when a person helps others at the expense of his or her spouse.

Furthermore, just like offspring beget further generations, so too do the good deeds of the righteous generate further good deeds in the world, in a chain that stretches into eternity. When a tzadik stands up for the elderly, it encourages, or "gives birth to," such a practice by those who see him do it. Similarly, when someone generously responds to an appeal, it creates an impulse in others to do the same.

Yet another way to understand the analogy between good deeds and offspring is the work and effort that should be expended in bringing a mitzvah to fruition. Just as a child emerges in the world only after nine difficult months of gestation and the pains of labor and delivery, so, too, much effort is often needed when trying to do a mitzvah in the proper way.

One might wonder why Rashi calls good deeds the "primary" offspring of a tzadik. After all, what about his children? Are they relegated to secondary status? Why didn't Rashi simply say that good deeds are *also* considered offspring? I believe that the answer is as follows: A tzadik's children are not exclusively his own products. Rather, they are the synthesis of his genes together with his wife's and the genetic coding of many of their ancestors. Furthermore, when the child reaches the age of intellect, he or she has his own bechirah (free will) and, as such, is not a pure product of his father's actions anymore. On the other hand, the good deeds that a righteous person fulfills are exclusively a product of his own making and remain so eternally.

Yet one more question needs to be addressed. If a person's good deeds are considered only his offspring, what constitutes his essence? I would like to suggest that his intrinsic essence is his study of Torah. As we say in Maariv, "*Ki heim chayeinu*—The Torah is our life."

May Hashem help us to live up to all of these lessons and, in that merit, may we enjoy both our spiritual and biological offspring all the days of our life.

What Goes Around Comes Around

A fundamental principle of life that the Torah teaches us from its start is the theme of middah k'neged middah, the method with which Hashem exercises justice, rewarding and punishing "measure for measure."

For example, the snake, who tempted Chava to indulge in the forbidden fruit by enticing her with reports of its awesome taste was punished with the decree, "*Ofer tochal kol yomei chaiyecha*—You shall eat dust all the days of your life" [*Bereishis* 3:14]. At first glance this is puzzling since, if you visit the zoo, you will find that the snakes are given strips of meat and not the contents of a flowerpot. Rather, the meaning of the curse is that Hashem punished the snake by taking away its taste buds. Thus, everything tastes like earth to him. See how the punishment matches the crime? He doomed mankind through the incentive of taste and therefore lost the ability to taste for all time. Similarly, through the snake's actions, he condemned man to die and return to the earth. Therefore his legs were permanently amputated and his fate was to always slither and hug the earth which he caused man to be buried in.

By causing Chava to sin and entice her husband, the snake created a wedge that would cause Adam and Chava to separate for a hundred and thirty years. Therefore, he was punished that mankind would loathe him eternally.

Let's now turn to Adam. The Chasam Sofer points out that Adam acted submissively to Chava, who was created from him. When she tried to convince him to sin, he allowed himself to be swayed. He was therefore punished measure for measure that he would have to be submissive to where *he* came from, namely the earth. Thus he was punished with the curse of thorns and thistles erupting from the ground and the accompanying toil and labor which would now be required to earn his daily bread.

When we come to the punishment of Chava, we find that not only was she guilty of poisoning her husband with the forbidden fruit but also, according to certain opinions, of giving the fruit to Kayin and Hevel as well. By exhibiting this lack of concern for her husband and children, she was punished with the decree of, "*V'hu yimshol boch*—He will rule over you" [*Bereishis* 3:16], and the travail and pains of childbearing, labor, delivery and raising children.

As we go further in the sedrah, we find that Kayin killed his brother Hevel before he had any children, thus wiping him totally from the face of the earth. Measure for measure, almost every last vestige and trace of Kayin's family was wiped out by the ravages of the devastating mabul.

Indeed, as we enter parshas Noach, we learn about the generation of the flood, which indulged with boiling passion in all sorts of licentiousness and were therefore punished with the boiling waters of the flood. They mixed and confused all species of man and animal with the sin of incest and were therefore punished with the Mabul's mixing up the entire world.

Finally, toward the end of the parshas Noach, when the people of the world collaborated sinfully with each other to rebel against G-d by building the tower of Bavel, they were punished with the total disruption of communication. Hashem suddenly introduced seventy languages among them, and this completely disabled their ability to act in collusion with each other.

All of these lessons are not merely an interesting perspective on ancient times, but a contemporary and practical message for our daily lives. The next time our patience is tested and we take a deep breath and listen silently, holding back a biting retort or resisting the temptation to stomp out of the room, we earn for ourselves that sometime in life, we too will be the recipients of someone else's patience and tolerance. If we act with anger, we can expect to be targets of others anger one day. If we cause our parents to have nightmares, then—YIKES!—our children might eventually do the same to us. If we want affection, let's be affectionate. If we want caring, let's be considerate. And if we want courtesy, let's be courteous.

Furthermore, we can utilize this attribute of Hashem to try to diagnose where we need improvement. If we are plagued with earaches, let's examine what we have been listening to. And if depression is our nemesis, then maybe we are using our minds for the wrong things.

In the merit of our trying to better ourselves, may Hashem give us the good health and time to enjoy an even better life for many years to come.

Surrounding Ourselves
With Positive Influences

One may wonder why parshas Mishpatim, a parshah that contains many of the Jewish civil laws, starts with the subject of slavery. After all, Hashem, who sees the future in its entirety, knew that there would be many generations during which slavery would not be applicable. Wouldn't it have been better to start the parshah with something like the laws of damages, which have pertinence for all generations?

I'd like to suggest that the reason the parshah opens with the topic of slavery is to emphasize the wisdom and kindness of Torah law.

Jewish slavery—when one Jew becomes the servant of another—occurred in only a limited number of situations. One of the primary cases was when a person stole a sizable amount of money and, after being brought to justice, was unable to recompense his victims. When this happened, the beis din, the Jewish court, would sell the thief for six years, turning the money from his sale over to the wronged party.

Let's examine the wisdom of this procedure. In modern society, one of the biggest problems is the burgeoning jail population. Society is saddled with sheltering and catering to the needs of its malcontents, and sadly, the system is largely ineffective. Here is a typical scenario: Joe steals a sum of money. We put Joe in prison, where he is in the company of criminals of all varieties. There, he acquires a multifaceted education: How to crack a safe and hot-wire a car, even how to obtain and use a deadly weapon if necessary. In short, he becomes a true "professional." To our chagrin, when he finally gets paroled, he has developed into a well-educated crook. Some rehabilitation that is!

And what happens to Joe's family while he's in prison? The system can't help them. They are without their bread-winner, and if he is in jail for a length of time, the wife and children will likely suffer for years. Also, what happens to Joe's victims? Most of the time, they are left without recompense for all the money that was stolen from them.

Now let's look at the Torah's way of doing things. Hashem's aim is to rehabilitate this criminal and teach him the right way to live. Therefore, the beis din looks for a well-rounded family, strong and secure enough not to be affected by this person's influence, who can take in this person so that he can learn how to work productively and absorb the correct way to live. The Torah mandates further that the family must take in the criminal's wife and children along with him, thereby ensuring that they will be cared for while the bread-winner of the family is making restitution for his misdeeds. As mentioned above, the money acquired from this "sale" goes to recompense the victim of the crime, thus ensuring that his life isn't ruined either. Finally, the system is beautifully designed so that the whole process does not fall upon the community to fund for years and years.

The Torah's concept of "slavery" is, in fact, a system founded on kindness. An examination of the various halachos (laws) involved makes this clear. For example, the halacha specifies that, if the master has only one pillow, he must give that pillow to his Jewish "slave." This law and many other such laws lead the Gemara to conclude that "*Kol hakoneh eved ivri, k'koneh adon l'atzmo*—Whoever acquires a Jewish slave, it is as if he acquired a master for himself" [*Kiddushin* 20a].

We can learn from this study of Jewish slavery several things: For one thing, it is a powerful example of "*Hamavdil bein kodesh l'chol*—The difference between holy and secular." The brilliance of Torah is clearly evident when we compare its criminal justice system with that of our surrounding society.

Secondly, we can begin to appreciate the importance of a nurturing and positive environment. While we may be well aware of how the wrong influences can negatively affect us, we may not as readily appreciate how powerfully transformative the right influences can be. The Torah teaches us that a criminal can develop into a productive member of society if only he is surrounded by the right type of people. We, too, should understand from this that only by surrounding ourselves with positive influences (e.g., good peers for ourselves and our children, kosher sources of recreation, etc.) can we hope to develop the spiritual potential that Hashem has given us.

In the merit of our sincere striving in this regard, may we be zocheh to become true "servants" of Hashem.

Discovering Guidance in The Strangest Places

The Torah requires us to remember six significant concepts on a daily basis. One of these is our receiving the Torah at Har Sinai. Yet in all the time we may have thought about this significant moment, have we ever analyzed the odd circumstances with which Hashem gave us the Torah? The Torah paints the scene at Har Sinai quite vividly. It recounts that the sky was black, with thick clouds and smoke.

Why would the stage for the Giving of the Torah be set in such a dark scene when the Torah is described with metaphors absolutely opposite this? The posuk teaches us, "*Ki neir mitzvah v'Torah ohr*" [*Mishlei* 6:23], that Torah is our light, illuminating our way in life and piercing the darkness and gloom of our earthly existence. Similarly, the *Baal HaTurim* [*Bereishis* 1:4] teaches us that the gematria of "*es ha-ohr*—the light" is equivalent to "*baTorah*—in the Torah," for Hashem infused the Torah with true light. So the question remains, why did Hashem give the Torah in the midst of darkness?

The *Tosefos HaRosh* on Chumash offers an insightful explanation. In reality, he teaches, the Torah should have been given in the presence of brilliant rays of sunshine, accompanied by magnificent rainbows and swirling orbs of radiance. But we did not merit this because Hashem knew that, shortly thereafter, we would sin terribly with the golden calf. Therefore we did not deserve to enjoy the incredible light of the Torah at its revelation.

This idea can be used to explain why some people do not glean the expected ecstasy from their Torah study. For if, for instance, we fight with our children, shout at our parents, or browbeat our employees—right after we learn—Hashem will not grant us the pleasure of basking in the true glow of Torah.

As we discuss elsewhere, the entire Torah was given to make peace in the world [*Rambam, Hilchos Chanukah* 4:14]. Since this is true, it's logical to assume that every time we learn we should come one step closer to becoming a mentsch. Yet many wonder, if I'm learning about sukkah or the *lechem hapanim* (the "showbread" in the Temple), how does this bring me closer to becoming a finer human being?

Let me share with you a few examples of how we can find mussar lessons in many unexpected places.

We are taught [*Brachos* 51b] that it was Beis Hillel's opinion that in kiddush, we should first say the "Borei Pri Hagofen" brachah and then the brachah about Shabbos. Similarly, the Gemara cites the opinion that when Shavuos falls on Shabbos, we should dole out the *lechem hapanim*— which is for every Shabbos—first, and only then the two loaves that are special for Shavuos.

To explain these practices, the Gemara shares with us the famous Talmudic ruling, "*Tadir v'sh'eino tadir, tadir kodem*—That which is more frequent takes precedence." This is one of the reasons men put on their tallis before their tefillin, because the tallis, which is worn even on Shabbos and Yom Tov, is worn more often than the tefillin.

Ah! Now, let me show you how this is not only a halachic concept but also an excellent mussar lesson! It teaches us that if your spouse needs you to do something—and your neighbor wants something from you as well, you should make sure to help your spouse first. Your spouse's requests are more "*tadir*—frequent." Similarly, if there are two phone messages waiting at your desk, return your spouse's first. See what I mean about using our learning to become more of a mentsch?!

In a similar vein, we cover the challah during kiddush Friday night. One of the reasons is so that the bread should-n't be "embarrassed" when we make the blessing upon the wine first.

Now, let me ask you, are we worried that the poor loaf will sprout another bump or two out of embarrassment? When we pound the dough, or bake it at a high temperature in the oven and then pull it apart to eat with our teeth, are we concerned about its feelings? Of course not, but by high-lighting sensitivity to even an inanimate object at our Shabbos table, we are expressing to our families how impor-tant it is not to embarrass another human being. It will be a constant reminder, every week, for spouses not to do any-thing to embarrass each other in front of their company, and for parents not to embarrass their children.

Another example is a lesson from the Gemara [*Bava Kamma* 94b]: Do not throw a stone into the well from which you drink water. This demonstrates the important lesson of showing appreciation even to inanimate objects. I recently read an example of this from one of the great sages of the previous generation.

R' Elya Lopian would fold his tallis using the surface of a bench. He used the bench so that the tallis would not drag on the floor, placing one end of it on the bench to facilitate folding it. Once, a student saw him get paper towels to dust off the bench. When the young man offered to do it for him, R' Elya declined, explaining that he wanted to show appreciation to the bench that helped him show respect to his tallis. Besides this being a new type of "bentching," it's a practical modern application of an ancient Talmudic principle. Once again this practice should inspire us, and help condition us to show appreciation to all those who do favors for us in life.

One more example: The Gemara discusses "rishei anovim," which is translated as "stunted grapes." Rashi explains that these are grapes left on the vine for too long and will never fully ripen. But the literal translation is "wicked grapes." This teaches us a powerful ethical lesson. We too sometimes let ourselves "hang on the vine" for too long. It is wicked of us to allow our spiritual growth to become stunted, never attempting to realize our great spiritual potential. The Gemara is teaching us the critical lesson that we should never allow ourselves to fall into spiritual stagnation, and merely coast through life. We must always be striving and looking intently for more ways to daven better, to study more, to engage in more acts of kindness, and to bring ourselves ever closer to Hashem.

In the merit of our taking the time to learn Torah and always search for its guidance, may we be zocheh to reach higher and higher in our service of Hashem.

Reaping Summer's Benefits

In our Maariv prayers we thank Hashem for being "*Machalif es hazmanim*—changing the seasons." Since change adds spice and variety to life, we acknowledge our appreciation for this on a daily basis. And although every season has its unique delights, no time of the year elicits as much anticipation and excitement as the happy months of summer. I'd like to discuss some ideas to ensure that our expectations for summer become all that we desire—and that the summer months are spiritually productive as well!

Couples should discuss with each other what they dream about doing for their summer pleasure. For men, summer dreams might mean a Sunday ball game, or 'conking-out' on the hammock. A woman's dream might be lounging by the pool with the ladies, some brisk country jogging, or driving through the nooks and crannies of the mountains in order to browse through quaint shops and malls. For some couples, all of these might be true in reverse. Whatever our spouse's summer hopes may be, let's try our best to bring them to fruition, for the Torah obligates us to try make our spouse happy, and besides, a happy spouse is much nicer to live with.

If we have some free time in the summer, we should reserve a nice chunk of it for "re-connecting" with our loved ones. Because of the frantic pace of life, and the difficulty of earning a living, many of us spend very little time with our spouses and children. Therefore, although we might be personally drained and washed out and need a breather, we must make sure that our spouses and children get some much needed attention as well.

Another way of utilizing our free time is to "discover" Torah this summer! As the verse in *Mishlei* [4:24] teaches us, "*Ki chaim heim l'motzeihem*—The Torah is life to those who find it." So, let's rediscover the delights of learning Mishnayos or reviewing the summer Torah portions. Or, let's consider sinking our teeth into a small masechta of Gemara and challenge ourselves to finish it over the summer. We might even think about tackling a few "*sugyos b'eeyun,*" learning a few particular topics in depth, something which many of us have absolutely no time for during the winter.

We might also try to help our children get a head start for the new school year by beginning to learn with them the masechtos they will be learning in the fall.

Another rewarding campaign is to make time to learn the meaning of those sections of our davening which we may not know as well (for example, the *shir shel yom, brich shmei, tachanun,* etc.). Since we say the prayers every day, our tefillah study has a built-in review schedule. We will also derive a terrific sense of accomplishment from this type of study, since it will help us pray more sincerely for the rest of our lives! So a tefillah campaign is certainly time well spent!

Let's keep in mind that summer is the season to recharge our batteries, and an excellent tool for this is Torah. This is stated clearly in *Tehillim* [19:8], when it says, "*Toras Hashem t'mimah, m'shivas nafesh*—Hashem's Torah is pure, it rejuvenates the soul." Indeed, there are a lot of frustrated people who find themselves eager to get back to work simply because they don't know what to do with their free time. Either they're not athletic, or they are not readers or socialites (not that these types of people shouldn't be concerned about their learning as well!). Yet, if they would take the initiative to engage in a Torah project, fulfillment and glorious pleasure would be close at hand! Let's remember, as we try to make our summer a happy one, that, "*Ein simcha k'simchas ha Torah*— there is no greater happiness than the joy of Torah!"

Many of us will be sending our children off to camp. One of the things parents should insist on (besides the brushing of teeth) is a weekly letter from children away at camp. We should explain to our children that it takes hard work and much sacrifice to send them to camp, and that it is a luxury. Thus, it is only proper that they willingly share their thrills and excitements with us on a regular basis.

This arrangement will accomplish many things. First, it will allow them to fulfill a beautiful mitzvah of kibbud av v'eim, honoring their parents, every week! In fact, R'Yehuda Zev Segal, zt"l, would encourage his talmidim to write home often to their parents. He would then ask them if he could bring the letters to the post office so he could have a share in their mitzvah. Second, it will force them to communicate with us, which will enhance our connection with them while they're away from home, instead of their time away causing us to grow apart. Third, this lesson in communication is great training for their marital careers. It will begin conditioning them to share their daily activities and feelings with others. Finally, these letters will be a vehicle through which we can keep up with their spiritual accomplishments in camp. In so doing, we can spur them on to greater heights in Torah and mitzvos.

We should also counsel our children on the importance of wisely choosing their friends, reminding them that we pray every day for Hashem to protect us from bad influences, and reiterating how the mishnah in *Pirkei Avos* [1:6] teaches us to acquire a good friend for ourselves. Let's also advise them to be on the lookout for the lonely and sad child, and teach them to strive to cheer up someone who is feeling down and melancholy.

I hope implementing these tips will prove helpful, and may Hashem bless all of us with many healthy, happy and spiritually productive summers!

Improving Our Relationships

Child-Raising Turbulence: What Happened All of a Sudden?

Children's suicides. Rebelliousness. Total dropouts from Yiddishkeit. An entire issue of *The Jewish Observer* about "Children on the Fringe," which was sold out and had to be reprinted.

What's going on? Where did this onslaught of adolescent problems come from?

First, it's important for us to attempt to diagnose the problem in order that we, as parents, can try to ensure that this plague doesn't affect our loved ones. Since this crisis seems to have cropped up only in the last ten to fifteen years, it would be safe to surmise that, if we can discover changes that came about in the last decade and a half, we might be able to pinpoint some causes that have led to this frightening situation.

I humbly believe that one of the most blatant changes is the fact that, in most Jewish homes, both parents have entered the work force. I remember starting out teaching twelfth-grade girls in Yeshiva Sarah Schneirer in 1985. At that time, when I took a poll among my students, approximately eighty percent told me that their mothers were full-time home-makers. When I ask the same question now, at Machon Beis Yaakov seminary, at Kesser Beis Yaakov, or at Beis Yaakov L'Banos, the situation is totally reversed, and approximately eighty percent tell me that their mothers are working to help the family make ends meet.

There is no doubt in my mind that this has a tremendous impact on the chinuch capabilities of the parent team. Not only because of a simple lack of time for the needs of the children, but also because of the physical and emotional burnout of parents. With husbands and wives shouldering the pressures of heightening economic demands on their fami-lies, they have less patience and concentration for the needs of their children. The limited amount of time that working parents have to themselves is dissected into little pieces for Torah study, shalom bayis purposes, household needs, and just plain downtime. Unfortunately, in many families, only a tiny sliver of time is left to cater to the needs of what is often, boruch Hashem, a large family.

Even the minuscule amount of time that a parent has for his or her children is often with a distracted state of mind. One who comes home with frazzled nerves is not in any condition to listen to and empathize with a child's classroom problems.

Furthermore, we have to find time to focus on the individual needs of *each* of our children.

As the Torah teaches us, "*L'maan t'saper b'oznei bincha*—In order that you shall relate in the ears of your child" [*Shemos* 10:4]. Note carefully the word "ears." It would seem to be superfluous. Obviously, we're going to speak into their ears and not their eyes. Rather, Hashem is emphasizing several important parental lessons. First, it's not enough to merely talk to your child. You have to make sure that it enters their ears, that they absorb what you are saying. The method of accomplishing this varies from child to child. To some children, you need to sing, while others, you may need to gently cajole. To some you need to occasionally speak harshly, while with others you need to play a game. We need to speak into the ears of each child separately, for every child is a world in his or her own right, as the posuk advises, "*Chanoch lanaar al pi darko*—Educate the youth according to his or her distinct ways and needs" [*Mishlei* 24:6].

Forewarned is forearmed. Just like a decade ago, when we were warned and advised by our leaders that busy parents must find quality time for each other on a regular basis in order to keep their marriages fresh, we must now make sure that we find special moments for each of our children. It is imperative that we find time to ask Yossi how he is doing at learning his first Tosefos. We must make it our business to see how much Shaindy's pimples are bothering her, or how Chaya did on her Navi test.

We need to plan private times for each of the children. Even a little drive in the car, when we could ask our son or daughter if they have any close friends, or whether they are feeling good about themselves, means the world to a child. Taking a child out to share a sandwich or a soup and having a heart-to-heart talk about their dreams and ideas and what they consider the fun part of life, is terrific parenting and the best preventive medicine.

Let's remember that children do not live in a vacuum. If they don't feel loved at home, (even though this might just be their mistaken perception!), they *will* look for love elsewhere. This explains the frustrating phenomenon where children of the most loving parents hang around with gangs or kids on the street, claiming that they have finally found love and acceptance.

Let's also remember that, as is with learning Torah and in shalom bayis, the yetzer hara tries to frustrate our success in the important area of child rearing. Busy parents need to plan ahead and structure their lives in a way that they can have private and focused time for each child. Let's not procrastinate, for our time with our children is more limited than we realize. Yeshivah bochrim who go out of town to learn come back home one day and suddenly ask us to help them with their wedding invitations. Our pretty little girls go all too quickly from their Osh Kosh B'gosh jumpers to their satin-white wedding gowns.

Wise couples plan together to find ways to connect with all of their children. This is also an aid to improve our shalom bayis. As the posuk tells us, "*Al kein yaazov ish es aviv v'es imo, v'dovak b'ishto, v'hayu l'basar echad*—Therefore, a man should leave his father and mother, cleave to his wife, and they will become one flesh" [*Bereishis* 2:24]. Rashi explains that this "becoming one flesh" transpires when they have a child and their flesh is united in the body of their child. The deeper lesson of this verse is that through their child they achieve a common focus, which unifies them.

To reiterate, just as it is important for parents to provide clothing for their children, formula for their baby's bottles, milk for cereal, shelter and schooling, their mental health needs much attention as well. The Gemara in *Kesubos* [111b] interprets, "*U-l'ven shinaim m'cholov* [*Bereishis* 49:12]," to mean that smiles are even more important than milk. This Gemara emphasizes the vital need for the psychological staples, for warmth and emotional support to round out a successful Jewish home.

We need to be creative and find ways to happily connect with each of our children. Of course, learning is the happiest medium, but it is not the only vehicle. Besides being a way for parent and child to bond, playing chess together with a child achieves many wondrous benefits. Chess teaches the wisdom of looking ahead, it trains one to consider all the angles, it teaches a sense of balance, and it contributes to many other life skills. Sports are also a wonderful way to share time with a child. Family outings (which need proper planning to ensure that activities are in consonance with the Torah) can be memorable events for a child. They also do wonders towards demonstrating to our children that, when we have free time, we like nothing better than spending it with them

One delightful and rewarding thing to do with the family is to take them to meet a Godol. Later in life, they will fondly cherish the memory of such an experience.

Now I'd like to focus on another parental vulnerability in modern times: namely, the lack of meaningful feeling in our fulfillment of many of the mitzvos. Call it "hislahavus;" call it "chasidishe bren;" call it spiritual passion; call it any other name you want. It's severely missing in many a modern life and home.

In Krias Shema we say, "*V'hayu hadevarim ha'ela, asher anochi mitzavecha hayom al levovecha, v'shinantom levanecha*—Let these words which I command you today be upon your heart, and teach them to your children." The saintly Chofetz Chaim, zt"l, may his merit protect us all, reveals a fundamental pedagogical lesson from these pesukim. He explains that Hashem is teaching us that only when the words of Torah are upon our heart, only when we relate to them with deep feeling and emotion, can we effectively transmit them to our children. Thus, the Torah links the heart to the proper instruction of our *kinderlach*.

It is for this reason that so many New Yorkers successfully pass on their love and passion for the Yankees, *l'havdil*, to their kids. The child picks up on the excitement in his father's voice when he talks reverently about Berra and Mantle, Mattingly and Billy Martin, Derek Jeter and Tino Martinez. So too, a mother often infuses her daughter with the thrill of shopping for a new outfit, and putting together a matching ensemble, because a daughter's interest is naturally ignited by the thrill and glint in her mother's eyes as she views the latest styles in outfits and jewelry.

It is this kind of passion that we must exhibit when we perform mitzvos in order to thoroughly fulfill our commitment to transmit our heritage to the next generation.

Perhaps this is one of the reasons we drink four cups of wine on the night of Pesach. Besides their symbolic message of the heady feeling of freedom that we try to experience on the night of the Exodus, the four cups might represent something else. Namely, that as we are warmed up by the influence of the ruby red spirits on this night dedicated to "passing over" the Jewish traditions to our families, our actions become more passionate and leave a more meaningful trace in our children's memories.

While it is obvious that a parent who doesn't talk in shul has a better chance of expecting his child to behave the same way, there is much more that can be achieved. If a father, for instance, sings Pesukei D'zimra, or says the Shema with a meaningful and reflective tone, it rubs off on a child that "Daddy is really *into* this." And he, too, will search for meaning in his prayer. The youngster who witnesses his father's mechanical gibberish in shul and notices how his father's head is moving to and fro—not with devotion—but to discover all the latest goings-on in the synagogue, will *not* be turned on to the importance of tefillah in life.

This subject of meaningful mitzvah observance is aptly illustrated by a beautiful thought from the Sfas Emes, zt"l. It says in *Megillas Esther* [8:16], "*Layehudim hoysa orah v'simcha v'sason vi-y'kar*—For the Jews there was light, gladness, joy and honor." The Gemara [*Megillah* 16b] explains that *orah* is Torah, *simcha* is Yom Tov, *sason* is milah and *y'kar* is tefillin.

The Sfas Emes asks, "Why speak in code? Why doesn't the Megillah simply state that the Jews had Torah, Yom Tov, milah and tefillin?" He answers that, even before the miracle of Mordechai and Esther, the Jews surely fulfilled all of these mitzvahs. The change, however, was that after the miracle, they realized that Torah was their light, Yom Tov was their happiness, milah was their joy, and tefillin was their honor. Prior to this, Haman had slandered them with the accusation, "*Y'sheinim heim min hamitzvos*—they are 'sleeping' from the precepts" [*Megillah* 13b]. This accusation meant that they were indeed doing the mitzvos, but they were doing them as if they were sleeping, bereft of any feeling or thought, performing each deed mechanically out of habit and routine.

This is a malady that plagues us terribly in modern times. Men slap on tefillin like a blood-pressure cuff, put on tzitzis while half asleep, mutter brachos incoherently, and perform so many rituals without proper meditation and spirit. While the outward appearance is still one of total *frumkeit* and religious adherence, if the inner core is spiritually empty, the consequences are clearly apparent in the next generation. The acutely perceptive eyes of our young ones discern the difference between what we do excitedly and warmly, and what we do merely to dispatch an obligation and get on with the more important things in life.

If we quickly take care of Mincha to get back to a ball-game, or frantically finish off the piece of Gemara to get outside, then what message are our children digesting about what is paramount in our eyes? Similarly, if we dash into the house right before Shabbos and take a one-minute shower and slap on our clothing, and then arrive late and emotionally unsettled to Mincha, what are we teaching them about respectfully greeting the Shabbos Hamalkah?

How appropriate do the words of R' Yaakov Kaminetsky ring, that in today's generation the challenge is not Shabbos observance, but how we prepare for Shabbos on Friday. A child that sees his father lovingly buff his shoes, taste the food, sharpen the knives, prepare the ice cubes, and help to make the home shine, absorbs an excitement for Shabbos that remains with him throughout his life.

We all know the familiar adage that the best way to teach is by example. The point I am trying to make is that children pick up even on those things that we think are hidden in our hearts. As R' Yitzchak Elchonon Spector tells us, "*V'shamru Bnei Yisroel es haShabbos, la'asos es haShabbos l'dorosom*"—Bnei Yisroel are charged to have a meaningful enough Shabbos experience to ensure that Shabbos will continue down through their generations, *"l'dorosom"* [*Shemos* 31:16]. This means that our Shabbos should be infused with enough true meaning that our children will want to experience the same Shabbos beauty in their own homes.

Without a doubt, one of the most dramatic changes in recent years is the encroachment of the ways of the outside world into the Jewish home. One can almost hear the yetzer hara scheming to himself, "How can I bring the decadence of America into ultra-Orthodox homes? They don't have television. Many of them don't even have a radio. They filter out offensive magazines. There must be a way to challenge even them with the 'advances' of glamour and romance, violence, immorality and the plethora of pleasures of the senses." So, in his devious and clever way, he latched on to the Internet.

Lo and behold, even the most sheltered families have a computer in their homes. They use them to e-mail their relatives in Eretz Yisroel, or see a live view of the Kosel, maybe even while saying tikun chatzos. They can have a vast array of fresh Torah thoughts for the Shabbos table ranging from discourses by R' Yissachar Frand to marvelous insights from Aish HaTorah and much, much more. The Internet has also provided isolated Jews in small towns and hamlets all over the world with easy access to Orthodox Jewish thoughts, ideas, and products—something which was unheard of a mere ten years ago.

Yet now, in the "connected" home, with the touch of a mouse, things which S'dom v'Amorrah never dreamed of are instantly accessible. The most graphic and deviant pornography is but a "dot-com" away and "www.blank" can expose our children to information and pictures which can leave not only a lasting mark upon their souls, but can be a fierce form of the most nasty type of addiction. "Chat rooms" have provided a way for the most sheltered and protected yeshivah boys and beis yaakov girls to be exposed to elements of society light-years away from what we want our children's social circles to include. All is not as it seems in the Internet world. "Shalom" in the sports forum might really be Sammy, a car thief recently released on parole. "Rivkah" might be Randy, a professional con-artist. This is the sewer that so many unsuspecting parents allow to pollute their homes without limit on a daily basis. How many brilliant fresh minds have been addicted to the lure of this frightening new vehicle?

Okay, I hear many of you saying to yourselves, Rabbi Weiss, we know the problem. Give us some solutions. Well, one great idea is to locate the modem-connected computer in an open place in the home, which does not lend itself to clandestine voyeurism. The fear of being surprised as someone suddenly enters the room will provide a good modicum of inhibition. Of course, if there are long stretches that a child is home before Mom and Dad get home from work, this method will not prove to be effective. Parental software controls also help a bit, but let's remember that many children are more savvy in the new technology than we are. All it takes is a few taps, and they are ready to explore the wild blue yonder of *shmutz*. A possible alternative is the use of filtered gateways such as Kosher.net, which a parent who ascertains that there is a real need for the Internet in the home should definitely explore. Principals and teachers should debate seriously amongst themselves the pros and cons of giving the children homework and projects that necessitate research on the

Internet.

In general, if a child locks the door when he or she is on the computer, take it as a red alert. Although he or she might say that they just don't want to be bothered while they are studying, in this case it pays to be suspicious. They don't need private time with their Compaqs.

The Internet is not the only area of exposure from the media that has had a marked effect on the attitudes and psyche of our youth. Many teenagers have the headphones of their disc players and Walkman's "glued" to their heads, with the provocative voices of female temptresses filling their ears. Furthermore, the kedusha of "kol Yaakov" with its lofty implications for refinement in our speech, gets an awful pounding from the bombardment of *nivul peh* (foul language), which abounds in modern pop music. A spirit of rebelliousness and arrogance floods the minds and beings of the young people who are addicted to the seductive rhythms of this music. The raunchy and risque lyrics of pop music singers belong to ideologies and lifestyles that are diametrically opposed to the *tznius* (modesty), *anivus* (humility), and *derech eretz* (ways of respect) which are hallmarks of Torah Yiddishkeit.

Even popular radio programs, such as the Bob Grant Show, the Jay Diamond Show, and others, can have a extremely dangerous effect on the minds of our youth. While many find it enjoyable to listen to Mr. Grant's aggressive manner and caustic wit, this behavior and treatment of others in the presence of hundreds of thousands of listeners is fundamentally opposed to the Torah's absolute insistence on sensitivity to others, especially in a public forum. After all, we are taught in no uncertain terms, "*Hamalbin pnei chaveiro b'rabim, ein lo cheilek l'*Olam Habah—One who (habitually) embarrasses his friend in public has no portion in the after-life" [*Pirkei Avos* 3:11].

The "call-a-therapist" programs, such as Dr. Joy and her ilk, can also be dangerous in a subtle way. Deciding people's futures by hearing only one side of the story in a span of two minutes is a lethal way of dispensing advice. In addition, the opinions that our children hear are many times totally foreign to the mores of Torah. Whether they are listening to confused conceptions of the parent-child relationship or hearing details of out-of-wedlock relationships, the voice on the radio, which inspires so much awe and bears so much weight for naive young listeners, can be awfully dangerous.

The gossip columns in our newspapers (besides the las-civious pictures found in the pages around them) are found-ed on the sins of lashon hara and rechilus. Furthermore, as we've already mentioned, revealing other people's secrets in a public forum is in total opposition to Torah Judaism.

These are just some of the dangers with which modern media presents us. We must become aware of these dangers, so we can take measures to help our children avoid these temptations.

Many of us have seen the glaring signs of an adolescent who has gone awry: the hair parted in the middle, the yar-mulke perched at the front, a dangling cigarette, an arrogant swagger, a disinterested look, a foreign vocabulary full of a scary new slang, and a penchant for behaving in a way that will shock us. These are all telltale signs of rebellion. Many a time, parents wonder in true puzzlement and shock, "What caused this transformation? How could this happen to our sheltered child, raised in a home dedicated to the ways of *ruach Yisroel*? Where did we go wrong?"

Sometimes, a huge part of the answer lies in one word: *peers.* Long ago, R' Yochanan ben Zakkai asked his five brilliant disciples to investigate and attempt to discover the single most important thing that a person should stay away from, the thing that can have the most detrimental effect upon his or her spiritual success. R' Yehoshua came back with the answer: a *chaver rah*, a bad friend. R' Yosi said a *shochein rah*, a bad neighbor [*Pirkei Avos* 4:9].

What a lesson! Of all the things to avoid in life, R' Yehoshua and R' Yosi felt that the negative impact of bad friends and neighbors is worse than anything else. Now, they said this about all of us. However, it is especially true when it comes to the vulnerable and impressionable young minds of our teenagers.

In a similar vein, the Rambam teaches us in the beginning of the sixth chapter of *Hilchos Deos* (Laws of Attitudes) that a person is affected by his environment, that it is natural for a person to think and act like his friends. What a scary thought! The people we hang around can affect even the way we think! This is also the sentiment of the famous statement of Chazal, "*Oy l'rasha, oy l'scheino*—Woe to the wicked, woe to his neighbor" [*Negaim* 14:7]. Even before the requests that we make in our Shemoneh Esrei, we make the following daily petition in our early morning brachos. "*V'harchikeinu mei-adam ra u-meichaver ra*—Hashem please distance us from an evil person and an evil friend." We see how vital this must be for our daily success if it is one of the first requests we ask Hashem for every day. Indeed, since we say it in the plural, we should certainly have in mind our spouses and children when we say this prayer.

It is known that the saintly Chofetz Chaim, zt"l, celebrated every year with a *seudas hoda'ah*, a meal of thanks, for recognizing and parting ways from potentially evil friends.

Now, you might claim that a discussion of the dangers of bad peers doesn't fit neatly into the category of "things that have changed in the last fifteen years." After all, detrimental peers have been around since the beginning of time. There is a big difference, however, in our present time. Twenty-five years ago, for instance, when a child fell in with the wrong friends, perhaps he concentrated more on Mike Shmidt's batting average than on Tosefos's *peshat*, or maybe he read some smuggled *Mad* magazines under the covers. Perhaps he listened to some tapes of the Beatles. These days, when a child falls in with the wrong crowd, the results are much more sinister. When a teenager is disillusioned and seeks a new set of friends, he can be exposed to the most lethal and heinous practices. They range from getting involved with some real "cool" and understanding member of the opposite sex to experimenting with the latest drugs.

We must do whatever we can to help our children acquire friends that are good for them. It is obvious that this is one of the critical factors that we should investigate when choosing a school. Who will our children's friends be? Sometimes, we tend to consider only geographical convenience when picking a yeshivah for our children. Other times, we are lured by a top-notch academic reputation. We must realize, however, that peer pressure influence may have the single biggest impact upon the minds and hearts of our loved ones in school.

We should make it our business to find out—before there are problems—who our children's friends are. We shouldn't be passive in this area. Especially if our child is somewhat introverted, we should help them cultivate good friends. Ask them, for example, if they would like to bring a friend over for the weekend. Usually they will pick one who will impress you, and this will help them forge healthy friendships. You can also ask them if they want to bring a friend along when you go on a day trip. Enlist the help of your child's rebbe or morah in trying to find a good friend for your child. Perhaps the teacher can give them a project to do together.

In this area, it is also important to choose the right camp for your child. Sometimes, lifetime friendships are forged in the less pressured environment of a healthy Torah camp. We must be aware of how dangerous the wrong kind of peers can be for our children. If you're like me, then you're saddened to see young yeshivah bochrim smoking as you leave a simcha. Know that this kind of behavior is infectious amongst friends. Younger ones try it out to see what it's like or to copy the older ones. This is but one example of how peers can have a very detrimental effect on our children.

May it be the will of Hashem that we and our loved ones always be surrounded by fine friends and may we all be zocheh to true yiddishe nachas from all those around us.

Raising
Wonderful Children

Hagaon HaRav Pam, shlit"a, once electrified a huge crowd with a quote from the Holy Gaon, the Steipler Rav, of blessed memory. The Steipler recommended the following two ingredients for raising wonderful children: Fifty percent tefillah and fifty percent shalom bayis (marital harmony). Imagine! Just *two* ingredients!

What a crucial message! But how can we translate this sage advice into action?

In our prayers, our children's futures should permeate our thoughts. In our Shemoneh Esrei, we should think of them when we say "*Atta Chonein la'adam daas...*—You bestow knowledge upon man...." How often have we frittered away this opportunity when we could have been praying for our children to understand their studies better?! Do we consider that fifty percent of our children's future rests on the quality of our prayers, in which we can plead with the Almighty for their happiness and success? With this mandate from the holy Steipler Rav, we should condition ourselves to utilize every possible opportunity to pray for our children.

Mothers should fervently beseech Hashem for children that are G-d-fearing. An especially suitable time for this is after lighting the Shabbos candles. Similarly, on Shabbos night before kiddush, fathers should bless their children with a deep prayer in their hearts that their *kinderlach* should merit Hashem's triple-corded blessings—of protection, grace, and peace.

Another auspicious time to pray for our children is every morning when we say birchas haTorah, which according to many poskim should be said by women as well as men. We should emotionally petition Hashem, "*V'nihye anachnu v'tze-etzo-einu… kulonu yodei Sh'mecha v'lomdei Sorasecha lishma*— May we, and our children and grandchildren, know your name and learn Your Torah for its own sake…."

In this blessing, we can plead every morning with Hashem that the Torah should be sweet for us and for our progeny. How important this request is! We are asking Hashem that the study of a piece of Gemara should be enjoyable and not a burden. We pray that learning should be a "geshmake" (tasty) part of our children's day, for if it is then we can be reasonably confident that they will continue to learn Torah when they get older. We also petition Hashem that our descendants will always have yiras Hashem (awareness of G-d). (Think about it! How many Jewish children around the world don't even known what the word "Hashem" means?!)

This concept, of praying "ahead," is highly recommended by the Gemara. In *Masechtas Brachos* [8a] we are taught, "*Al zos yispallel kol chasid l'eis m'tzoh*—For this every pious person should pray towards the time of finding." The Gemara interprets this verse homiletically as telling us to pray in advance of our time of need. We should even pray that when we leave the world it will be through an easy death and that, even when they throw, and even after they throw, the last clod of earth upon our graves, there should be no terrible mishaps (e.g., coffins being accidentally switched or graves caving into one another). Talk about planning ahead!

We must also obviously pray fervently that our young children find good mates and be able to have children, and that our future grandchildren should be entirely healthy. When we hear so many stories of people dying young, *lo aleinu*, it behooves us to remember the extraordinarily important Talmudic dictum, "*L'olam yispalel adam shelo yecheleh*—A person should always pray not to become sick!" Once again the stress is on *preventive* prayer.

A good comparison to this type of tefillah is as the act of putting on a seat belt, something we often don't worry about until it's too late! The stakes are too high for us to be careless about these measures! Just as we must condition ourselves to put on that belt, we must learn to pray in anticipation!

We should also focus when bentching, and saying the section, "*Harachaman, Hu yishlach lanu brachah m'ruba b'bayis hazeh*—Merciful One! Please bless our home!" What greater blessing of their home can couples contemplate when praying this tefillah than Torah *nachas* from the children?

Similarly, we should intensely concentrate when we pray in U'vo L'tzion, "*L'maan lo neega larik v'lo neiled labehola*—That we should not weary ourselves in vain, nor give birth for naught!" We pray that all the hard work we do to earn a living and raise our children should elicit only positive results—that our children should all grow to become G-d-fearing Jews.

What are we to make of the other fifty percent of the holy Steipler's recipe, namely, shalom bayis? It goes without saying that if we are caring and affectionate to our spouses, our children will likely become caring and affectionate adults! If we show patience, exercise flexibility, and know how to apologize and compromise, our children will follow suit. But if we scream and fight, our children will make a nasty little kal v'chomer (inference): If Daddy and Mommy are this way with each other (even though they're married), we can surely scream and fight with people who are only our friends. Let us realize we are on constant display, and make the most of our opportunity as parental role models.

And may Hashem bless all of us with good health and wonderful Torah nachas from our children and grandchildren.

Maintaining a
Healthy Marriage

Ask yourself the following blunt questions:

How much thought do I give before I react to my spouse? (Do I pause for even a second or two?)? Am I acting in a caring way? Am I fair? Do I think before saying no? Do I pay sincere attention?

If you find that the positive responses to these questions are just not part of your normal behavior, then happily there is much room for improvement in your marital relationship!

Let me share a wonderful story with you. When the great Gaon, R' Shlomo Zalman Auerbach, zt"l, said a eulogy for his Rebbetzin, he commented that it is customary to ask forgiveness from the deceased. However, he continued, for fifty-four years they had lived together according to the *Shulchan Aruch* and he had nothing to ask forgiveness for, except that he did not have enough merits to save her from death.

R' Ezriel Tauber (as quoted in the *Jewish Observer*) related another story about R' Auerbach. One time, a ben Torah noticed that R' Shlomo Zalman was grooming himself before entering his home. When the young man questioned him about this, the Gaon explained that when one has shalom bayis (marital harmony), his home is blessed with the Shechinah's presence. Therefore, before entering his home, he was preparing to greet the Shechinah that dwelled inside!

I believe that this episode offers a deeper insight into the strange conversation between the angels and Avraham in parshas Vayera. The angels asked Avraham where his wife was. He answered that she was in the house. This seems to be a relatively mundane dialogue for the Torah to record for all eternity. Rashi points out that the angels wanted to heighten Avraham's awareness and appreciation of the incredible modesty of his wife Sarah. Note that, although they were already married way over half a century, there were still more praises that even someone like Avraham Avinu could learn about his spouse!

We might wonder, though, that at first glance it seems strange that Sarah chose to remain inside at this juncture, when there was so much going on outside.

First, Hashem himself came to be *m'vaker choleh* (visit the ailing) Avraham on the third day after his circumcision. Then, Avraham took leave of Hashem and went to greet his guests. This act, we are told, is even greater than greeting the Shechinah. Then, the guests revealed their identity as angels and—through all of this—Sarah remained inside! It was in response to this that Avraham answered that, (to paraphrase) "Sarah is inside *our* tent, which has been blessed with shalom bayis for decades!" In such a place, with an unparalleled presence of the Shechinah, Sarah Imeinu was not missing anything by remaining inside!

Indeed, Avraham was reminded at other times as well of Sarah's incredible powers. The Gemara in *Bava Metzia* [59a] teaches, "*Ein habrocha shru'ya b'soch beiso shel adam ela bishvil ishto*—Blessings reside in a person's home only because of his wife." The Gemara learns this fact from the verse, "*Ul'Avraham heitiv ba'avura*," meaning that Hashem assisted Avraham for her (Sarah's) sake [*Bereishis* 13:16].

The reason we are specifically taught this lesson from Avraham is to accentuate that even someone like Avraham, who dedicated his whole life to kindness and spirituality, and who we would think had enough merits of his own, still needed the merits of his wife. Certainly we should realize that we are all in need of the merits of our spouses!

In the Torah portion that discusses the sotah, the posuk states, "*Ish ish ki sisteh ishto*—Any man whose wife turns aside" [*Bamidbar* 5:14]. The medrash, in *Bamidbar Rabbah*, asks why the Torah repeats the word "*ish*—man." It explains that there are times that a man should behave one way and other times that he should act in a totally different way. The repetition indicates: like one man and like another man. The medrash elaborates that if one's wife accidentally spills his wine he should look away. If he does so, it is written of him, "*L'hanchil ohavay yeish*—I will reward those that love me with substance" [*Mishlei* 8:21]. If she spills his oil (which in those days was like having Con Ed shut off the electricity), and he looks away, Hashem says "*V'otzroseihem amalai*—And Hashem will fill their storage places" [*Mishlei* 8:21]. If she rips his clothes, he should look away, and Hashem will fulfill all his requests! But if she acts unfaithfully, he should rise like a lion and take her to the kohen with alacrity.

We see from this medrash that when we refrain from

reacting harshly to an act of negligence, thoughtlessness, or unfairness on the part of our spouse, the Ribbono shel Olam calls that person "ohavay," one who loves Me! For, when we look away, we are deciding that the avoidance of a confrontation and a fight is worth it, no matter what just happened, in order to keep the Shechinah in the home. An eagerness to retain the Shechinah demonstrates love for Hashem.

Furthermore, Hashem promises that we will never lose out from such behavior. Rather, Hashem will fulfill all our requests for practicing restraint with such fortitude! Conversely, when the fabric of the home is threatened by unfaithful behavior, it is equally as important *not* to look away, but to take a stand, because the Shechinah cannot reside in a home of immorality either.

In *Taanis* [21], the Gemara relates that the disciples asked R' Ada bar Ahava why he merited unusual longevity. He answered them, "*L'olam lo hikpad'ti b'soch beisi*—I never acted upset in my home!" We must realize that since R' Ada was taking credit for *never* being angry, this suggests that there must have been times that warranted his becoming agitated. Otherwise, there would be nothing to take credit for. Yet he always stoically looked away, and this earned him something we would all deem worthwhile to strive for—the gift of long life!

Indeed, the *Keren Orah* (in *Masechtas Taanis*) beautifully elucidates that when studying the common denominator of all the Talmudic prescriptions for long life, one thing emerges. If one makes the body a pleasant place, the soul is not anxious to return to heaven, resulting in a long existence down here for that smartly conditioned body!

Let's work to change the routine of our marriages, and

break out of the doldrums of habit that threaten our unions with dullness and stale spirit. Make a date with each other, as you did many moons ago when you were first courting, and strive to make each other more happy. After all, you're both more mature now and have a deeper understanding of yourselves and each other. You'd be surprised that a long walk might bring to light new ways to enhance each other's lives in some incredibly important ways.

Let's strive to continually improve our shalom bayis and may Hashem Yisborach bless us all with the presence of His Shechinah in our homes always.

Tips for a Happy Home

Often, when I speak to single people, I caution them not to judge a prospective mate simply by their outward appearance. I compare it to shopping for a car. Foolish is the consumer who chooses a car merely by its color and sleek look. What a careless way to buy a car. Savvy buyers know that they must take into account gas mileage, engine size, safety, price and many other variables.

The parable of a car illustrates some important marital lessons as well. The responsible automobile owner knows that to succeed with his car, he must take care of it. Every 3,000 miles or couple of months, he must bring it in for an oil change. Every couple of years, he makes sure to get a tune-up. In a similar vein, our marriages also need diligent attention. If left without regular maintenance, they deteriorate.

The knowledgeable car owner rotates his tires in order to ensure that they last longer. In marriage too, "rotating" one's behavior—adding variety and spice—ensures that the ever-present dangers of boredom and habit do not erode the magic of marriage.

When one rides one's car over unusually bumpy terrain, or hits a succession of nasty potholes, one knows one must carefully inspect the car and give it special attention. So too, if a couple is going through "bumpy" times, such as a period of financial difficulty, a sickness in the family, or the trial of a wayward child, lo aleinu, we must devote more attention to the health of our marriage. As a vehicle ages and the signs of age begin to show, it needs special attention. So too, as the years go by, a wise couple invests more and more time in working on the success of their relationship.

A fundamental principle of a good marriage is the belief and realization that your spouse is the most important person in your life. As R' Pam explains, when a woman walks around her husband seven times under the chupah, she is proclaiming that from then on he is the center of her universe. Similarly, the Torah states that upon marriage the husband leaves his mother and father, until then his most important allegiances on earth (besides Hashem), in order to cleave to his wife. Further, in the marriage kesubah, he pledges to honor her (and according to Jewish law, he must honor everyone, so this pledge must mean that he will honor her even more than that!).

This commitment, to make one's spouse "Number One," manifests itself in a multitude of areas. It means that upon hearing good news we will not share it with someone else (mother, best friend, etc.) before telling our spouse. It also means we must not make the mistake of declining our spouse's advice on a given issue, and then take it to heart when someone else gives us the same advice.

Considering our spouse "Number One" involves loyalty, a trait that is unfortunately threatened with extinction in America today. When standing under the chupah, the chasan and kallah pledge lasting loyalty to one another. This is the first virtue that Shlomo Hamelech extolled about the Woman of Valor, "*Botach boh leiv ba'alah*—Her husband's heart is sure of her" [*Mishlei* 31:1]. While he does not know which of his friends is talking behind his back, and he is never sure who is really on his side in the office politics, one thing he should be certain about—his wife will always stand by him.

This is the model of a loving couple that puts their marriage first, and for this reason it is a cardinal error of the highest proportion to ever embarrass your mate publicly. It is a terrible sin, for instance, for a wife to say amongst friends, "I'm glad someone else finally told him he's a slob. I've been saying it for years." While the statement might be completely true, loyalty has just been chucked out the window.

How we answer the phone when our mate calls is extremely telling. If we pick up the receiver with a sweet hello and, upon hearing it's our spouse, we respond sullenly, "Oh, it's you. What do you want?" we are not demonstrating the "Number One" philosophy. Similarly, if when our mate enters the room we fail to even momentarily give recognition, but continue our "important" conversation on the phone, we are clearly lacking in this crucial area of marriage.

It is unconscionable for us to pay attention or show affection to anyone more than we do to our spouse. If this happens regularly, your mate will surely begin to dislike the recipient of your attention simply because they feel that they deserve it more. This explains why it is common for people to dislike their spouse's best friend or sibling. It is not the friend or sibling that the spouse dislikes, but the fact that because of them they feel they aren't receiving their deserved treatment and attention.

In the merit of our working on making our marriages sweeter, may Hashem bless us all with success and true shalom bayis.

Respecting Other People

Throughout the long history of the Jewish people there have been a lot of acute, cataclysmic, and catastrophic trauma. We are now on the heels of one of the worst times in Jewish history; namely, the terrible holocaust of European Jewry. In the more distant past, the destructions of our two Temples were each accompanied by the unspeakable loss of millions of Jewish lives as well. Yet there was another event that resulted in a much more intense period of national mourning on the Jewish calendar than any of these disasters. I am referring to the horrific death of the 24,000 disciples of R' Akiva. To recall this horror and keep us aware of the pertinence of its message in our daily lives and collective consciousness, we mourn as a nation for more than a month, by abstaining from marriages, music, haircutting, and other expressions of rejoicing. How astounding, then, that the destructions of the two Temples, accompanied by millions of Jewish deaths, only merit a nine-day mourning period on the Jewish calendar! Furthermore, countless plagues, pogroms, inquisitions, and crusades, which resulted in the decimation of hundreds of thousands of Jews, do not even elicit a single day on our religious calendar. Yet the relatively small number of 24,000 disciples of R' Akiva warrants over a month of national mourning every year.

Let's try to understand why we commemorate this event in particular.

If we would envision in our minds, G-d forbid, the decimation of all the yeshivah boys we have now in the late twentieth century, from Lakewood to Ponovezh, from Telz to Brisk, by a plague which pinpointed only the dedicated yeshivah students, we would realize that such a blow would leave the Torah world reeling in a state of shock. Imagine too, chas v'shalom, the thousands of grieving families, and thousands of Bais Yaakov girls faced with no match to marry. Imagine the next generation bereft of Torah leadership. Imagine the awful depression that would result from seeing the cream of the crop of our society buried by the thousands. This was precisely the effect of the acute catastrophe that befell our people during the days of R' Akiva. Nor did they die peacefully. They died in the most horrible way, from askara (dyptheria or croup), which the Gemara in *Brachos* [8a] informs us is the most painful of all deaths.

Unlike now, in the aftermath of the recent holocaust—where we have no Sages with the ability to explain the reasons for the occurrence—during the time of R' Akiva there *were* gedolei Torah who had the ability to explain exactly why the tragedy had transpired. And so, having been advised of its cause, we observe this period of national mourning in order to learn how to be vigilant against the possibility of such events ever recurring.

In six short words, the Gemara [*Yevamos* 64b] explains the reason for the fate of R' Akiva's disciples: "*Mipnei she'lo nahogu kavod zeh l'zeh*—Because they did not give honor to one another." How scary! The Gemara doesn't say that they didn't honor their Rebbe. Perish the thought. Nor does it say they disgraced each other. Rather, they were at fault for not giving *each other* honor and, as a result, met a most dreadful end.

What a lesson! Proper respect, even to one's equals, is truly a matter of life and death! When our children ask us why we abstain from music and other forms of enjoyment during sefirah, we must stress this powerful concept. We must proclaim the grave importance of respect for the sages, our spouses, our parents, the elderly, teachers, colleagues, and yes, for every single human being.

I will illustrate with one example. Let's say you're a single person out on a date. You notice your prospect summoning the waiter rudely, as if the waiter is his or her serf. Such behavior is a strong indication that a person lacks respect for others. Bear in mind that respect is critical in a successful marriage and, indeed, is one of the major promises that a husband makes to a wife in the Jewish kesubah (marriage contract). As we advise couples of all ages, "If you treat her like a queen, she will treat you like a king, but if you treat her like a cleaning lady, she'll treat you like a shmata" (and vice versa).

However, I would like to add a further caveat. R' Akiva was a master teacher. He himself authored the Talmudic dictum, "'*V'ahavta l'reiacha kamocha, zeh klal gadol baTorah*'— 'Love your fellow man like yourself' is a primary principle of the Torah" [*Yerushalmi, Nedarim* 9:4]. Why didn't R' Akiva put a stop to the carnage? Why wasn't he able to stem the disaster's tide and educate his disciples about the errors of their

ways? The answer, I believe, is that he must have tried valiantly, but they did not listen to or absorb his teaching.

This is a key lesson and warning for many of us. A rabbi
can talk himself "blue in the face" about the lethal dangers of
fighting with others. He can lecture for decades about the
grave consequences of talking in shul. He can advise, plead,
cajole, and pontificate about the importance of spousal affection and attention. Yet there are many people who will simply never change, not even one iota. Such was the fate of the
students of R' Akiva. Thus, it is crucial that every one of us
bluntly ask ourselves whether or not we fall into the same
category. Do we, too, ignore the lessons we learn, or do we
seek to change and better ourselves in response to the Torah
we are taught?

We can question further: Why didn't any of R' Akiva's
twenty-four thousand talmidim do teshuvah? Why didn't
they take it to heart once they saw their friends dying? After
all, the *Medrash Rabbah* [4:8] says, "*Mays echad min hachaburah,
tidag kol hachaburah*—If one of the group dies, the whole
group should worry." The individuals in the group must
search their own deeds and correct what is askew. How did
all those great Torah scholars not realize this and correct
themselves before it was too late?

We must seek, therefore, to understand the error of R'
Akiva's talmidim on a subtler level. Perhaps the explanation is
as follows: These students all had the same teacher, the same
rebbe. They all learned the same lessons, heard the same lectures, and had the same notes. So each one felt there was no
reason to honor his peers. After all, what did one talmid have
that his colleague didn't? His friend had Torah, but he had the
same Torah, the same notes, and the same teacher. So why
should he honor any of the other talmidim?

Perhaps, on this deeper level, their sin is to be found. "*Shelo nahagu kavod zeh lazeh*—They did not give honor to each other." They all had the same reasoning: Why should they honor each other when they all had the same accomplishments?

However, this is a crucial mistake in the concept of *kavod haTorah*, honoring the Torah. When we honor a *talmid chochom*, a Torah scholar, we are not merely honoring the person. We are honoring the Torah contained within the person. A person who has acquired Torah knowledge contains a lofty cheilek (portion) of Hashem. It is that essence of Hashem that demands respect.

We can learn this concept from the posuk, "*Ozvei Hashem yichlu*—Those who forsake Hashem will be destroyed" [*Yeshaya* 1:24]. The Gemara in *Brachos* [8a] interprets the posuk in the following manner: "Who forsakes Hashem? *Zeh hamaniach Sefer Torah v'yatza*—Someone who walks out of shul during the reading of the Torah." This person is called an "ozeiv Hashem." We see from this that the Gemara equates the Torah with Hashem, for one who walks out during layning is considered as having walked out on Hashem Himself. Hashem and Torah are one.

With this in mind, we can seek to understand the posuk, "*Uvo sidbakun*—And you should cleave to Him" [*Devarim* 10:20]. How is it possible for a physical human being to cling to Hashem, Who is completely intangible? The Rambam answers that we can fulfill this posuk by cleaving to talmidei chachomim, because a talmid chochom has Torah in him. He is a living Torah scroll, and the Torah itself is viewed as an "appendage" of Hashem. Therefore, when you cling to a talmid chochom, you are indeed clinging to Hashem.

The Gemara [*Brachos* 6b] tells us that Shimon Ha'amsoni

explained homiletically all the es's (the often untranslated word spelled simply "aleph-sav") in the Torah. He would expound on the specific meaning of each appearance of this mysterious word, explaining what it added to the meaning of the sentence it was in. However, when he came to the posuk, "*Es Hashem Elokecha Tira*—You should fear your G-d" [*Devarim* 6:13]. What could that "*es*" possibly be coming to tell us? What could it possibly add or include? What else could be on the same par as fear of Hashem? As a result of being confounded by this posuk, R' Shimon was ready to discard all his work and to conclude that all the es's in the Torah do not come to teach us anything. That is, until R' Akiva came along and explained, "*Es Hashem Elokecha tira, l'rabos talmid chochom*." The reason for the "*es*" in that posuk is to specifically include a talmid chochom. You must fear a talmid chochom like you fear Hashem.

How could R' Akiva equate fear of a talmid chochom with fear of G-d? As we've already explained, the Torah of the talmid chochom is a cheilek of Hashem. When we show respect for a talmid chochom, it isn't simply for the man. Our respect is for the Torah he has within him.

And this was the mistake the students of R' Akiva made. They felt that, since each one had exactly the same Torah knowledge as the next, there was no reason to honor one another. Now if the point was to honor the person, they might have had a valid argument. However, it's not the person that has to be respected, but the *knowledge of Torah* that the person possesses. So even though they all had the same amount of learning and the same amount of Torah in them, each and every one of them, nevertheless, contained a special cheilek of Hashem. Therefore, it was incumbent upon them to honor one another.

Again, we can see this concept in the posuk, "*Mipnei seivah tokum, v'hadarta p'nei zakain, v'yaraisa mei-elokecha*—Stand up for an elderly person, show honor for a zakain, and fear your G-d" [*Vayikra* 19:34]. "Zakain" stands for, "*zeh konoh chochma*—One who has acquired wisdom" [*Kiddushin* 34b]. Why should we stand for a talmid chochom? The posuk answers us—because you should fear your G-d. When you stand up for a talmid chochom, you are illustrating your fear of Hashem.

In *Koheles* [8:13] it says "*V'tov lo yih'yeh l'rasha, v'lo yaarich yamim katzeil asher einenu yarei milifnei Elokim*—It will not be good for the wicked man. He won't live long, like a shadow, because he does not fear G-d." What exactly is Shlomo Hamelech referring to when he says that the *rasha* will not live long because he does not fear Hashem?

The Gemara in *Kiddushin* explains (using the midrashic principle of substitution) that a rasha will not live long because he does not stand up for a talmid chochom. Based on the posuk of "*v'hadarta p'nei zakain*" [*Vayikra* 19:34], in which the idea of fearing Hashem is also mentioned, the Gemara proceeds to translate the posuk: "It will not be good for the wicked man. He will not have length of days, because he does not stand up for talmidei chachomim."

So we can see that the wisdom of Shlomo Hamelech foretold the future fate of the disciples of R' Akiva. Because they did not honor one another, because they did not stand up for each other, they forfeited their lives.

We can all learn an important lesson from this incident. When it comes to showing honor, those who learn in kollel all day must also show proper respect for other people who learn Torah, even for a regular "balhabus" (literally, "home-owner," a working man, a regular Yossi). It makes no difference if that person didn't learn as many masechtas as you, or if that person learns "only" Chumash. We are not honoring the person's prowess in learning. Rather, we are honoring the fact that the person *is* learning, and that as a consequence the person contains a special part of Hashem.

The *Divrei Chaim*, the Sanzer Rav, zt"l, would always honor people who knew far less than he did in Torah. R' Moshe Feinstein, zt"l, would partially stand up for people who were much younger and certainly not as great as he was in Torah. These two tzadikim did not look at a person's accomplishments. They respected someone for whatever Torah the person knew, even if it was so much less than what they themselves knew. For they understood that the person who learns Torah contains an elevated cheilek of Hashem.

In *Masechtas Megillah* [27b], the Gemara tells us that R' Elazar ben Shamua enjoyed an extremely long life. When his students asked him why he merited such a length of days, he replied, "*Mi'yamai lo pasati al roshei am kodesh*—In all my days, I never walked over the heads of people that belong to a holy nation."

What does this mean? In those days, the talmidim would sit on the floor around the rebbe. R' Elazar had a great many talmidim and, if he came late, he had to step over his students in order to get to his place in the front. R' Elazar always made sure to be there early, *before* his students arrived, so that he would not have to subject them to that kind of humiliating treatment.

So here we demonstrated how a rebbe went out of his way not to dishonor his talmidim. R' Elazar respected his students, not for what they knew, for he was their teacher and thus knew much more than they did. He honored them because they learned Hashem's Torah. They were living sifrei

Torah, each containing a lofty piece of Hashem.

That is the reason that R' Elazar merited such a long life. He was a *mechabed* (an honorer of) Torah. We can see from here that, not only will one who does not respect the Torah not live long, but the reverse is also true.

Indeed, this was the *derech*, the philosophy, of R' Elazar's life. In *Pirkei Avos* [4:13], it says that R' Elazar used to say: "*Yehi kavod talmidcha chaviv alecha k'shelach*—Let the honor of your student be as dear to you as your own honor."

We now know that if we don't show the proper respect, it can be deadly. The talmidim of R' Akiva reasoned logically that there was no need for one to honor the other. However, they should have realized that they had to honor the Torah inside each other, the holy cheilek of Hashem that they all contained.

No matter what time of year it is, but especially during sefirah, we have to ask ourselves: Do we practice this important concept? Do we give honor to all those who learn Torah? Or do we honor only those who are outstanding in Torah? If we find fault with ourselves in this area, now is the time to correct it.

The Rambam in *Hilchos Talmud Torah* [6:11] states, "*Kol hamevazeh es hachochomim, ein lo chelek l'olam habah*—One who embarrasses a talmid chochom does not have a share in the world to come." That's a pretty absolute punishment: To lose forever. To lose eternity.

But now we can understand why. People who embarrass a talmid chochom are not only embarrassing flesh and blood (which is bad enough in itself), they are embarrassing a part of Hashem. And that deserves a most severe punishment.

We have to realize that Hashem went to great lengths to teach us this concept. "*Yakar b'einei Hashem, ha'mavsa lachasi-*

dov—It is extremely hard on Hashem, the death of his righteous ones" [*Tehillim* 116:15]. And Hashem had to part with not
one tzadik, but twenty-four thousand tzadikim, in order to
teach us this lesson.

But Hashem did this in order to impart to us just how
essential this lesson is. Let us take it to heart and pass this all-
important message on to our children.

May it be the will of Hashem that we, together with our
children, learn and show respect for one another and, in that
merit, may we be zocheh to long life, Torah nachas, and
everything wonderful.

Avoiding the Envy of Others

"**D**on't give me an ayin hara."

"I'm afraid of an ayin hara."

"*B'li ayin hara.*"

These are all phrases and expressions we've heard, and probably use, often. But what exactly does "ayin hara" mean? Is there any Torah validity to it? Is it just superstition, or a real force of evil?

The first thing we need to establish is: ayin hara is definitely a valid concept from a Torah point of view, and it can pose a threat. The mishnah in *Pirkei Avos* [4:11] tells us, "*R' Yehoshua omer, 'Ayin hara, v'yetzer hara, v'sinas habrios motzi'in es ha'adam min ha'olom'*—R' Yehoshua used to say 'Three things lead to a person's expulsion from the world: an evil eye, evil desires, and hatred of others.'" Here the mishnah teaches us in black and white that not only is ayin hara real, but it can cause a person's early demise. Even more astounding is the order that the mishnah specifies. R' Yehoshua must have felt that an ayin hara was a most perilous thing if he listed it first!

We can readily understand that the yetzer hara can cause someone to be expelled from the world. The yetzer hara incites us to sin, thereby giving license to the malach hamavess (angel of death) to do his job. (The Gemara actually tells us that the satan, yetzer hara, and malach hamavess are one and the same.) *Sinas habrios* (hatred and anger) can cause someone to become physically ill and thus also bring about an untimely death. Hatred also leads to lashon hara and rechilus (slander and tale bearing) which we know shorten a person's life. However, by mentioning ayin hara first, the Tana is telling us that he considers ayin hara more deadly than both the yetzer hara and sinas habrios!

Further indication of the dangers of ayin hara can be found in *Masechtas Bava Metzia* [107b]. Rav once went to a small cemetery. The Gemara tells us that he knew how to divine the cause of the deaths of those buried there, and he remarked as he left the cemetery, "*Tishim v'tisha b'ayin hara, v'echad b'derech ha-olom.*" Out of the one hundred people buried there, Rav concluded, ninety-nine died because of ayin hara, while only one died of natural causes.

For instance, when we hear that Teflon pots may cause cancer, or that the U.S. Surgeon General warns us of the possible dangers of this product we're quick to pay attention. So it goes without saying that when the Torah cautions us about something, we should *really* be concerned. A further example of the lethal potential of ayin hara can be seen from the posuk in Eikev, "*V'heisir Hashem mimcha kol choli*—Hashem will remove all sickness from you" [*Devarim* 7:16]. The Gemara in *Bava Metzia* [107b] elucidates, "*Kol choli, zu ayin hara.*" What does the posuk mean by "all sickness?" It means ayin hara! Rashi explains further that the number one cause for all disease is ayin hara.

What is the nature of this deadly danger and how do we go about avoiding its lethal consequences? The Rishonim tell us that if someone has a talent or an advantage over the average person and flaunts it, people become upset and envious. Hashem sees this flaunting, and does not want this person to upset the natural flow of things, so He takes away that person's special gift or privilege. And if that gift is too ingrained within the person to remove it, Hashem, *chas v'shalom*, takes the person away entirely. So if people do not take care to modestly use the talents or gifts they may have, they are endangering their gift—and maybe even their life. This is the threat of ayin hara.

Now it is clear what Chana was davening for so fervently, when petitioning Hashem for a child, "*V'nasata l'amasecha zera anoshim*—Please, Hashem, give to your maidservant a '*zera anoshim*'" [*Shmuel I* 1:1]. The Gemara [*Brachos* 31b] explains, "*Zera hamuvla bein anoshim*—A child accepted among people." Chana actually prayed for a son who would be "*lo chochom v'lo tipeish*—not too wise and not a fool."

How astonishing! Doesn't every mother want her son to be an extraordinary talmid chochom? Rashi explains that Chana didn't want a son that was too wise, because he would stand out. People would envy him and he would be in danger of an ayin hara.

Throughout the ages, our brilliant ones always tried to protect themselves from ayin hara. When the shevatim (twelve tribes; in this case, ten of the twelve brothers) went down to Mitzrayim to buy food, Yaakov told them to split up and not enter the land together through the same entrance. Why did he do this? Because the shevatim were ten of the most perfect specimens of the human race, and if they would have all come in together, they would have attracted attention to themselves. Then, upon noticing them, people would have become jealous, and this would have made them extremely vulnerable to an ayin hara [*Bereishis* 44:5, *Rashi*]. (Incidentally, this is how Yosef was able to plausibly accuse them of being spies. Since they came in through different gates, and not together as a family would have come, he argued that they must have been spying on the land, seeking to identify its vulnerable points.) So, we see from this that even Yaakov Avinu was concerned about ayin hara!

How can we protect ourselves from the dangers of ayin hara?

"*V'hatz'nei-a leches im Hashem Elokecha*—Walk modestly with Hashem your G-d" [*Michah* 6:8]. Do not flaunt your advantages. Do not call attention to a special talent that you have. Or, if Hashem has given you something wonderful, don't brandish it in front of those who haven't been so blessed. For example, if you meet someone who doesn't have any children after years of marriage, don't start "carrying on" about how your little one is starting to walk, and don't make them spend the entire afternoon looking at your baby pictures. (This sensitivity demands a sense of balance and tactfulness, since the childless couple does not want to feel deliberately left out either.)

There are many Jewish customs that reflect fear of ayin hara. In Europe, many families would never sit for a family portrait. We are taught that a son shouldn't be called up for an aliyah to the Torah immediately before or after his father. One reason for this is that the two of them are *posul l'eidus* (invalid witnesses) together. But another reason is to avoid generating an ayin hara. Similarly, we break a glass at a chasanah (wedding) under the chupah (canopy). This is primarily an act which is a *zecher l'churban* (remembrance of the Temple's destruction). It is to symbolize that no simcha is complete in our time, as we still do not have a Beis Hamikdash. However, we also break a glass, the *SM"AH* informs us, to slightly blemish the perfect happiness of the new couple, so all the hundreds of people watching should not become jealous—and cast an ayin hara on the chasan and kallah!

The custom of putting on a "red bendela" (a red string usually worn around the wrist) is fairly common even today. It is possible that it was adopted to serve as a "red alert" to remind someone to be modest, and wary of the ayin hara.

The *Pele Yoetz* tells us that even when we say good things about someone, we should say a tefillah that no harm should befall him or her. From this we can see that we must protect ourselves not only from receiving an ayin hara, but from giving one to others. In fact, the mitzvah of *lo sachmod* (not to covet what someone else has) includes this prohibition. For by being envious of a neighbor's lot, one can bring one's neighbor harm through ayin hara.

Now, we might ask ourselves, "If ayin hara is so dangerous, how can someone *darshan* (expound on the Torah) to the masses? How can one risk doing any good deed publicly?"

The *Pele Yoetz* tells us that this is the exception. When a person is doing a mitzvah, he does not have to worry about ayin hara. "*Shomer mitzvah lo yada daver ra*—One who performs a mitzvah will not be harmed by evil" [*Koheles* 8:5]. So when they ask you to be a guest of honor at a yeshivah din-ner, don't use ayin hara as an excuse to decline. "*Mitzvas Hashem barah meeras ainayim*—The commandments of Hashem are clear, brightening the eyes" [*Tehillim* 19:9]. Chazal tell us that this posuk teaches us that Torah protects us from the evil eye.

Interestingly, there is one group among Klal Yisroel entirely immune to the ayin hara—shevet Yosef. "*Ben poras Yosef, ben poras alei uyin*" [*Bereishis* 49:22]. The Gemara [*Brachos* 20a] interprets this posuk homiletically, and tells us not to read it "*alei uyin*," but rather "*olei ayin*," above the eye. The tribe of Yosef is above the evil eye, the ayin hara.

The Gemara tells us that if we are afraid of an ayin hara we should say (as an incantation), "*Ana mi-zera d'Yosef ka-asina, d'lo shalta bah eina bisha*—I am from the seed of Yosef which is immune to the ayin hara." (The use of incantations, it should be noted, is not common nowadays.)

Why was Yosef so special, that not only he but even all of his descendants were and are immune to the ayin hara? If we take a look at the life of Yosef Hatzadik, we can understand why he has this special merit. Yosef flaunted his *k'sones pasim*, his coat of many colors, in front of his brothers. That coat was an extraordinary gift from Yaakov, who gave it to him to serve the function of *bigdei kehunah* (vestments of the priesthood), as a sign that Yosef would inherit the firstborn right to perform the Temple Service. Because their father singled Yosef out in this manner, the brothers became envious of him. He also told them about his dreams, in which he occupied a position of rulership over them.

This situation landed him in a pit of scorpions, and, soon after, slavery. Later, Yosef became overseer in Potiphar's house. Once he began to get comfortable, he combed his hair and brought notice upon himself. This brought him under the desirous gaze of his master's wife, and because he wouldn't bow to her wishes, he ended up in jail. So we see that during his early life, Yosef was plagued by ayin hara. He flaunted his talents, his gifts, and did not take them for what they were, G-d-given. Yosef stayed in jail two additional years because he told Pharaoh's butler to mention him to Pharaoh. Yosef thought he could get himself out of jail, that it was within his power to do so. To show him otherwise, Hashem made the butler forget about him for two years, and Yosef remained in jail during that time. (We must note that in Yosef these flaws were actually quite microscopic. The Torah brings them to the surface in a clear way, even though they were subtle, so that we may learn to be wary of these issues in our own development, on our own level. Yosef's failings, as it were, were only punishable because of the incredibly lofty level he occupied.)

People who say, "*Kochi v'otzem yadi*—My success comes through my own strength and power" [*Devarim* 8:17], and not from Hashem, will find themselves under the power of an ayin hara.

Hashem gave Yosef two years of intense thought to realize his error. With all of his suffering, he managed to completely eradicate this flaw in his soul! After this period, we find Yosef's attitude drastically altered. When Pharaoh said to him, "I hear you know how to interpret dreams," Yosef corrected him, saying, "*Elokim ya'aneh es sh'lom Pharaoh*—G-d will reveal Pharaoh's welfare" [*Bereishis* 41:15, 16]. So too, when his brothers came down to Mitzrayim, Yosef told them, "Not you, but Hashem sent me here." Because he rectified the same flaw in himself that caused him to be harmed by ayin hara, he and all his descendants can never be harmed by it again.

To summarize, in order to avoid ayin hara, an extremely dangerous threat to us, we shouldn't flaunt anything we have; not our talents nor our riches, or anything else we have that others may not. We must recognize that everything we have is a gift from Hashem, to be used in accordance with His desires. In this way, we will not cause others to feel badly or be envious of us, and we will be safe from the ayin hara.

Timeless
Timely
Lessons

Elul: *Wrapping the Year Up Right*

The month of Elul presents exciting opportunities for the religious Jew. Elul is an acronym for, "*Ani L'Dodi V'dodi Li—* I am to my Beloved (a reference to Hashem), and my Beloved is to me," which means that during Elul Hashem will focus on us—in direct proportion to the amount that we focus our thoughts and actions on Him. While this is actually true the entire year, it is particularly pronounced during Elul.

Thus Elul is the perfect time to sharpen our prayer skills. It is also a time to cleave to Hashem by learning more Torah, by working to create and maintain shalom bayis and by honoring our parents.

Elul is also the last month of the year. In Yiddishkeit, this concept assumes significant prominence. We are taught, "*Hakol holeich achar ha-chesom*—Everything goes according to the finale" [*Brachos* 14]. Thus, failing to pause for a moment at the end of our prayers, out of respect for Hashem, can cause our entire tefillah to be torn up and discarded. So, too, we are taught to repent, if at all possible, an hour before our death.

Another example of this concept is contained in our Sukkos prayers. When Sukkos falls on Shabbos, we say, "*Hoshannah, yosheves u'mamtenes ad klos haShabbos, Hoshannah*," which means, "Please save us, in the merit of our sitting and waiting until the end of Shabbos, please save us." This is a rather strange petition. Is it meritorious that people sit and look at their watches, waiting until Shabbos has ended? Rather, I think this prayer signifies that it is the final moments of Shabbos that are the most critical. In fact, the character and integrity of the entire Shabbos are defined in these last moments of Shabbos. So too, since Elul is the final month of the year, it affords us an incredible opportunity to correct and refine our entire year, if we use it properly.

There are, of course, a myriad of ways to do this and each of us has his or her own strengths and weaknesses. However, I would like to focus on one area that could greatly improve our chances for a beautiful New Year. This is the area of *shmiras halashon*—guarding one's tongue. We all know the famous dictum: "*mi ha'ish hachofetz chaim*—Who wants life? Guard your tongue from speaking evil" [*Tehillim* 44:13]. Since Elul is the time of the year when we petition Hashem for life and happiness, it is clear that we must reevaluate our manner of speech and work to improve it.

In a most astonishing statement, the Vilna Gaon revealed (in the *Iggeres HaGra*—the letter he wrote to his family before he departed for Eretz Yisroel) the vital importance of guarding our tongues. He writes that the most powerful factor in determining our Olam Habah is proper speech. This is such an awesome statement and fundamental life-lesson that it's astounding that it doesn't grace everyone's refrigerator and office desk! Similarly, at this time, when we try to purge ourselves from sin, how important it is to remember the words of the Yerushalmi in *Pe'ah*, that as Torah is equal to all mitzvos, so too, lashon hara is equal to all the aveiros.

Furthermore, the *Zohar* reveals that the Satan cannot prosecute us by himself. As the Torah says, "*Al pi shenaim eidim, yakum davar*—Evidence can be established only with two witnesses" [*Devarim* 19:15]. So how does the Satan corroborate his accusations? As an example, let's suppose that Shmuel talks a lot during davening. The Satan wants to prosecute him, but can't do it by himself. However, he hears that there is a chasanah at El Carib and decides to attend. He hovers around the smorgasbord and listens to the swirls of conversation. Suddenly, he hears Chaim telling someone how terrible it is that Shmuel is always talking in shul. "What a crass fellow!" Chaim says. "I don't know why the Rabbi puts up with it!" The Satan pounces on this opportunity—now he has the partner he needs to prosecute Shmuel. Thus, Chaim—even though what he said was true—his sinful chatter actually caused punishment to descend upon another Jew.

The *Zohar* continues: The Satan doesn't stop there. He then asks Hashem, "Since Chaim helped me prosecute another Jew, can I, measure for measure, now audit Chaim's records to see if he's due for any prosecution?" And Hashem says, "Absolutely."

Thus, we see how imperative it is for us to avoid speaking ill about each other, especially so close to the judgment day of Rosh Hashanah. Furthermore, by not listening to lashon hara about others, we gain a powerful protection, *mid-*

dah k'neged middah [*Shabbos* 105], that Hashem won't listen to any bad things people may say about us.

Elul: Preparation Is Crucial

Each year, when the month of Elul arrives, we often find ourselves trying to squeeze the last drops of juice from our vacations before we return to the yearly grind. Our minds fill with thoughts of school supply lists and new bus routes.

Yet, to an observant Jew, the month of Elul means so much more. We are taught that Moshe Rabbeinu went up on Har Sinai to appeal to Hashem to forgive the Jews for the sin of the Golden Calf on the first day of Elul. After staying there for forty days and forty nights, he descended on Yom Kippur, having achieved atonement for Klal Yisroel.

Moshe Rabbeinu thus injected into this time of year a powerful opportunity for us to repent and mend our ways. This is why this time of the year is known as the *y'mei rachamim v'selicha*—days of mercy and forgiveness. The *Chayei*

Adam (ch. 138) tells us that it is incumbent upon a G-d-fearing Jew to prepare at least thirty days before Rosh Hashanah for the Day of Judgment. The Alter of Kelm suggests that, without ample preparation, it is absurd to say the verses of Kingship in the Rosh Hashanah davening. How can we realistically accept Hashem as our King, without understanding what Hashem's Kingship is all about?

So how do we prepare? Of course, the answer is to do teshuvah. But, what exactly is "teshuvah"? The meaning of this word is not as simple as you might think. You see, teshuvah has two seemingly contradictory meanings. In the verse, *"Vayashov Avraham el na'arov"* [*Bereishis* 24:19], the word "vayashav" (which shares the same root as the word "teshuvah") means "to return." However, in the verse, *"Shuv meicharon apecha"* [*Shemos* 34:14], the word "shuv" (which has the same root) means "to abandon" or "to forsake."

The Rambam explains teshuvah in the latter sense, interpreting it as the abandoning and forsaking of our sins. However, both the Maharal of Prague and the Mabit explain it in the sense of "return," understanding it to mean the attempt to return to Hashem.

In reality, there is no contradiction. *Returning* to Hashem means that we must *abandon* our past misdeeds. By doing so, we fulfill the verse, *"V'shavta ad Hashem Elokecha*—and you should return to Hashem your G-d" [*Devarim* 30:2], and we give meaning to the concept embodied by this month's name—ELUL—**A**ni **L**'dodi **V**'dodi **L**i (I am to my Beloved and my Beloved is to me). It is up to us to turn our thoughts to Hashem during this critical month.

Elul is also a time for deepening our awareness of Hashem. We have a positive command—*Es Hashem Elokecha tirah*—to fear G-d [*Devarim* 6:13; 10:20]. How, on a practical basis, do we fulfill this? The Rishonim teach us that if, for example, we are tempted to speak lashon hara, scream at our spouse, or gaze at improper things, and we abstain because we realize that Hashem is watching us, this is the essence of *"Es Hashem Elokecha tirah."* This behavior is consistent with the deeper focus of Elul, which is simply becoming more aware that Hashem is around.

But Hashem is not only an inhibiting factor. He should also be our primary motivation for positive action. The posuk teaches us, *"B'chol d'rachecha da'eihu*—In all your ways you should acknowledge Him" [*Mishlei* 3:6]. Thus, for instance, when we are debating whether to get up early for selichos or sleep another half an hour, whether we should travel an entire hour to visit a sick person or browse the latest sports page, whether we should pay attention to our spouse or continue shmoozing on the phone, and we decide to do the right thing because we want to please Hashem, this is an embodiment of the real meaning of yiras shamayim. It shows that the determining factor in our decision-making process is fear and love of Hashem.

In our Yomim Noraim liturgy, we say, *"teshuvah, tefillah, u'tzedakah ma'avirin es ro'ah hagezeirah*—Repentance, prayer and charity abolish the evil decrees" [Unesaneh Tokef from Mussaf]. Thus, we see that *prayer* is also an immensely important item on which to work at this time of year. Working on our davening is certainly consistent with the theme of returning to Hashem, for success in prayer depends on the proper realization that everything depends upon Hashem and that, when we are praying, we are really talking to Him, and believe with certainty that davening can really help.

So many people think that working on davening means to learn the meaning of the words and concentrate on them.

While this is a noble pursuit, it is not the first step. Rather, we must first learn to realize that whenever we pray, we are talking to G-d. Once we tailor our davening with this realization, everything else will just come naturally.

Let us remember that, in direct proportion to how much we feel *Ani l'Dodi*, (I am to my beloved [i.e., Hashem]), that is how much Dodi Li, my Beloved, will pay attention to me. So, let's make an effort, during the countless times we pass mezuzahs every day, let's pause just for a millisecond, to feel Hashem in the room with us. Let's think "Thank you, G-d" every time we say a blessing. And let's make it a firm practice to start off our day with a meaningful "thank you" in Modeh Ani, and end our day with gratitude as we say in the important brachah of Hamapil.

As we pepper our day with constant acknowledgments of Hashem, we will then truly be ready, on Rosh Hashanah, to crown Hashem as our King. In this merit, may Hashem show us, His loyal subjects, special favor, and bless us all with good health, happiness and everything wonderful.

Elul: *Avoiding Discouragement*

It is the way of the yetzer hara that, when the stakes are high, he pulls out all the stops. Therefore it logically follows that before the Day of Judgment, when we are naturally motivated to be introspective and repent, he tries in a plethora of ways to distract us. Let's not be fooled for even a moment into thinking that it is coincidental that distractions like shopping for school supplies, dealing with long lines at the shoe store, struggles in establishing car pools, packing and unpacking, all fall out smack in the middle of the month of Elul. This is just one of the ways in which our evil inclination attempts to steer us away us from the path of self-analysis and teshuvah.

But this is only the start! The yetzer hara has many more tricks up his ingenious sleeve. First, he tells us in a calming and soothing voice, "Don't get so nervous about Yom Kippur. After all, you made it through this year just fine—and last Elul you weren't so well prepared. So, you'll make it through this year too!" In reality, this is a dangerous way of thinking. Who knows? Perhaps this year we were just hanging on by our fingertips, surviving only because of some *zechus avos* (some merit of our ancestors).

Let's not assume that we can just coast through the season! Instead, let's stir ourselves to action and prepare properly for judgement.

The yetzer hara has other tactics, as well. He tries to dishearten us by pointing out that last year, in the passion and fervor of the High Holy Days, we acted properly contrite about our various misdeeds. Indeed, we may have even committed ourselves to pray better, to study more, to give more attention to our loved ones, to answer more "amens," and a host of other nice things. But as always, a mere few weeks later, all those promises and commitments were like a wisp in the wind, gone as if they never existed.

So the yetzer hara challenges us, "Who are you kidding?! Why are you trying to fool Hashem? Drop the charade and stop trying to put on a show!"

Unfortunately, if we succumb to such talk, we are only fulfilling the desire of the yetzer hara who desperately wants to stop us from thinking thoughts of teshuvah. Let's remember that even momentary contrition and regret, and even fleeting thoughts of self-improvement are much better than nothing. Furthermore, when Hashem sees that we are moved by the seriousness of the season to make an effort to improve, He will surely come to our aid.

Another strategy of the yetzer hara is to try to get us to say to ourselves, "I'm a hopeless case. I have so many faults and flaws that Hashem must be totally fed up with me." And when he succeeds from this angle, he causes many people to despair from doing teshuvah, thinking that they are lost causes. The late Satmar Rebbe, zt"l (as quoted in the *Hanhogos Tzadikim*), taught us that people who think they are too far gone for Hashem's forgiveness is guilty of saying a *brachah l'vatalah*, a blessing in vain, when they say three times daily in the Shemoneh Esrei, "*Chanun hamarbe lisloach*," that Hashem is the gracious One Who forgives exceedingly. Hashem forgives without limit, so—no matter how guilty we feel—we must never surrender to the feeling that we are beyond hope.

In the chassidic masterpiece, the *Pele Yoetz* (in the essay on the word "teshuvah"), the author describes yet another technique of the yetzer hara. He cautions us that the evil inclination often downplays our misdeeds to us, until we think they are not really so bad.

Examples of this are people who habitually don't think about the meaning of their prayers, and don't even focus on the fact that they are talking to Hashem, can come to feel that they are not doing any grave injustice. They might rationalize by musing that they go to minyan three times a day, that they say every single word, and that anyway there's an opinion that mitzvos don't require kavanah!

What a cover-up job! The yetzer hara can thus blind people like this to their own brazenness, in thinking that they can stand before G-d and not even pay attention! In this way, they can continue committing this offense daily for years and years!

This, says the *Pele Yoetz*, is hinted to us in the verse, "*V'chol yeitzer mach'shavos leebo rak ra kol hayom*—And every product of the thoughts of his heart is but evil all day long" [*Bereishis* 6:5]. The *Pele Yoetz* explains that the word "rak," which means "but," always indicates a limitation. Thus, in this verse which speaks about the evil one, the word "rak" stresses that the yetzer hara often tries to *limit*, or minimize, in our minds the offenses and transgressions we commit.

In another example, a man who hardly spends time with his children can fool himself into thinking that this is normal and acceptable, or at least excusable. Or, a woman who is inattentive to her husband can convince herself that there will be plenty of time later to make up for her lack of affection. Children often believe that disrespectful behavior toward their parents is the social norm, and that Hashem will understand.

Now that we know many of the techniques of our evil inclination, we must be wary. The human tendency is to go easy on ourselves. "*Ein adam roeh nigei atzmo*—a person does not easily recognize his own faults" [*Negaim* 2:5], and overcoming these natural tendencies is not easy. Having a mentor, such as a Rebbe or Rav, helps us to discern our imperfections. The study of mussar is also extremely beneficial in helping us to ferret out our mistakes and spiritual shortcomings.

A successful formula with which to approach Hashem on the Day of Judgment is to come before Hashem with the commitment that we will try to overcome our evil inclination more often this coming year than we did last year. With this promise, we can rightfully ask Hashem to give us a better year than the previous one.

But how can we "convince" Hashem that we will succeed in this endeavor? There is only one sure way. The Gemara tells us in *Masechtas Kiddushin* [30b], "*Barasi yetzer hara; ubarasi lo Torah tavlin*—I (Hashem) created the evil inclination and I made the Torah as an antidote to it." Thus, for example, families should sit together before Rosh Hashanah and figure out how they can add more Torah to their homes in the coming year. Unmarried people should also assess how they, too, can do the same. This is an effective way to show Hashem that we will defeat the yetzer hara more often since we will be "drinking" more of the "Torah potion," which Hashem assures us will always work.

There are many (good) ways to increase a family's Torah output: a commitment to have divrei Torah at the Shabbos table, a designated time for Torah study on Sundays, a nightly review with the children about something that they just learned in school that day, a husband's commitment to review the sedrah each week, or a couple's decision to study the laws of lashon hara together.

Mothers should commit themselves to working harder at creating a Torah environment in their homes. Wives should motivate their husbands towards Torah excellence by showing their pride and happiness with their spouse's Torah accomplishments. Even a resolution to learn the meaning of our prayers (the study of which is also considered Torah learning) is a powerful commitment to bring before the Kisei HaKovod (the throne of Glory) on the Day of Judgment.

In the merit of our attempt at self-improvement and our trying to avoid the pitfalls of the yetzer hara, may all of our efforts prove successful.

Rosh Hashanah:
Emulating Hashem's Compassion

During the Days of Awe, we strive to examine ourselves honestly. When we do this deeply and sincerely, we are forced to admit our shortcomings. Whether it is a lack of dedication to Torah study, impatience with our children, careless davening, or a thousand other things, we usually do not approach this time from a position of strength. Thus, our only practical and logical petition to Hashem when praying that we be judged "*latov*—for good" is to ask for mercy, rachamim. Even though we know we're not deserving, we can always ask Hashem to forgive us.

Before Moshe Rabbeinu died, he begged Hashem to let him enter Eretz Yisroel. What type of tefillah did Moshe use?

The Medrash tells us that there are ten different methods of prayer a person can utilize. In this instance, Moshe chose "Va'eschanan" [*Devarim* 3:23]. Moshe did not ask Hashem to grant his request because of his zechuyos (his merits). Nor did Moshe complain to Hashem. Moshe's form of prayer was derived from the language of "cheyn," which denotes the idea of getting something for free ("chinom"), solely due to Hashem's mercy.

The *Matnas Kehunah* tells us that this is, in fact, the best possible way to pray. However, utilizing this mode of prayer comes with a price. If there was no price tag attached, then any sinner could just beg for Hashem's mercy and be forgiven. In *Masechtas Shabbos* [15la], the Gemara specifies the criteria needed in order to daven for rachamim. "*Kol ha'm'rachaim al habrios, m'rachamim alov min ha'shamayim*—Whoever has mercy on other, G-d will have mercy on him." One must be compassionate towards others for Hashem to be compassionate towards them. So it is crucial that we prepare ourselves *before* we pray in this manner, to make sure we have the ammunition we need on the Yom Hadin.

When Bnei Yisroel committed the *cheit haeigel*, Hashem taught Moshe a most powerful tefillah—the tefillah containing the Thirteen Middos of Rachamim. Hashem then told Moshe that whenever Klal Yisroel would cry out to Him with this tefillah, He would listen. In this tefillah, when we say "*Kel Rachum V'chanun*," we declare our belief in Hashem's abundant mercy. At the same time, this very same proclamation can work to our detriment. The Torah commands us, "*V'halachta bid'rachav*—follow in His ways" [*Devarim* 28:9]. Similarly, we say in Az Yashir, "*Zeh keli V'anveihu*—This is my G-d and I will glorify him." The Medrash tells us that "*Anveihu*" is a contraction of two words, *ani* and *Hu*—I and

He. I will glorify Him by trying to be like Him. Both of these verses teach us to emulate Hashem by copying His middos, His attributes. Consequently, if we pronounce the Thirteen Middos of Rachamim, but we don't embody them as we are commanded to, it could very well turn the tide against us. Can't you just hear the prosecuting angel address the Holy Tribunal, "Listen to that person! He is begging for Hashem's mercy. He is admitting that Hashem is full of rachamim, full of compassion, and that is obviously true! Hashem is! But *he* isn't! On what grounds does *he* deserve such mercy?" This is why we have to truly arm ourselves with rachmanus, compassion towards others.

A perfect example of a true rachaman was R' Shmuel Salant, who used to receive people in need at all hours of the day and night. As the years passed, his family saw the physical toll this was taking on him, and wanted to limit appointments to certain hours of the day. But R' Shmuel refused, citing what it says in Birchas Hamazon, "*U'm'farneis osanu tamid b'chol yom, u'v'chol eis, u'v'chol shaah*—Hashem supports us always, every day, every time, at every hour." Hashem is always on call, R' Shmuel protested, and we are supposed to emulate Him. Since Hashem is always available, R' Shmuel felt that he had to be available always as well.

The degree to which we behave with mercifulness toward others to a large extent determines the effectiveness of our tefillos. In *Devarim* [33:12], the posuk tells us, "*L'Binyomin amar: Y'did Hashem yishcon lavetach alov*—To Binyomin [Moshe] said: Friend of Hashem, Hashem will dwell in security in his portion." Rashi explains that this refers to the fact that the Beis Hamikdash would be built in the portion of Binyomin. The *Yalkut Shimoni* explains why the tribe of Binyomin was chosen for this unique honor. For all the years of its existence, people would come to the Beis Hamikdash to daven to Hashem and to beg for mercy. In order for their prayers to be effective, the place that they came to needed to be a place of compassion. Hashem therefore selected the portion of Binyomin, the most merciful of the twelve brothers, since he was the only one not involved in the cruel act of selling Yosef.

In short, the more merciful one is to others, the more merciful Hashem will be to him. If we personally concentrate on strengthening ourselves in the middah of *rachamim*, we can have confidence that Hashem will show mercy to us.

Hashem, in fact, has given us a number of practical mitzvos to kindle, awaken, and develop the priceless attribute of rachmonus within us. Hashem, Who of course desires only the best for us, wants to help us in developing this essential trait. In order to do this, He gave us mitzvos that kindle feelings of empathy within us and help us feel compassion for others. One such mitzvah we have is *shiluach hakan*, sending away the mother bird before taking her eggs or her offspring, so she is not there to witness her children being taken from her. The *K'sav Sofer* stresses the importance of this mitzvah as an act of mercy. It is a drill, an exercise to help us feel the suffering of another. The Gemara [*Pesachim* 13b] tells us that, if we are sensitive to the suffering and feeling of others, we will merit the blessing of "*L'maan yitav Loch v'haarachta yomim*— It will be good for you and your days will be lengthened" [*Devarim* 22:7].

The Torah tells us: "*V'nasati esev b'sadcha livhemtecha, v'achalta v'savata*—Hashem will give you grass in the fields for your animals, and you will eat and be satisfied" [*Devarim* 11:15]. The Gemara [*Brachos* 40] explains that here the Torah is telling us that we must feed our animals before we feed ourselves. The meforshim further explain that this posuk speaks to us not only about animals, but about all those who are unable to help themselves. Before we sit down to breakfast, for example, we should make sure to give the baby a bottle, or see to it that an elderly person in our care has eaten.

The fact is, we often do the right things, but for the wrong reasons. When our child cries in the middle of the night, we get up, change the baby's diaper, and give her a bottle. Why do we do it? Because we want to be able to go back to sleep as quickly as possible?! Because we don't want the neighbors to think we don't tend to our children?! In truth, we should do it primarily for the most important reason: The child is uncomfortable and is suffering. We should feel that discomfort as if it were our own and rush to ease and soothe it. This is the madreiga we must all aspire to, that "greatest principle of the Torah," the fulfillment of "*V'ahavta la'reiacha komocha*—love your brother as you do yourself" [*Vayikra* 19:18].

The root letters of rachamim—"reish," "ches," and "mem"—correspond to the ramach aivarim, the 248 bones each human has in his or her body. If one behaves mercifully, Hashem will be merciful in return and save one from bodily harm.

Those letters are also the same as the letters in the word "rechem," meaning womb. For in no other place is the caring for another human being so complete and fundamental. The baby is totally dependent on the mother, and she supplies its every need.

The same letters also comprise the word "chamor," donkey. A donkey goes through life carrying people's burdens. A person who is merciful also carries the burdens of others.

And what of someone who does not care at all for anyone beside himself? For such a heartless individual, the letters of rachamim can also be rearranged to spell "cheirem," expulsion.

Rachmanus is absolutely necessary for us to have a hope for success in our prayers on the Yom Hadin. A lack in this department is assuredly lethal. In the Gemara [*Yuma* 80b], R' Alazar Ben Azarya tells us that teshuvah and Yom Kippur can atone for all aveiros, all sins, except for those bein adam lachaveiro, between one person and another. No degree of teshuvah will erase that type of deed until the person who was harmed has been appeased.

The Gemara illustrates just how dangerous it is to cause pain to another person. It tells us how Avdon caused R' Yishmael Bar R' Yosi some distress. Because of that, Avdon became a leper, two of his sons died, and two other sons suffered divorce from their wives. The Gemara in *Kesuvos* [62b] tells us of R' Rechumi, who was a talmid of Rava in Mechuza. He learned there all year round and only came home once a year, on Erev Yom Kippur. One year, however, he was so engrossed in learning that he forgot to go home. His wife, who was eagerly awaiting her husband's visit, started to cry when he did not appear. As her tears flowed, the roof that her husband was learning on collapsed, and he was killed.

A person has to feel rachmanus for all Jews, but it is especially important that we feel compassion for our spouses. We are not on guard when we are with them. We don't have to impress them. We subconsciously rely on the fact that they are stuck with us irregardless of our behavior. Our tolerance level is very low with them, especially when they repeat the same offense more than once. But we should know that we have to be very careful. A wife's tears could be deadly.

We might have the best excuse there is, even that of learning Torah. Indeed, we know that Torah usually protects us from evil. But no excuse in the world will protect us from the consequences of hurting another human being. R' Rechumi certainly did not mean to make his wife cry. He was engrossed in Torah study. But such are the consequences of insensitivity.

In another famous example from the book of *Shmuel* [chapter 1], Penina taunted Chana relentlessly about her childlessness, but only so that Chana would turn to Hashem and pray more fervently for a child. Her intentions were *l'shem shamayim* (for a good purpose). However, because of what she did, all of her children tragically died during her lifetime. Hurting someone is like putting your hand in a fire. No matter *why* you put your hand in it, no matter what the excuse is you cannot come away unscathed.

In another Gemara, we are told that R' Kahana had a defect in his lips that made it seem like he was always smiling. R' Yochonan was once giving a shiur. R' Kahana attended the shiur, and when R' Yochanan looked at him, he thought that R' Kahana was laughing at him. R' Yochanan felt hurt and, because of that, R' Kahana died. R' Kahana certainly intended no harm, yet he still caused someone pain, and was unfortunately punished as a result.

We must train ourselves to be extremely sensitive to the needs of others, especially those closest to us. We should not keep our spouses waiting. We should not exclude them from conversations, and we should be even more careful during times when they are under more stress, such as when a woman is expecting, or when a husband is experiencing difficulty at work. It is at these times that we are called upon to be sensitive because they are usually even more sensitive.

The Gemara Yerushalmi *Pe'ah* [3:1] tells us of R' Pinchas Ben Yair and his talmidim. They were traveling on a road when a flash flood hit, creating an impassable river in front of them. R' Pinchas called out to the river to let him pass. The river split, and R' Pinchas crossed to the other side. His talmidim called to him and asked that he make the river split for them as well. R' Pinchas replied that whoever had never hurt another person in their entire lives could approach the river, and it would part.

We are not perfect from birth, but, perhaps, we can strive for perfection in this middah from now on. The Chazon Ish tells us that we should be careful not to hurt another human being, not just because of the immediate consequences, but also because of the long range consequences. Even if no present harm is done, some harm might come from it in the future.

Take, for instance, the naming of a child. Names rise and fall in popularity. Thus, in a situation where a name is being contemplated, even if it belonged to a wonderful and righteous person, if that name is no longer used, if it is out of style, so to speak, it should not necessarily be given since the child, as he grows older, may suffer from it in school or elsewhere.

We must all work on ourselves to develop the sensitivity we need to be merciful and compassionate—to our spouses, to our children, and to every yid in Klal Yisroel, so that when we ask Hashem for His mercy, He will look at us and see that we are merciful like Him. In the merit of our increased sensitivity to others, may Hashem bless us all, with His Infinite rachamim, with peace at home and a life of good health and happiness.

Rosh Hashanah:
Heeding the Shofar's Blast

We say in selichos, "*K'dalim u'chrashim, d'faknu d'losecha*—
Like the needy and the poor, we bang on Your door." This
seems to be a paradoxical statement. When a person is needy
and destitute, he is meek and timid, and not likely to be bang-
ing on anyone's door. The commentators explain that, when
one is desperate enough, he bangs, even if he is embarrassed.
Thus, the person who has not eaten for five days will pound
on the door for food, no matter how timid he is.

So too, although we realize that we are poor in deeds and
weak in Torah, we are also aware that, as we come closer and
closer to the Day of Judgement, we are desperate. Therefore,
we knock loudly on Hashem's doors of mercy.

The posuk says, "*K'nesher yo'ir kino*—Like the eagle who

awakens her nest." Rashi explains that the eagle does not swoop down suddenly upon her nest, for if she would do so, she would severely startle her young. Instead, she rustles the neighboring branches with her wings to alert them that she is on the way. So too, Hashem in His kindness does not suddenly spring the Yom Hadin upon us. Instead, metaphorically, He "rustles the branches" during the month of Elul, giving us a chance to prepare properly for the day of reckoning.

The rustling branches are the sound of the shofar blast every morning. As the Rambam teaches us, its message is, "*Uru yesheinim m'sheinaschem*—Awaken, you sleepers from your slumber." Thus, the shofar heralds the urgent message that we must prepare wisely for the critical day of Rosh Hashanah.

There are, in fact, many messages of the shofar. The *Ksav Sofer* says that shofar reminds us, "*Shapru* (consisting of the same letters as shofar) *ma'aseichem*—Improve and beautify your deeds." It is reminding us that throughout the month, we should analyze our good deeds and try to make them even better. For example, we should try to pray more meaningfully, to be more attentive to our spouse's needs, to spend more quality time with the children, and so on.

The *Ksav Sofer* also advises us that the correct order of business during Elul is, "*Sur meira va'aseih tov*—Turn away from evil and do good." Thus, we must first concentrate on removing the bad from within us. This includes anger, foul speech, destructive gossip, gazing at forbidden things, laxity in kashrus, and so forth.

The Gemara in *Rosh Hashanah* teaches us that we specifically use the horn of a ram as a shofar because it is bent. This reminds us of one of the most important callings of life: to bend our evil inclination to the service of Hashem. We know we are succeeding in life when we manage to break our natural sinful tendencies. When we awaken with alacrity for prayer or study, we "bend" away from our tendency toward laziness. When we give tzedakah or a loan, we thereby overcome our natural selfishness. When we hold back a biting, sarcastic reply, especially on a tense erev Shabbos, or when we come home tired and washed out and nevertheless help out with the dishes, do homework with the children, and keep ourselves fresh for our spouses, we have succeeded in "bending" away from the calls of our yetzer hara.

I have heard yet another fascinating message of the shofar from R' Zev Leff, shlit"a. He points out interestingly that the shofar cannot ever go up on the mizbe'ach, nor can it be eaten with religious intent as the kohanim or its owners eat other parts of the sacrifices. Yet, on Rosh Hashanah, it is catapulted into the forefront, becoming the centerpiece of our atonement process. R' Leff explains that one of the key points of the shofar is where it is located on the ram. The horns are situated above the head, and they symbolize that which is beyond our understanding. In other words, since the shofar is placed above the brain, it represents the mitzvos of Hashem that we do, even though we cannot grasp the reasons for them.

Perhaps this is why the posuk says, "*Tiku bachodesh shofar …Ki chok l'Yisroel hu*—Blow, this month, the shofar…For it is a statute for Yisroel." Statutes are the commandments of the Torah that we fulfill even though we don't understand them. We do them only to follow Hashem's will. Thus, we avoid wearing shatnez, we don't mix meat and milk, and we strive to fulfill all six hundred and thirteen mitzvos, even when we don't understand why.

This is one of the primary reminders of the shofar: That Hashem is our Boss and we are committing ourselves to follow Him always—whether or not we understand. This is why, on Rosh Hashanah, when we crown Hashem as our King, we do so with the vehicle of the shofar. How fitting that we pay homage to the King with that which symbolizes that we will always follow Him, even when His directives are above and beyond our understanding.

May we merit to follow the messages of the shofar: avoiding evil, improving ourselves, bending our inclinations to Hashem's ways, and following Him at all times.

Yom Kippur:
Tipping the Scales

When the chazan intones, "*Mi yichyeh umi yamus*—Who will live and who (chas v'shalom) will die," we all quake in our boots, and rightly so. So what can we do to improve our chance for a positive judgment on Yom Kippur?

The Gemara tells us that Hashem initially creates every husband and wife as one. Indeed, forty days before a child's conception, a Bas Kol, a heavenly voice, announces that child's bashert [*Sotah* 2a]. So in fact, we are preprogrammed to complement our spouses, and it is Hashem's desire that we should live out our lives together with our predestined match. Thus, even if we are otherwise undeserving, if we fulfill our marital responsibilities, we give Hashem a strong reason to view us as indispensable. It is a powerful defense, on the Day of Judgment, to pledge to Hashem that in the coming year we will try harder to make our spouse's life sweeter, happier, and more fulfilled.

This is what the Gemara means when it informs us that Nadav and Avihu (the two saintly children of Aharon who passed away tragically during the dedication of the Mishkan) died because they were not married and didn't have children. This is rather mystifying, considering that the Torah tells us explicitly that they died because they offered a "foreign fire" (one that Hashem had not commanded them to bring) in the Mishkan. The commentaries explain this puzzle by pointing out that it is true that their sin was bringing a foreign fire. However, if they had been married, then having wives would have saved them. If they had had children, then having children would have saved them. They would have been too needed by their families for Hashem to take them away.

This is the advice that the *Orchos Chaim* offers: "*Harotzeh l'ha'arich yamim, hevei marbeh b'achim v'rei'im*—If someone wants to live long, he should try to have many relatives and friends." Thus, we see that the more we make ourselves needed, the more secure our lives become, for even if we don't deserve to live for other reasons, nevertheless, these other people don't deserve to lose us. And, although Hashem has no lack of available helpers, no one can fully replace a biological father and mother, a loving child, or an attentive and helpful spouse.

Therefore, a husband should carefully consider whether or not he is properly fulfilling his wife's needs. The Gemara [*Pesachim* 109a] informs us that clothing creates a special joy for a woman. The wise husband will be diligent in attending to his wife's happiness in this way. Many middle income people fall into the trap of squirreling away any "extra" income. The yetzer hara hoodwinks us into thinking that in order to feel secure we must have whopping nest eggs. He deludes us into thinking that if we save every extra dollar, one day we'll be really wealthy. So when our wives ask for a new dress, sheitel, or shoes, our response should not always be, "Things are tight right now." In reality, this is shortsighted and completely contrary to the truth. For, while the money sits dormant for years in the bank, it could better be used to protect its owner. If we would use our resources to make our spouses happy, Hashem would see how needed we are and keep us around a little longer.

A wife should ask herself if she can improve in those areas where she alone can bring happiness to her husband, for in that way she makes herself truly indispensable and fulfills her very essential role of being an "eizer k'negdo."

Indeed, during the Aseres Y'mei Teshuvah, spouses should ask each other not just for forgiveness, but for concrete suggestions on how they can make each other happier in the coming year.

When it comes to our children, we should consider how to connect with them more frequently despite the fast pace of our lives. We should learn the favorite nosh of each of our children in order to treat them occasionally, and thereby create a twinkle in their eyes. We should try to make a commitment to Hashem that we will increase our efforts at trying to emulate Avraham Avinu by inculcating awareness of Hashem into our children.

When it comes to our parents, nothing beats visiting, calling, and writing to them more often. They don't have to live in Eretz Yisroel for them to enjoy a letter from us. A postcard sent from Boro Park to Flatbush is just as touching and might be read and reread many times. Let's make a commitment to ensure that they are clothed properly for the winter, and that they have the correct food and medical attention, and everything else they need.

Let's try to be there for our friends. Let's make a commitment that whenever we notice one of our acquaintances has taken sick, we will make sure to call, for we know how much we appreciate a phone call when we are under the weather.

Let's make sure to tell Hashem: Hashem, we don't want anyone to be punished on our account. We don't want someone to be put into traction, to lose his job, or to get depressed because they might have hurt or insulted us. So, we forgive them before this Holiest of Days. But let's make a deal. We are forgiving them even though they don't really deserve it. So You, Who reward measure for measure, should please forgive us for our many faults, even though we don't deserve it either. Burying the hatchet, overcoming grudges, and abolishing feuds all create a setting conducive to a positive middah k'neged middah, measure for measure, where Hashem will in turn forgive *us* and bury our misdeeds. As the Gemara teaches us, "*Kol hama'avir al midosov, ma'avirin mimenu al kol p'sha'av*—Whoever looks away from the ills that others do to him will have his sins removed" [*Yoma* 23a].

When we come to the fresh start of another year and proclaim Hashem our King, we must define and crystallize our mission in life. Firstly, we must try to be more cognizant, on a daily basis, that we are Hashem's subjects. It is for this reason that throughout this season we say twice daily, "L'Dovid Hashem Ori" [*Tehillim* 27] for we try to live by this motto of Dovid's—that Hashem is my Light, my Guidance, my Illumination, and the key factor in my day-to-day life decisions [*Orach Chaim* siman 581, seif katan 4].

When we live with constant awareness of Hashem, it is

Hashem's pleasure to keep us around for a long, long time. After all, like we say in the wedding blessing, "*Shehakol bara lichvodo*—He created everything for His honor." If we fit in with Hashem's plan, Hashem will allow us to remain here for a while.

We know that "*M'zonosov shel adam k'tzuvin lo meirosh hashanah*—A person's livelihood is fixed for him on Rosh Hashanah" [*Beizah* 16b]. Therefore, besides the obvious responsibility to pray fervently for a sufficient annual income, this is also the time to work on incorporating the attitude that our parnasah is from Hashem, and to embrace a lifestyle that embodies that outlook.

To illustrate what this means, let me share with you a beautiful parable from the Dubno Maggid. He tells the story of a pauper who is trudging along with a heavy backpack. A wealthy coachman drives by and offers him a ride. Gratefully, the pauper climbs in, but even though he is sitting he keeps the heavy burden on his back. The driver says to him in consternation, "Why are you still schlepping your heavy pack? Put it down." The poor man replies that it is enough that he is giving him a ride, he doesn't want to trouble the coachman with the burden of carrying the package too. The coachman laughs and says, "Either way, it's in the coach. You might as well put it down and enjoy the ride."

The Dubno Maggid says that it is the same with one's efforts at making a living. Of course, we can't rest on our laurels, saying that whatever we are supposed to get will come along anyway. Rather, we must make the proper hishtadlus, the proper effort, to get our annual stipend, but it is foolhardy to spend more time working than Hashem expects from us. If we work long hours, and as a result forego things like praying with a minyan, a fixed Torah learning session, or studying with our children, then we know that we have taken "hish-tadlus" too far. After all, Hashem is giving us a ride anyway. Why don't we put down our bags and trust in Him? As the posuk says, "*Hashleich al Hashem y'havcha, v'hu yechalkilecha*— Cast upon Hashem your burden and He will sustain you" [*Tehillim* 55:23].

So let's commit ourselves to spending more time with the family, more time in shul, more time learning, and more time on chesed, and let's leave the extra hours of income for Hashem to take care of.

Let's be proactive when it comes to Yom Kippur: "*L'olam y'vakeish adam rachamim shelo yecheleh*—A person should always pray not to become sick" [*Shabbos* 32a]. Let's not take any of our good fortune or Hashem's kindness for granted. It is also a wonderful idea for people to pray for each other. This method of tefillah is precious in Hashem's eyes. As we are taught, "*Kol hamivakeish rachamim al chaveiro, v'hu tzarich la'oso davar, hu ne'eneh techilah*—Whoever asks for mercy on behalf of his friend when he shares the same need will have his own prayers answered first" [*Bava Kama* 92a].

In fact, I try to make it a point to pray for the health and well-being of my wonderful readership—for those who need a cure, for those who want children, for those who are seek-ing a mate, for those who seek wisdom in dealing with their children, for those who need employment, for those who wish for increased marital bliss, for those who need peace of mind, and for everyone seeking a new year of good health and prosperity. It is my hope that all of you will find a few minutes to do the same for me.

Sukkos:
Stop Kvetching!

Chazal teach us [*Sukkah* 11] that the sukkah is primarily symbolic of the Clouds of Glory that protected us during our long journey through the hostile Sinai desert. These clouds were miraculous in multi-faceted ways. They protected us from the lethal desert heat and the severe nighttime chill. They leveled the ground for us, and exterminated the venomous and extremely dangerous desert wildlife. From these clouds came cosmetics for the ladies, a cleaning service for our garments, and wonderfully effective climate control for millions of people. The clouds also unerringly guided us through the maze of the desert on a precise path. Indeed, when we were in these miraculous clouds, we were transported royally, like one who is traveling first class on a luxury liner. The Chidah says that, when Bnei Yisroel traveled in the clouds, they felt like they were in a boat.

But, as miraculous as the clouds were, they were only a small part of the incredible story of this era in the desert. Hashem also provided munn (the manna) to feed Bnei Yisroel, and even delivered it right to the front door of those who were deserving. For those who were not as deserving, it was delivered at varying distances from their homes, depending upon their worthiness. So, besides being a food that was wholly nutritious and absorbed completely by the body (thereby making it unnecessary to go to relieve oneself), it also served as a barometer for one's day-to-day spiritual progress.

The munn also miraculously tasted like any food that one fantasized. It was a complete restaurant menu in one compact food. It had a self-regulating expiration date. It only lasted for twenty-four hours. It was fresh and then it was gone, to ensure that we put our trust in Hashem every day to provide us with a new supply.

Yet, we make no remembrance of this miracle. Nor do we make a remembrance of the miracle of the Well of Miriam, which, by the way, wasn't a little well. Actually, it was an enormous reservoir, enough to quench the thirst of millions of people.

The Chidah, in addressing why we make no mention of these miracles, introduces a fundamental lesson. He explains that both the munn and the Well of Miriam came about through complaining. Bnei Yisroel murmured and cried out, and only then did they receive the munn and the well. On the other hand, the Clouds of Glory were not precipitated by any complaining whatsoever. The Chidah concludes that anything that comes about through complaining is *not* worthy of commemoration throughout history. It was only the Clouds of Glory—that came to us without any complaint on our part—that are worthy of being commemorated through-out the centuries.

The Gemara says in *Masechtas Avodah Zarah* [3] that sukkah is a "mitzvah kala," an easy mitzvah. Rashi explains that it is considered easy because it doesn't cost money. (Sukkahs used to be constructed from the refuse of the harvest and the winepress, which didn't cost anything.) What is puzzling about all of this is, why did Hashem design the mitzvah that symbolizes the Clouds of Glory to be free? After all, we spend plenty of money on most other mitzvahs. I'd like to suggest that, since the sukkah symbolizes the Clouds of Glory, which came without complaining, Hashem made sukkah a free mitzvah to ensure that no one would complain about it.

This is a message that we should preserve and internalize. Complaining is not the way to advance in life. There are people who spend entire decades of their lives listening to krias haTorah, not to soak in the words of the Torah, but just to catch the reader on a mistake. There are people who, when the chazan chants "Hamelech" on Yom Kippur, are not contemplating Hashem's Kingship with awe, but are busy noticing that the chazan is off-key. Oh, how many people come home to their spouses with complaints of what's missing in their marriage, and how many parents complain to their children that they should be doing much better in school!

Yaakov Avinu lost many years of his life because he complained to Pharaoh, "*M'at v'ro-im hoyu y'mei shnei chay-yai*— Few and bad were the days of the years of my life" [*Bereishis* 47:9]. Indeed, the Mishnah tells us, "Who is wealthy? He who is satisfied with his lot" [*Pirkei Avos* 4:1]. It follows logically, therefore, that the unsatisfied, habitual complainer will end up a poor and unhappy person. This is one of the reasons

Sukkos is *z'man simchaseinu*, the time of our happiness, because this lesson of the Clouds of Glory emphasizes one of the crucial keys to personal happiness.

So, let's check it out! Are we always in complaining mode at home, at work or in shul? If so, it's time for us to make a U-turn, and in that merit may Hashem always bless us with much happiness.

Sukkos: "Drinking In" the Sukkah

Why do we celebrate Sukkos for seven days? After all, the sukkah commemorates the Clouds of Glory that shielded us in the desert for a full forty years after we left Mitzrayim. So why did Hashem establish Sukkos for seven days?

The *Sefer Matamim* answers succinctly that the seven days symbolize the seven sets of clouds that surrounded us in the desert. There were four clouds encircling us on the four sides of the compass. There was another above us which protected us from the sun during the day and the frost at night. A sixth cloud was below us in order to level the ground and kill the venomous snakes and scorpions. Finally, the seventh was a column that preceded us, to direct us and lead the way.

We find the theme of seven repeated often on Sukkos. Besides the seven days and seven clouds, there are seven parts of a lulav and esrog: one lulav, one esrog, three hadasim, and two aravos. There are seven Ushpizin (spiritual guests that visit us in the sukkah): Avraham, Yitzchak, Yaakov, Moshe, Aharon, Yosef and Dovid. There are seven special mitzvahs: the four species, the sukkah, simchas Yom Tov (enjoying the holiday), and the water offering. All of these "sevens" allude to the central theme of Sukkos—the commemoration of the seven Clouds of Glory that accompanied and sheltered us throughout our stay in the wilderness.

This commemoration is considered so vital that, while for most mitzvos it is sufficient simply to have in mind that one is doing the command of Hashem, that is not good enough when it comes to the mitzvah of sukkah. The *Bach* [*Tur Orach Chaim* 625] rules that, since the Torah expressly states, "*L'man yeidun doroseichem ki ba-sukkos hoshavti es Bnei Yisroel*—In order that your generations shall know that I sheltered Bnei Yisroel in booths (i.e., in the Clouds of Glory)," it is insufficient to merely sit under the s'chach with only the thought of fulfilling G-d's will. Rather, one must specifically consider Hashem's miracle of the Divine Clouds while eating in the Sukkah.

Why such an insistence on recalling this event? The *Mishnah Brurah* explains that since the Clouds of Glory were the first miracle that occurred as we left Mitzrayim, this miracle became the springboard that caused us to remember all the other miracles. Therefore, we should indeed commemorate and discuss, while sitting in the Sukkah, all the miracles that occurred in the desert. Indeed, the Gemara in *Sukkah* tells us that they used to hang clusters of grapes and other fruits as well as garlands of wheat and other items upon the s'chach. This was only partially to symbolize that Sukkos is the Chag Ha-asif, the Festival of Ingathering Crops, during which we thank Hashem for the bounty that we are able to gather into our homes for the winter. I believe this is done also to highlight the miraculous *munn*, which could taste like any food one desired. (If you want to be adventurous, you might even hang some cosmetics from your s'chach, since the Medrash tells us that Hashem miraculously made "*tachshitei noshim*," adornments for women, rain down with the *munn*. How revealing that Hashem considered marital harmony so important that, in a place where there were no cosmetic shops, He miraculously sent beauty aids down from Heaven.)

Here is another vital point to ponder while enjoying the rarified and joyous atmosphere of the sukkah. When people go to a diet center for a three-week program, they are not trying to lose all the weight in three weeks. Rather, they are engaging in a training program to condition themselves to acquire new habits and attitudes that they hope will remain with them long after they finish the program. Similarly, when we sit in the sukkah, contemplating that we are together with the holy Ushpizin, under the "*tzeila d'heimnusa*," (the *Zohar's* phrase for the s'chach's symbolism of Hashem's Divine protection), we should be extremely careful not to get angry, not to speak about others, and not to even indulge in wasteful chit-chat. This is because one of the goals of the sukkah is to help us internalize the heightened level of spirituality which sitting in the sukkah makes us feel. Nor is it an option to say, "It is too holy in here. Let's go inside," for during the Sukkos festival we are charged to make the sukkah our primary place of residence and live in it as if it *were* our home.

Thus, we are compelled to look for productive activities to do in the sukkah. Reading the daily newspaper about the

Mets or upcoming sales just doesn't feel right in the presence of Avraham Avinu. So, we are "forced" to take out a sefer, study with our children, or spend meaningful time with our spouse. After living this way for seven days, the hope is that, through the conditioning we had in the "airlock" of the sukkah, we will continue this careful behavior throughout the rest of the year.

The sukkah thus exactly parallels our sojourn through the wilderness. There, where Hashem put us in the training camp of the desert, we studied Torah uninterruptedly for forty years as an intensive preparation for our entry into normal life in Eretz Yisroel. After forty years of learning, the Torah would become part of us and continue to be with us even after we had left the desert. We use that same system now every year on Sukkos.

So, we have much to think about in the sukkah. May we find success at "drinking in" the sukkah atmosphere and using it wisely, and so merit the blessings of a healthy and joyous Sukkos.

Simchas Torah: Approaching Torah with Joy

Hashem created the world to do kindness, as it says "*Olam chesed yiboneh*—the world will be built with kindness" [*Tehilllim* 89:3]. Avraham Avinu arrived at this conclusion when he contemplated the purpose of the rose. Its powerful sweet fragrance convinced him that it is obviously the Will of the Creator to bring happiness to humans.

We also know that Hashem commanded us to learn Torah at every available time, as it says, "*V'hagisa bo yomam valayla*—And you should meditate in it day and night" [*Yehoshua* 1:8]. It is therefore quite clear that Hashem, our Manufacturer, is letting us know that there is no better way to attain happiness than through Torah study, since this is what He recommends (and indeed demands) that we do whenever possible.

It is this important realization that we celebrate on Simchas Torah. Annually, on Simchas Torah, we reiterate this theme of, "*Ein simcha k'simchas haTorah*—There is no joy like the joy of the Torah." We do this in unison with all of Klal Yisroel, emphasizing that Torah is our national pastime. Those of us who live in America can make an interesting parallel, and learn some important lessons, by comparing Torah to the American national pastime of baseball. Across the country, fathers eagerly await the time when their children will be old enough to bring them to a game, to share the excitement of a pennant race, the edge-of-the-seat drama of a ninth-inning comeback, and a gritty pitcher's duel. How they enjoy arguing with their friends over the respective merits of Mets or Yankees, quibbling for hours over whose team has better players!

This level of enthusiasm is really what Hashem expects from a true Ben Torah. He should excitedly introduce his children to "*Torah tziva lanu Moshe*—Moshe commanded us with the Torah" [*Devarim* 33:4], from a very young age. He should eagerly await the day when he will be able to introduce his child to Abaya and Rava, and other giants of the Talmud. He should experience intense excitement over taking his children to Torah shiurim and introducing them to the wonders of a R' Chaim's p'shat (explanation) in a Rambam.

In Krias Shema, we say, "*V'dibarta bam*," that our talk should be about words of Torah. We should be sharing new thoughts about Kayin and Hevel, the wonders of Noach's Ark, and the fascinating complexities of the Seven Days of Creation much the way others speak about the latest accomplishments of baseball players like McGuire and Sosa.

The aforementioned joy of Simchas Torah is expressed by Jews all over the world embracing the Torah and dancing with it in celebration. But when we do this we should be aware of our relationship with the Torah. We don't want the Torah to look at us and say, "Who are *you*?! Am I supposed to know you? Why are you dancing with me with such enthusiasm? I don't think I even recognize you." If we want to meaningfully rejoice with the Torah, we must make a commitment to spend time throughout the year with our "dance partner." We should make up our minds that we will review the parshah weekly as we are supposed to. We should try to prepare some Torah "food-for-thought" to bring to the Shabbos table, and thereby elevate it spiritually. Perhaps, we will consider getting on the daf yomi bandwagon, or learning a daily regimen of *Mishnah Brurah* or *Kitzur Shulchan Aruch*. With this commitment in mind, we could then warmly embrace the Torah and say, "Come let's dance! We're going to have a superb year together!"

Let's get back to our baseball analogy. A true baseball fan doesn't let a day go by without keeping abreast of his team's latest accomplishments. In the same way, a true Torah devotee should never let twelve hours go by without learning some Torah. Indeed, we are taught that when we get to the next world, every aspect of our lives will be weighed and considered. But, from the vast array of pursuits of a lifetime, we will *first* be judged about our Torah study. As the Gemara in *Shabbos* [31] tells us, we will be asked, "*Kovatah ittim l'Torah?*—Did you establish regular times (both day and night) to learn Torah?" This is what we should be thinking about as we dance and sing on this special day.

On Simchas Torah, there is another unique custom, something we do that is not done at any other time of the year. Every Jewish adult male gets his own aliyah (being called up to make a blessing on a portion of the Torah reading) to the Torah. This is an opportunity to clearly realize that we believe that the true aliyah, literally "uplifting" and advancement of life, is through Torah study. This custom also offers every male the opportunity to voice the blessings over the Torah, which thank Hashem for bequeathing us, His special nation, with this National Treasure, and express appreciation to Hashem for allowing us to experience a taste of the pleasures of the afterlife, and prepare for the afterlife, in this world, through Torah study. This is what we refer to when we say in the prayer of *Uva Letzion*, "*V'chayei olam nota b'socheinu*—The everlasting world You planted in our midst."

For many Jews the Simchas Torah celebration is unfortunately usually a wearisome and trying day that they watch with a mixture of tiredness and frustration, feeling that they are going through the motions of joviality without feeling any authentic sense of happiness. With a renewed commitment to Torah study and Torah life, may we all merit to feel enormous inner joy on Simchas Torah and be blessed by Hashem with many Torah blessings.

Simchas Torah:
Discovering the Many Facets of Torah

Our Sages have shown us a glimpse of the plethora of lessons hidden in the word "Bereishis," the first word of the Torah. In the *Zohar*, R' Shimon Bar Yochai declares that this word contains many secrets. The great chassidic master, the Bnei Yissaschar, relates 194 different concepts contained in various combinations of the word "Bereishis"! And the great sage R' Yosef Nissim ben Adahan cites 720 different lessons, including references to all 613 mitzvos in the Torah and the seven rabbinical ones as well! Like these tremendous chachamim, let us try to delve into a few of the secrets of "Bereishis"!

    1. When rearranged (in Hebrew), the letters of the word

"Bereishis" spell *"bris aish*—a covenant of fire." On a simple level, this teaches us that the Torah is a covenant of fire, as it says elsewhere, *"mee'y'mino aish das lamo*—From His right hand, a fiery law to His people" [*Devarim* 33:4]. This comparison to fire, on the basic level, is designed to convey that one should not trespass the dictates of the Torah—for that is like playing with fire! This is the way Rashi explains the mishnah in *Pirkei Avos* [2:10] which advises us to beware of the "coals," the words, of the sages, lest one be burned!

The analogy to fire is also meant, in a positive sense, to convey the warmth of the Torah, as it states, "to warm oneself from the 'fire' of the sages" [*Pirkei Avos* 2:1]. For the ways of the Torah are pleasant and sweet and foster warmth in a person—an all-important ingredient in our relationships with others!

This message of *bris aish*, a covenant with/of fire, also teaches us that, when we embark on the study of Torah, our studying protects us from the fires of Gehinnom [*Chagiga* 27a]. In *Sanhedrin* [92a], the Talmud relates that "any house which has no Torah in the night time will be consumed by fire." This is perplexing! Many Jewish homes are bereft of Torah study, unfortunately, but (thank G-d) they are not consumed by fire. Now, if the Gemara had said, "any house that has Torah will be spared from fire," it would have been easier to understand. However, instead the Gemara makes the emphatic statement that without Torah, there will be fire. This is truly amazing!

I believe an explanation is that fire manifests itself in many ways aside from the obvious one. There are also the fires of rage, of fighting, or of fever and sickness. The study of Torah (the covenant with fire) will protect us from all of these other manifestations of fire as well.

2. The Torah starts with the letter "beis," which has the numerical value of two. This, says R' Yehuda ben Pazi in the Medrash, is to teach us that there are two worlds—this world and the afterlife. Thus, in the first letter of the Torah is one of the primary messages of the Torah, for the knowledge of the existence of the afterlife points us towards the most desirable direction and ambition for our lives. We must prepare for the infinite years of afterlife by making the sacrifices necessary to live as an observant Jew.

3. It is beautiful to note that the word "Bereishis," when jumbled, spells "*Barasa shai*—you created 310 worlds." The last mishnah in *Uktzin*, which is the last masechta in the entire Talmud, teaches us that every righteous person is destined to inherit 310 worlds!

4. The word "Bereishis" also spells "*Rashi tavo*—Rashi will come." Here it is foretold in the Torah that the brilliant commentator, Rashi, who explained the Torah to the whole world like no one else had ever done before would come to our aid!

5. One of the most severe crimes in the Torah is to embarrass someone publicly. Indeed, it's one of the few crimes that carries the penalty of the loss of one's afterlife! It is therefore fitting that the first word of the Torah carries a warning against this heinous crime. The word "Bereishis" also spells "*Y'rei boshes*—Be fearful of causing embarrassment!"

6. The *Sefer Rokeach* comments that the word "Bereishis" is an abbreviation of the following words: "*Amen, y'hei Shmei rabbah b'kol tefillah*—(that one should say) "*Amen, y'hei Shmei rabbah*," at every prayer." This underscores the amazing importance of the prayer of kaddish, and our participation in it. Indeed, the saintly Chofetz Chaim, of blessed memory, writes in the *Mishnah Brurah* that those who respond "*Y'hei*

Shmei…." loudly and with feeling will have any bad decree regarding them (G-d forbid) torn up. Thus, if, for example, Hashem decreed that someone be hit by a car, but comes to shul in the morning and makes this statement with passion, it can literally save his life. Therefore, if we wake up a little late and figure, "Why go to shul? I've surely missed kedushah," we should still not hesitate, and should run to shul just to be able to answer "*Amen, y'hei…*" Doing so is extremely worthwhile in its own right.

7. The Torah ends with the words, "*L'einay kol Yisroel*—In the eyes of all of Israel." Rashi says this is a reference to Moshe's breaking of the Ten Commandments. I'd like to suggest that this is alluded to in the first word of the Torah as well (the Sages have various ways of connecting the end of the Torah to the beginning), since "Bereishis" also spells "*Es yud shavar*—he broke the Ten!"

8. As mentioned previously, our major life goal is to constantly improve ourselves through the process of *teshuvah* (repentance). Thus, it's no surprise that the word "Bereishis" spells "*ashrei tav*—Fortunate is he who repents!"

9. The Vilna Gaon offers us this incredible acrostic:

ב—"beis"—*bitachon* (trust in Hashem)

ר—"reish"—*ratzon* (having the will to do what's right)

א—"alef"—*ahava* (love for Hashem, one's spouse, parents, children, other people, etc.)

ש—"shin"—*shtika* (silence—knowing when to keep our mouths shut!)

י—"yud"—*yirah* (fear of Hashem)

ת—"tav"—*Torah*.

It is especially noteworthy that, for the letter "reish," the Gaon passed over a word like "*rachmonus*—mercy," and chose instead "*ratzon*." The Gaon is undoubtedly pointing us in the direction of the Talmudic dictum *"B'derech sheadam rotzeh leileich bah molichin oso*—Hashem helps a person along the path he chooses for himself" [*Makkos* 10b]. The overwhelming importance of silence can be seen in *Chullin* [89a] where it says, *"Ma oomnaso shel adam b'*Olam Hazeh? *Yasim atzmo k'ileim*—What should a person's profession be in this world? He should train himself to act (when appropriate) like a mute!" Similarly, for "shin" he declined to choose the powerful words *"shalom*—peace," or *"simcha*—happiness," and instead chose "silence."

Let me conclude with words of encouragement to everyone. We must make it a priority to review the weekly Torah portion. Make this the year that you're going to finish the Torah from beginning to end. Don't let this week slip away and then say, "Oh, I missed it already. I'll do it next year."

Here are some helpful tips in this regard:

1. Many people wait to review the parshah on Shabbos, and this is their undoing! Shabbos is at the end of the week and, if they get busy or are too tired (a common occurrence), the week is over and it's already time for the next parshah. Therefore, start the parshah on Sunday. (If there is time Sunday morning for the *Daily News* or *New York Times*, there's definitely time for the parshah.) If you are too busy on a particular day, you still have the rest of the week ahead of you.

2. If you miss a week, don't give up! Mark down the parshah you missed. You can make it up. In any case, it's better to complete forty parshiyos than none at all!

3. Get yourself a new sefer with which to review each week's portion. It will provide you with something new and challenging to whet your appetite.

Hatzlachah rabbah! May we all be *zocheh* to finish the Torah each year and merit all of its many blessings.

BHA"B: *Fasting For a Reason*

In two locations [*Masechtos Kiddushin*, 81a, and *Bava Kama*, 82a], Tosefos mentions the custom of fasting on the first Monday and Thursday, and the second Monday of the months of Marcheshvon and Iyar. This series of fasts, which is also mentioned several times in *Shulchan Aruch* and the *Tur* [429], is commonly known as the "Fast of BHA"B." Though most of Klal Yisroel does not observe this practice, and many do not even say the accompanying selichos (forgiveness prayers), many congregations still "bentch BHA"B" on the Shabbos before the fast days begin. And, while many of us will not fast, it behooves us to understand the reasons for these fasts so that we can still pray for the messages that the fasts represent, and give tzedakah towards their specific significance.

One reason given by the *Elya Rabba* [492:3] for these fast

days is to atone for the possible sin of doing work on the Chol Hamoed of Sukkos or Pesach that just passed. One can immediately see how pertinent and timely this reason is, for in our times many are forced to work on Chol Hamoed and must determine what halachically constitutes a *davar ha'avud*, i.e., a situation where financial loss, and not a mere avoidance of profit, would occur if work wasn't performed. The stakes are extremely high, for the mishnah tells us, "*Kol ham'vazeh es hamo'ados, ein lo cheilek l'Olam Habah*—All who ignore the 'moeds' have no portion in the World to Come" [*Pirkei Avos* 3:11]. Rashi explains this as referring to those who work unnecessarily on Chol Hamoed. We must therefore beg forgiveness if we mistakenly worked in an unnecessary way during these holy days.

Another reason for this series of fasts can be found in the *Sefer Matamim* (page 131), in the *Ta'amei Minhogim* (page 250) and in the *Mataeh Moshe* (page 747). They explain that we fast because at these two points in the year, after Sukkos and after Pesach, there is a sudden change in the weather, which tends to cause people to get sick. Therefore, in anticipation of this danger, we fast and pray for the welfare of Klal Yisroel. This is yet another vivid example of how applicable this is to contemporary times. In fact, I was once trying to get a hospital room for someone who was stuck in the emergency room of a New York hospital. The person had already been there for over thirty hours, but the nurse explained to me that there were no ICU or CCU beds available. When asked why the hospital was so congested, she explained to me that, at the change of the seasons, the hospital is always fully booked, because many elderly people just can't cope with the sudden change of weather. Similarly, a druggist told me that his busiest time comes when the seasons change.

During the BHA"B fasts after Succos is an opportune time for Rabbonim to alert their congregations to the advisability of inquiring about a flu shot for their elderly parents. The flu (a nuisance for younger people) can be, chas v'shalom, fatal to elderly people. So arranging a simple preventive flu shot before the onset of a harsh winter can be a marvelous opportunity for kibbud av v'eim, honoring our parents. (Nevertheless, please consult your physician to know if this is the correct approach for any specific person.)

It is also around the time of BHA"B that, in many synagogues, the age-old argument of whether to open or close the windows rears its ugly head. One must realize that it is not coincidental that such a problem occurs in our shuls. It would seem to be a challenge to us to see if we have absorbed the divrei mussar that we hear and hanhogos tovos that we see regularly in shul, to see if we can focus more on giving and caring for another person than taking for ourselves. Precisely when we pray that no one should be caught off-guard by a sudden change of weather, we should certainly be concerned about causing our friend a sudden draft.

Yet another reason for these fasts can be found in the *Mordechai* on *Masechtas Taanis* [629] and in the *Sefer Chasidim* [227]. They explain that at the onset of Marcheshvan we begin to wait for the yearly rainfall on which earning a livelihood once depended. In the month of Iyar we are concerned that devastating natural disasters such as wind blast or crop jaundice should not ruin the fresh crops. Hence, these fasts are, in essence, prayers for success in parnasah, which is as much today as it has always been a source of concern.

Finally, *Tosefos* in *Kiddushin* and in *Bava Kama* explain that we fast because, during Yom Tov, both men and women go to hear the droshah from the brilliant sages and the men are exposed to many women dressed in their Yom Tov finery. Therefore, in order to atone for any sinful thoughts this might have generated in the men, Chazal instituted a period of fasting and selichos.

When we learn these *Tosfos*, we should reflect with fright on how far we've deteriorated. In the olden days, when men and women came in contact with one another, even though they were going to shul for the sole purpose of listening to Torah from the mouths of Torah giants, it was enough to prompt the drastic reaction of a three-day fast. Imagine how our wise Sages would have blanched at the exposure to arayos, immorality, that some of us receive from the movies, television, and advertising. It is an important lesson for us to remember how high our standards should really be.

As to why no fasts were instituted after the festival of Shavuos—according to most of the above reasons, it is self-explanatory for, if the fast is because of work on Chol Hamoed, there is obviously no Chol Hamoed of Shavuos. If the fast is because of the change in seasons, likewise there is no such change around Shavuos time. There is also, at that time of the year, no significant threat to the crops for they are already fully completed. After all, Shavuos is also known as the *Chag Hakatzir,* the festival of harvesting. And, even according to the reason of Tosefos, although the people also gathered on Shavuos to hear a droshah, since the festival is only one day long there was less of a threat from men being distracted by women. Hence no fast was deemed necessary.

In the zechus of our praying for Klal Yisroel's health and wealth, may we merit that these great blessings permeate our homes until the coming of Moshiach, may it come speedily in our days.

Chanukah: *Spreading The Light of Torah*

Chanukah seems to be a puzzling Yom Tov. We have no issur melachah (prohibition of work), and we have no obligation to make a grand seudah (festive meal). We might think that the only times of significance during this holiday are when we light the menorah and when we say Hallel in shul. Nevertheless, Chanukah is a Yom Tov in the fullest sense, and it encompasses much more than the few minutes of kindling lights.

The *Levush* tells us that no eulogies are allowed on Chanukah except in the case of a talmid chochom, a Torah scholar, who is eulogized in front of the aron kodesh. The reason for this, he explains, is so that our minds will not stray from the spirit of Chanukah. During every moment of every day of Chanukah, our minds should be immersed in thoughts of this special time.

It is difficult to think only thoughts of Chanukah throughout the holiday since, as we have said, we go to work or we're busy with our daily lives. We also have no specified festive meals, and there are no long davenings and no kiddush. It seems as if these eight days are regular days except that, when we come home at night, we light the menorah. And even though on Purim we have a similar situation, with no kiddush and no extensive davening, we do have mitzvos that are specific to the day. We have the mitzvos of megillah, mishloach manos, matanos l'evyonim, and seudas Purim. So even if we go to work on Purim, there are so many mitzvos to do that our minds stay focused on the festival all day. On the other hand, Chanukah has no obligations aside from lighting the menorah, which occurs at the end of the work day. We have no commandments to help us keep Chanukah on our minds throughout the day.

It behooves us, therefore, to first understand what Chanukah is and then, perhaps, we will see what this special time is teaching us and how we can keep these thoughts with us throughout its eight days—and afterwards as well.

The Rambam tells us about the mitzvah of ner Chanukah, "*mitzvah chaviva hi ad m'od*—[The mitzvah of lighting Chanukah candles] is a mitzvah that is extremely precious" [*Hilchos Chanukah* 4:12]. The lashon (expression) he employs of being "precious" is not used to describe any of the other mitzvos of our Yomim Tovim. It does not say this about the mitzvah of lulav, or matzah, or sukkah. Only the lighting of the menorah is a "precious" mitzvah—and "*ad m'od*," exceedingly so.

Why is the light of the menorah, something from which we are not allowed to derive any personal benefit, considered so precious?! The Radamsker Rebbe offers a reason. We say "Haneiros hallalu kodesh heim—These candles, they are Holy." The gematria (numerical value) of the word "heim," or "they," is equal to that of "adam," meaning man or humans. Therefore, we can substitute the word adam for heim. Kodesh adam—A person is holy. By lighting the menorah, we can uplift ourselves, and fill ourselves with holiness.

The reward for fulfilling the mitzvah of ner Chanukah properly is great indeed. The Gemara in Shabbos tells us, "Haragil baner, havyan lo bonim Talmidei Chachomim—Whoever is careful with the mitzvah of ner Chanukah will have children who are Torah scholars." What a terrific reward! It doesn't say this about the mitzvah of eating matzah, nor does it say this about the mitzvah of tefillin or the mitzvah of tzitzis. However, if you light the menorah, your posterity is ensured—your children are guaranteed to be talmidei chachomim, Torah scholars. Of course, we must surely realize that there is more to this than simply lighting some wicks.

We all know that, at the time of the miracle of Chanukah, the Chashmonaim, after cleaning out the Beis Hamikdash from all the idolatry left there by our enemies, wanted to rededicate the Temple. They wanted to light the menorah, but could not find any oil that had not been rendered impure by the Greeks. After searching high and low, they finally found one small jar of pure olive oil, stamped with the seal of the Kohen Gadol. The oil was only enough to light the menorah for one day, but Hashem made a neis, a miracle, and the oil burned for eight days. This is the story as we all know it. Now let us look into it and understand it more deeply.

We are used to taking the story of Chanukah at face value. Let us remember that there is no such thing as coincidence. Hashem is in charge and nothing is left to "chance."

So what happened to all the other oil? Did Antiochus and his men just happen to contaminate it when they moved their idol into the Beis Hamikdash? Clearly, Antiochus must have ordered his men to make all the oil impure. He did so because he wished to extinguish the ner tamid, one of the menorah's lights that always burned in the Beis Hamikdash. This was the way in which Antiochus knew he would win his war and destroy the Jews forever. However, Bnei Yisroel still succeeded in finding one small jar, and not just any jar, but a jar that had the seal of the Kohen Gadol on it.

Over the years, the enemies of Klal Yisroel have been formidable foes, and they have unwittingly taught us powerful truths about ourselves. They have shown us our weakest points. Pharaoh made us work b'avodas perach (in excruciatingly hard labor) so that we would not have time to think about wanting to go and serve Hashem. He knew that if we were too busy with our physical survival, we would not have time to think about our spirituality. This is surely a weak point that we possess. We are often so involved in the drudgery and routine of everyday life that we don't have time to devote to our spirituality.

Haman, our enemy at the time of Purim, said about us that we were "M'fuzar um'furad bein ha'amim—scattered and separate among the nations" [Esther 3:2]. There was no unity among Bnei Yisroel. To this day, if Bnei Yisroel do not stand together, our downfall is imminent.

So too, at the time of Chanukah, Antiochus wanted to extinguish the light of Bnei Yisroel. He wanted to quell the inner light of what the menorah represents, the light of Torah. Antiochus attempted to Hellenize us, to lure us with the temptations of the human body. The contamination of oil represented the diminishing of the light of the Torah during this period. The holy Chashmonaim saved the day by carrying the torch of Torah and igniting its spark once again in the hearts of our people. Thus the glow of our menorahs represents the illumination of Torah, and it is when we embrace this glow, rather than the glow of video, television, and the internet, that we can be assured of success in raising a generation of Torah Jewry.

We can learn much from the nature of the oil that we use to light our menorahs. Oil is obtained through pressing olives. Similarly, the flaxen wicks are only made possible through the beating of the flax. So too, a successful career of Torah study does not come easily! Since *"Talmud Torah k'neged koolam—Learning Torah outweighs everything else"* [Pe'ah 1:1], the yetzer hara works overtime to thwart us from pursuing this lofty goal. As a result, we too must "press" ourselves to create the time for Torah study and "beat" away the many distractions that always surface to frustrate our Torah aspirations.

Indeed, just like the Chashmonaim, who were faced with the problem of not having enough oil, many of us feel we are not wise enough, or patient enough, or young enough to succeed in the world of Torah study. We look at the massive tomes of the Talmud, the thousands of chapters of Tanach, shake our heads longingly, and conclude that, unfortunately, they are beyond reach. The message of Chanukah is to persist—even if we don't see how we could possibly obtain our goal—and Hashem will bless us with the fulfillment of our Torah dreams, just as He miraculously gave the single jar of oil the ability to remain lit for the full eight days of Chanukah!

Some of the commentators ask the question: Why is it that a Torah scroll, which is the symbol of life and pleasantness, can only be made by killing an animal (since the Torah is written on klaf—parchment—obtained from the hide of an animal)?

The answer, perhaps, is that we cannot achieve Torah greatness without "killing" some of the "animal" within ourselves! As the Gemara teaches us, "*Ein divrei Torah mikayamin ela b'mi shemeimis atzmo aleha*—words of Torah are only retained by those who 'kill' themselves over it" [*Brachos* 63b]. The more we deny the materialistic distractions of television, novels and so forth, the more we will enable ourselves to climb the great ladder of Torah success! In this way, Chanukah provides encouragement for our Torah learning. Just like the optimum time for lighting the candles is from the setting of the sun until people cease to be in the streets, so too, the challenge of learning Torah manifests itself forcefully when the breadwinner comes home tired and weary at the end of a hard work day, yet still makes it his business to open up a sefer and learn a little.

Let's all gird ourselves to grow greater in Torah study, and may we all earn the great reward of children who are wise in Torah.

Purim: *Giving The Day to Children*

If we compare and contrast the Yomim Tovim, we might wonder which Yom Tov has the closest connection to children. At first glance, we might answer Pesach. After all, many things that we do, especially on the night of the seder, are solely to keep the children interested and awake. Some people hand out sweets so the children will stay alert, and we do all sorts of unusual things throughout the seder, such as washing our hands and not making a brachah, "stealing" the afikomen, and so on. So, the seder night seems to be strongly directed towards children.

The *Korbon HaAni*, however, tells us something most of us are probably not aware of about Purim. He tells us that he saw in a dream the reason we bang and make noise when reading the Megillah—so that the children will stay awake and alert during the reading.

There are four pesukim that we read aloud from the Megillah. The *Mishnah Brurah* [*Orach Chaim* 590:58] says that this is because our hearts are so full of joy and enthusiasm at these parts that we cannot help but burst forth with the words. Others tell us that we say these pesukim out loud because of pirsumei nisa, to publicize the miracle, and these four pesukim specifically publicize the miracle of Purim. The *Levush*, however, tells us something akin to the *Korban HaAni*'s explanation. He says that the reason we say these four sentences out loud is in order to wake up the children who might have dozed off during the reading of the Megillah.

When we think of Purim, Esther and Mordechai obviously come to mind as the central figures in the story. But the Medrash tells us an interesting part of the story, which gives us a whole new perspective on the miracle of Purim. The Medrash tells us that, when he realized the depth of the threat to the Jews, Mordechai took drastic action and gathered 22,000 "*tinokos shel beis raban*," Jewish schoolboys. He dressed each of them in sackcloth and ashes and made them fast. He then sat them around him and began teaching them Torah.

When Haman saw this, he immediately put chains around their feet and told Mordechai that first he would kill all the children and then he would kill him. The children's mothers ran out to them with food, begging them to have one last meal. But each refused to eat, saying that he would die fasting for Hashem. Together, they all let out a heart-piercing scream that reached the heavens. Hashem, turning to Moshe and inquiring as to the source of all the noise, asked if the scream had come from goats and sheep. Moshe answered that this was not the cry of animals but of His own children. At that moment, Hashem took His gezeira, His decree against the Jews, which was written in clay, and destroyed it. That moment spelled the downfall of Haman. So we see how our salvation came about through our children's prayers. With revelations like these, we begin to see how much children are a part of the story of Purim.

It is quite sad that in today's world many people have sterilized Purim. They don't want to be bothered sending out shalach manos to so many people and so, instead, after giving the one obligatory shalach manos, they send out cards that declare that a donation has been made to a charitable organization in lieu of the shalach manos. Now, tzedakah is a beautiful thing, but not at the expense of Purim. Let's think back on our own childhood memories of Purim—the candy, the mess, the tumult, and how we loved every minute of it. What memories are our children going to take with them and transmit to their own children? They will remember Purim as the day we sent out cards and licked stamps and their parents went off to work. Indeed, children are the ones who dress up in costume, and they are the ones we appoint as our messengers for our shalach manos. Let's not cheat our children of their legacy in the involvement in a day which, if not for them, we would not be here to celebrate, for they are the real heroes of Purim.

Purim: Keeping The Mitzvah Responsibly

Imagine the following nightmarish scenes: A husband dashes out to the neighborhood grocery store to get some diapers and, rachmana litzlon, becomes the victim of a fatal hit and run. A mother leaves the apartment to pick up the kids and falls down an elevator shaft. A child trips in front of a moving school bus. How their lives would change so drastically and permanently in such a short span of time. How that family would wish so fervently that they could turn back the clock just a few brief minutes! When we reflect like this, we shudder, feel a tingling sensation crawl up our spine, and thank Hashem that we and our families are healthy and whole.

However, such frightening momentary meditations can

help us to better appreciate, and fully comprehend, the spirit of "*venahapoch hu*—turnabout" [*Esther* 9:1], which should permeate our very being on Purim. Look how Hashem changed everything around for us! In just a short span of time, G-d brought us from the brink of total annihilation at the hands of Haman, to the delirious joy of salvation and triumph over our enemies.

However, we must make a strong effort to ensure that it's only this joyful type of turnabout that we experience on Purim. Purim should not, chas v'shalom, become a tragic yahrzeit for a family member because someone foolishly entered a car and got behind the wheel while intoxicated. It is imperative for parents and teachers to charge their children and students not to so much as touch the ignition once they've attempted to—even minimally—fulfill the mitzvah of "*Ad d'lo yoda*—drinking until we are oblivious to the difference between Haman and Mordechai" [*Megillah* 7b].

It is crucial for this to become ingrained beforehand as much as possible, for even the most level-headed person will not make a logical decision once inebriated. We must remind those who partake of alcoholic beverages what they learned when they studied for their driver's permit, that coffee, exercise, and cold showers have almost *no* effect on diminishing the dangers of alcohol. We must caution our dear ones that it's not enough to stay away from driving themselves; they must make sure the driver is someone completely sober, a rare commodity on Purim.

As for ourselves, let's be on the alert to avoid those last minute shalach manos deliveries we forgot to make to a close friend or relative (who just won't understand, and whom we suddenly remembered) after we already started the seudah. Don't justify these trips by thinking that they're only a block away. Keep in mind that many car accidents happen within a few blocks of home.

If we are making a Purim seudah for a group of bochrim or several families, let's take responsibility for the wine people may drink while in our house. Let's make sure nobody who leaves will have to drive while under the influence of alcohol. (It might be a good idea for the host to politely collect the car keys at the outset to ensure this. A host might even want to invest a few dollars on a car service at the end of the evening and save someone a lifetime of grief.) Bear in mind that even if an accident does not occur, there is the real possibility that a slightly erratic vehicle will be stopped by the local police (who are well aware of the special observances of Purim). Just think of the horrendous chilul Hashem which would ensue! We must not forget, while attempting to fulfill the exciting and joyous rabbinical mitzvah of *"Ad d'lo yoda,"* to keep the even more important Biblical mitzvos of safeguarding our lives and preventing chilul Hashem

In the merit of our taking this issue seriously, may Hashem keep us all healthy and safe.

Purim: *An Interview with the Yetzer Hara*

Reporter (from the Torah Gazette): Mr. Yetzer Hara, the last time we had an opportunity to talk with you was before Pesach [see *Passionate Judaism*, pp. 143–148], and that interview was certainly enlightening. Thank you for agreeing to speak with us again.

Yetzer Hara: It's my pleasure. I'm always happy to challenge people's bechirah (free will) with more sinful ideas.

Torah Gazette: Well, I have the preventive angle more in mind, but in any event let's proceed. Purim is such a pleasant and fun-filled holiday. How do you manage to do any business on such a relaxed day?

Yetzer Hara: Are you kidding me? People start sinning weeks in advance for this holiday!

Torah Gazette: What do you mean?

Yetzer Hara: Well, you know, Mordechai and Esther instituted the mitzvah of mishloach manos for Purim, in order to create an atmosphere of friendship and warmth among Jews.

Torah Gazette: So, what's wrong with that?

Yetzer Hara: What's wrong is that the opposite often occurs. Everyone is busy trying to show everyone else up. A mitzvah which was intended as a spiritual pursuit—to cement achdus, unity—has become a furious rat-race of who can outdo whom.

Torah Gazette: Can you give me an example?

Yetzer Hara: Sure! Just the other day, I was in the wine store. The proprietor was complaining that Purim is his most frustrating festival. He explained that while before Pesach everyone comes in wanting to buy wine that just tastes good, on Purim people want their wine to fit a certain motif. They want to know if he sells a bottle of wine with the word "sunshine" on it. Or they tell him that some particular wine is nice but they need to have it in a red box. Or get a load of this—they tell him that they're going to bring in their Purim baskets so that he can find them a bottle that will fit into a particular crevice of their shalach manos basket.

Now, wouldn't you agree that I've done a spectacular job at confounding the spirit of this mitzvah?

Torah Gazette: At least they're trying to do the mitzvah in a beautiful way.

Yetzer Hara: Well, that's not all. I'm just getting started. For instance, when people make their lists of whom they're sending shalach manos, they usually include all the wrong people. What they should really do is send shalach manos to everyone whom they left off their list, the people they don't necessarily get along with and with whom they really need to make peace!

Torah Gazette: Oh. I'm sure that not everyone does these things.

Yetzer Hara: You're right. Some people don't even want to put up with the whole shalach manos parade. So they give one shalach manos in order to fulfill their obligation, and then they send cards to the rest, saying that, in lieu of shalach manos, they are giving tzedaka to a certain worthy organization.

Torah Gazette: What's wrong with that?

Yetzer Hara: All of a sudden they're so charitable! Mishloach manos is the mitzvah about which the Rambam says, "*Kol hamarbeh, harei zeh meshubach*—Whoever gives more (shalach manos) is to be praised," and they decide to turn it down?! Methinks that it has a lot more to do with not wanting to go through the trouble of shopping and preparing and delivering; or not wanting to be saddled with the problem of having mounds of nosh right before Pesach. But, you know how it is. I fool them into thinking self-righteously that mishloach manos is a mitzvah that's gotten out of hand and that they have to buck the trend and do the "right" thing.

Torah Gazette: Well, is the card route such a bad idea?

Yetzer Hara: Tzedaka is never a bad idea! But in this case, it comes at the expense of robbing our children and our family of the spirit of giving and depriving them of a house full of sweets and the joy of people coming and going in the house on Purim.

Torah Gazette: Is there such a problem with the modern day Purim?

Yetzer Hara: Are you kidding? In many American Jewish homes, I've succeeded in making Thanksgiving much more of a family day than Purim.

Torah Gazette: You're exaggerating.

Yetzer Hara: Definitely not! You see, on Thanksgiving, both husband and wife have off from work. They might even serve a traditional meal to the family. On Purim, however, many people have to go to work, so they leave their children home and tell them not to answer the door because they don't have any shalach manos to give back. How sad that so many Jewish children are lonely prisoners in their homes on Purim.

Torah Gazette: At least they all go out together to listen to the Megillah.

Yetzer Hara: Now that you bring that up, you know that the halacha says that you must hear every word of the Megillah. I cause all kinds of havoc during the Megillah reading by seducing parents into not paying attention to their children. Since many parents don't even attempt to keep their children quiet, the children make such a racket that many people miss their opportunity to fulfill the mitzvah.

Torah Gazette: I guess parents really should be more careful about this.

Yetzer Hara: I have another nasty trick. In some shuls I incite people to use cap guns and other loud noisemakers that really disturb and pain the older people. It's amazing what you can get people to do under the guise of a mitzvah!

Torah Gazette: Sure, but a lot of people do manage to fulfill the beautiful mitzvah of hearing the Megillah.

Yetzer Hara: That's another thing. Some people are so wrapped up in their Purim plans that they daydream during the Megillah and don't pay attention to every word. You see, even when a mitzvah comes just once a year, I find ways to disrupt them.

Torah Gazette: You can't do anything about the wonderful Purim mitzvah of matanos l'evyonim (gifts to the poor).

Yetzer Hara: That's what you think! First, I get people to procrastinate. You don't know any needy people, I tell them—so they figure they'll give later when they find someone poor to give to. Once I get people to push off doing a mitzvah, I've basically won the battle.

Then there's the pitiful way that some people perform this mitzvah. You know, the *Me'am Loez* mentions a beautiful practice for Purim: Calculate all the money you spent on the Purim feast, on shalach manos, and on costumes for the children, and give an equivalent amount to the poor. Now, that's the way to do a mitzvah. After all, the Rambam says there is no greater joy than to bring happiness to the hearts of orphans, widows and the poor.

Torah Gazette: So, I guess that about covers it, huh?

Yetzer Hara: Why, are you running out of time?

Torah Gazette: No, I just figured that was everything.

Yetzer Hara: No way! This was only the small stuff.

Torah Gazette: You can't be serious.

Yetzer Hara: (chuckling) Fortunately for me, I am serious. You see, Purim is a time of incredible joy in Judaism. At the time of the Gemara, when people were much holier, they were able to achieve, with the drinking of wine, uninhibited spiritual ecstasy. Nowadays, however, when people try this route, I am able to cause the most incredible spiritual havoc and devastation.

Torah Gazette: What do you mean?

Yetzer Hara: I get the boys to drink and then behave in public in ways that are truly a chilul Hashem (desecration of Hashem's name).

Torah Gazette: Such as?

Yetzer Hara: Making noise in the middle of the night. Staggering around in public like drunkards. And even sometimes going into a car while intoxicated.

Torah Gazette: How does that happen?

Yetzer Hara: Well, they're not used to drinking, so they don't realize how dangerous it is. They want to go to one more Rebbe's house, to deliver one more shalach manos, or just to get home. Imagine the chilul Hashem when they are stopped by a policeman, or even worse if they, chas v'shalom, get into a tragic accident with other helpless boys in the car.

Torah Gazette: I hope parents are reading these words intently and have a serious talk with their sons well in advance of Purim.

Yetzer Hara: You know, recently, I added a new trick to my Purim arsenal.

Torah Gazette: I don't think I like the sound of that.

Yetzer Hara: You know how dangerous cigarette smoking is? It's a real no-brainer, what with all the carcinogens, not to mention the risk of heart disease and emphysema. A lot of our youth wisely stay away from this ugly practice. But, you know how addictive cigarettes are. They're like Lays potato chips—Nobody can take just one. So, I'm always looking for the opportunity to get kids to take a few puffs, in the hope that I can hook them into this sinful practice.

And then, presto, I found Purim! Under the guise of Purim revelry, many unsuspecting youths are lured into this lifelong habit of ruination.

Torah Gazette: Mr. Yetzer Hara, I can't thank you enough for this very informative and frank discussion about your methods and machinations. It is our hope and prayer that Hashem will help us combat your tricks and plots, so that we should all have a very healthy, happy, and joyous Purim.

Pesach: Remembering Those in Need

A̲s Pesach approaches, we suddenly find ourselves over-whelmed by all the necessary preparations. Scouring the house to eradicate chometz, taking down the dishes, selling the chometz to the Rav, buying dresses and suits for the family—all of these obligations and many more seem to converge upon us all at once!

However, another aspect of Pesach preparation which is also important gets only our fleeting attention. I refer to the mitzvah of kimcha d'pischa, better known as maos chittin—providing matzah (and other foods) for the needy on Pesach.

The *Sefer Hatodaah* [page 321] relates that on Motzei Shabbos Parshas HaChodesh (the Shabbos when we bentch Rosh Chodesh Nissan), the Rav and the city council used to meet to divide all of the inhabitants of the town into two categories: those who could give and those who needed to receive. (Talmidei chachomim were also required to give for this mitzvah even though the Gemara in *Bava Basra* [6b] teaches that sages are exempt from most taxes [*Shulchan Orach, Orach Chaim*, siman 429].) Then, on the next day, they themselves went to collect from the first group. Anytime a well-to-do person would try to shirk his responsibility by saying, "Things are tight now," or, "I've given all my tzedakah for now," they would sternly reply that if he didn't give, he would be placed on the list of people who were to receive. Out of embarrassment, he would give.

The *Sefer Hatodaah* [page 321] explains that this is not regular tzedakah, for tzedakah is a requirement we must meet throughout the year. Rather, we are ensuring that when we say to our families at the seder table, "*Kol dichfin yeisei v'yeichol*—All who are hungry, let them come and eat" [*Pesach Haggadah*], the statement will not be a falsehood. Furthermore, Pesach is the holiday of freedom and redemption. Since we are celebrating that we are a kingdom of priestly people, we behave at the seder with a regal air. However, we cannot feel completely royal and free if our neighbors are suffering from need and hunger.

One might wonder why there is so much emphasis on "*kimcha d'pischa*—*flour* for Pesach." Furthermore, why is it called "*maos chittin?*—money for *wheat?*" Why don't we call it "money for Pesach?" After all, there are many other needs at this time of year, like wine, meat, and other expensive items for the seder. I believe the name "*maos chitin*—money for wheat" stems from an event dating back to the time the first matzah was made. This was when the angels came to visit Avraham's house.

Remember? Avraham said to Sarah [*Bereishis* 18:6],

"*Looshi v'asi oogos*—Knead and bake wafers." The *Sefer Ta'a-mei Minhogim* queries why it was necessary to tell the ninety-year-old quintessential balabustah, Sarah, to knead bread. Naturally, she was already quite experienced and skilled in hosting guests. But in this instance, Avraham was telling her to knead it continually, without stopping, "*l'sheim matzas mitzvah*—for the purpose of having matzah for the seder," so that it wouldn't become chometz, for the angels came on the first day of Pesach.

This is the source of using three matzos on the night of Pesach. The Tzadik of Zidichoiv asks, "Why is it that everything [in Judaism] is four—four parshios in tefillin, four tzitzis, four species of the lulav on Sukkos, four questions and four kosos (cups) of wine at the seder—but of matzos there are only three?" The Tzadik cleverly answered that when the middle matzah is broken, there are four here also. But the question remains, why do we start with three? The reason is because of the three *sa'ah*—a Biblical dry measure—of flour that Sarah Imenu used to prepare matzah for the three angels [*Bereishis* 18:6]. And when we think about it in this light, we realize that these first matzos were specially baked to be given to the needy! They were made for travelers who were (at least to all appearances) in need of food to eat.

The Medrash says that when Avraham was slaughtering the cattle to feed to the angels, one cow separated from the herd and bolted. Miraculously, it sprinted all the way to the Me'aras Hamachpelah which, at that moment, was revealed to Avraham as his final resting place. One must wonder why Hashem specifically chose this busy instant to show Avraham his burial plot. In the preceding hours he had just cut short Hashem's visit, and now he had three hungry angels waiting at his home to be served their meal. Does that sound like the proper time to inspect a future resting place? I believe that Hashem was connecting themes, teaching Avraham (and us) that the merit for what we serve to guests, and give to others, we will take to our graves. Perhaps this is one of the reasons men wear the kittel, our future burial shroud, on Pesach night.

Many people don't realize that on Pesach we are judged on our tevuah, our produce, which is directly related to our parnasah, our livelihood [*Rosh Hashanah* 17a]. Thus, sharing with others during this season is the best way to ensure that Hashem will give us a good judgment. Consistent with this theme is the fact that the word "matzos" is occasionally written defectively, i.e., missing a letter, in the Torah. It is sometimes written missing the letter "vav." That leaves us with "tzadee"-"suf"-"mem," which is an abbreviation for "*tz*edakah *t*atzil *m*imaves—Charity saves from death." In the same vein, if you take out the "tzadee" from **matzos**, you're left with the word **meis**, to teach us that without tzedakah, there is only death.

The word **matzah** also stands for, "*m*ikol *tz*ara *h*atzileini—From every pain, save me." Thus, we find that Avraham was miraculously healed from the pain of his circumcision when he arose and began serving the angels. Likewise, Lot and some of his family were saved when Lot served matzos to the angels in Sodom.

The *Zohar* calls matzah "*Michlah d'asvasa*—food of healing." Indeed, the *Sefer Ta'amei Minhogim* relates that even non-Jews used to purchase matzos in order to cure themselves of headaches.

Thus we see that giving kimcha d'pischa promises to help us in many beneficial ways: toward a bountiful judgment on our produce, toward our health, toward saving us from danger, and toward success in the world to come. Knowing all this, it behooves us to give more attention to helping others before Pesach.

A good way to perform this mitzvah is to go to the Rav or Rosh Yeshivah and ask him if there is a family that can be helped with matzah and wine, and maybe even with pairs of shoes for the children. Perhaps the Rav would want to give it to the family in our stead, in order to avoid embarrassing them. Even though this means giving of what we have, we will see how much richer we'll feel, and what a terrific lesson it will be for the family. Let's create an enduring legacy by directing our entire family's attention to this important mitzvah when Pesach comes around.

In the merit of this giving, may Hashem always provide us with the ability to give, and never the need to receive.

Pesach: **Educating the Next Generation**

"**B**aruch Hamakom, Baruch Hu. Baruch she'nosan Torah l'amo Yisroel, Baruch Hu. K'neged arba bonim dibra Torah. Echad chochom, echad rasha, echad tam, v'echad sh'eino yodei'a lishol— Blessed is Hashem, Blessed is He. Blessed is He Who gave the Torah to His Nation Yisroel, Blessed is He. The Torah addresses itself to four types of sons: the wise one, the wicked one, the simple one and the one who doesn't yet know how to ask."

With this passage, the Haggadah introduces the issue of, and establishes the central importance of, educating all types of children on the night of the seder.

Pharaoh tried, with many strategies, to exterminate the Jewish children. He asked the midwives to abort them, he commanded that they be drowned, he slaughtered them and drained their blood to treat his leprosy, and he buried them alive in the walls of Pisom and Ramses. He also embarked on a campaign to prevent Jewish births. The term "perech," literally translated as crushing labor which the Torah uses to describe the ways that Pharaoh tortured us, bears a connection to the Hebrew word 'paroches,' or curtain. The word teaches that Pharaoh attempted to interfere with family relations by keeping the men busy with intense labor in the fields while the women were at home, thereby separating them the way a curtain separates, so to speak. Furthermore, he also banned the use of mikvaos, in a further attempt to impede the birth of Jewish children.

Yet, miraculously, he failed miserably, and we experienced a population explosion unparalleled in history, increasing within 210 years from a family of seventy to a nation of many millions. This is one reason that, on the seder night, the children are the stars of the show and the focus of our primary attention.

Even more important is the fact that Pesach is the anniversary of the birth of the Jewish nation. Hashem said of Avraham Avinu that He knew that Avraham would transmit to his family and household Hashem's ways, and this is why he and his descendants, Bnei Yisroel, were chosen to be Hashem's nation. Thus, from year to year on the anniversary of our becoming a nation, our custom is to focus on inculcating in our loved ones the fundamentals of our beliefs.

The *Kol Bo* and the *Shibolei Haleket* clarify that the four parts of the blessing *Baruch Hamakom*, quoted above, correspond directly to the four types of children. Here we find an important lesson for our day and age. From the juxtaposition of *Baruch Hamakom*, which blesses Hashem, with even the wicked child, we learn that parents should be grateful even

for a wicked child. At first this sounds shocking. But R'
Tzadok Hakohain points out that, in the same section in sefer
Shemos [14:26, 27] which refers to the wicked child, it says
that the Jews bowed down to Hashem [*Shemos* 14:26, 27].
Rashi explains that the reason they bowed was to thank
Hashem for giving them children. R' Tzadok then asks,
"Who gives thanks for having a wicked child?" He concludes
from this that even for a wicked child one should be grateful—firstly, for being entrusted with the duty of turning this
child around and leading him to the way of the Torah and
secondly, for the vote of confidence from Hashem. For we
know that Hashem doesn't give anyone more than they can
handle. Obviously, this means that Hashem knows that these
parents have the many necessary talents to help such a child!

In this light, it is no coincidence that the seder night was
the night when Yitzchok gave the blessings to both Yaakov
and Eisav, thereby demonstrating that he loved Eisav, too
[*Rashi, Bereishis* 27:9]! Indeed, those who shower love on a
wayward child have tremendous bargaining power when they
pray to Hashem. They can say to Hashem, "Just as I love my
child unconditionally, please love your children unconditionally." It is for this reason that, in the future, Yitzchok will be
able to intercede and successfully petition Hashem for our
nation's welfare, while Avraham and Yaakov will not succeed.

The *D'var Aharon*, of blessed memory, (may Hashem
avenge his blood that was shed at the hands of the accursed
Nazis) states that the lesson of the sh'eino yodei'a lishol, the
child who does not know how to ask, is that we shouldn't
think that chinuch, education, begins only when the child is
old enough to ask questions. Rather, we must begin instruct-
ing and educating our children well before their questions
begin to emerge. The story is told of a family who presented

a young boy to a Rebbe and when they asked when they should start teaching him, the Rebbe replied, "You've already missed the best years."

The message of the tam, the simple son, is that, to be effective, lesson plans do not always have to be profound, novel, or complex. Sometimes you can achieve much more with people by simply stating clearly and then just constantly reviewing the basic tenets and fundamentals of Jewish belief.

The chochom, the wise son, is praised for his acquisition of wisdom. Indeed, it is to him that we refer when we say, "Blessed is Hashem that He gave the Torah to His Nation Yisroel." After all, Hashem told Moshe that the reason we merited the Exodus from Egypt was that we would accept the Torah at Har Sinai in the future. There is an incredible gematria (calculation using the numeric values of Hebrew letters) which alludes to this fact. "*Yetzias Mitzraim*—Exodus from Egypt," equals 891. This is the exact equivalent of "*na'aseh v'nishma*—We will do and we will hear," the statement with which the Jewish people accepted the Torah unconditionally.

The Steipler Gaon, of blessed memory, teaches that the supreme acquisition in life is that of wisdom. As proof, he cites the fact that the Gemara [*Kiddushin* 34b] explains that the Hebrew word "zakain," elder, also means a Torah sage. This is because **za**k**a**in is an abbreviation of "*Zeh kanah chochmah*—This one acquired wisdom." The Steipler continues, **za**k**a**in is really only a contraction of "*zeh kaneh*—This one acquired." So how do we know it refers to chochmah, wisdom? Maybe it refers to wealth, or friends, or cars, or a yacht? He concludes, it must mean chochmah because the only meaningful acquisition in life is the acquisition of wisdom. Thus, the chochom has succeeded in discovering life's most important pursuit. Perhaps this is one reason why "cho-chom" has the same gematria (68) as "chaim"—life!

An obvious question asked by the commentators is, "Why does the Haggadah say "*Echad chochom, echad rasha,*" etc., repeating over and over again the word "*echad*—one" each time a different son is specified. It could have just said, "The wise son, the evil son," and so on. The simple answer is that the repetition of the word echad sometimes indicates "whether one is this or one is that." This conveys the important lesson that we should give equal attention to all of our sons and daughters, regardless of whether a child is wise or wicked, simple or unable to ask.

R' Chaim Shmulevitz delves into this more deeply and offers a profound answer. He explains that the repetition of the word "one" indicates that we are not necessarily speaking about four different children! Sometimes all of these four attributes are present in the same child, manifesting themselves in different areas of his or her life. He bolsters this with the fact that the gematria of echad is thirteen which, when multiplied by four sons, equals fifty-two, which is the numerical value of "ben—son," or "child," namely a *single* child!

I would personally like to suggest that the quadruple mention of the term *echad* stresses the importance of empha-sizing achdus, family unity, even where there are several dif-ferent types of children. Chazal tell us that we were redeemed from Egypt when we repented for the sin of selling our brother Yosef as a slave. Thus, we should emphatically pro-claim to our children, "*Hinei matov u'mah na-im, sheves achim gam yachad*—How good and how sweet when brothers (and sisters) dwell together in unity" [*Tehillim* 133:1].

In a day and age when parents have their live-in maids

sign their children's homework sheets, and then, when repri-
manded by the teachers, "outsmart" the educators by giving
the maids a rubber stamp of their signatures, Pesach is the
time to commit ourselves to spending more of our own time
educating each and every one on our children. In the merit
of this attempt, may we live long and healthy lives, in order
that we may witness much Torah nachas from all of our
descendants.

Pesach: **Opportunities For Inspiration**

Pesach is our national birthday. It is the day on which Hashem bestowed upon us the ultimate gift—our status as His chosen people. This is, in fact, one of the reasons that we eat an egg at the seder, to symbolize our collective birth. It logically follows that on this momentous occasion we should eagerly seize the opportunity to impart our heritage to our children by introducing them to what is so special about being chosen as Hashem's people. Thus we have the mitzvah of v'higadta l'bincha, to teach our children the lessons of yetzias mitzrayim, our departure from Egypt.

Especially in today's society, we understand the enormous importance of connecting with our children. We readily realize the need to keep open the lines of communication with the rasha, the alienated child, giving him or her attention so they don't get lost. We must keep the chochom, the wise one, sufficiently challenged intellectually. We must stimulate the tam, the simple one, and start making inroads with the sh'eino yodei'a lishol, the child who doesn't even know how to ask anything, while he or she is still quite young.

Pesach is therefore a wonderful time to make a fresh start at spending more time with our children and working on infusing them with the spirit of Torah and the attitude of yiras Shamayim, awareness of Hashem. Let's remember a great rule: (this is a good one to keep on your desk, refrigerator, or in the car) "To our children all the presents in the world can't compare to more of our presence."

I recently saw a study in which over fifty percent of wives, when asked about their husband's work habits, replied that they were workaholics. Many of us would ruefully admit that we fall into this category. Indeed, because of spiraling medical costs, tuition increases, and other expenses, many of us need to juggle two or three jobs. Unfortunately, the ones to be lost in the shuffle, all too often, are our children. When many men finally get home in the evening, we are primarily thinking about grabbing some much needed relaxation or perhaps talking with our spouse. What we usually have the least inclination to do is spend time with an impatient, demanding child, or an often disinterested adolescent. However, we must realize that the most powerful achievements in life are also those that are most challenging!

It is of the utmost importance not to succumb to the whisperings of the yetzer hara, who torments us with thoughts that we might have already failed with our children. The evil inclination would like nothing better than to see us throw in the towel and give up on our kids. The truth is, though, that it's never too late to start. Pesach, which so strongly emphasizes the theme of education, is a wonderful time to begin recharging and revitalizing our commitment to our family!

So, let me share with you a few suggestions for ideal time-slots during the seder during which we can transmit some fundamental Torah principles to our children:

1. *Karpas:* During this ritual, in which we eat a vegetable dipped in salt water, we can point out to our family that it represents the suffering and pain of the Jewish people. The salt water into which we dip the herb symbolizes the tears and sweat of our ancestors in Egypt. Those who use parsley are commemorating that we proliferated like the green of the land and, when we dip it in the water, we are recalling how Pharaoh drowned our children in the water. We are also taught that karpas, when reversed, is a contraction of two words: "*Samech perech*—meaning that sixty myriads of Jews (i.e., 600,000 Jews) worked in conditions of crushing labor in Mitzrayim.

After painting this dismal picture of suffering and anguish, we can dramatically present to our family that there is a way to avoid pain and affliction. We can show them that karpas spelled backwards is the word "*sifrecha*," Your holy books! Furthermore, the numerical value of karpas is 360 which is the gematria of *shas*, the entire Talmud! We teach children that the members of the tribe of Levi were not enslaved and escaped affliction because they embraced the study of Torah. This, we should tell our children, is the way to avoid travail in life—by adopting a lifestyle of Torah study.

2. "*Afeelu kulonu chachomim, kulanu nevonim, kulanu z'kein-im, kulonu yodim es HaTorah, mitzva aleinu l'sapair b'Yetzias Mitzrayim*—Even if we are all wise, all full of understanding, all elderly (so there aren't even any children to teach), and all

knowledgeable of the Torah, it is incumbent upon us to talk about the Exodus." The obvious question is: Why rehash over and over again something which we already know? It is here that we can introduce our children to a critical lesson. There are two steps to living a Torah life in the optimal way. "*V'yadata hayom v'hasheivosa el l'vavecha* [*Devarim* 4:39]—a. Know today and, b. internalize it in your heart." It is one thing to intellectually accept something. It is an entirely different level to get to the point where you feel it in your heart. For example, we all believe intellectually that Hashem listens to our prayers, but how many of us really feel He is listening while we say the words, "*ki ata shomei'a tefillos kol peh*—You listen to the prayers of all mouths"? Now, we must tell our children, the way to make something a part of our feelings is to repeat it over and over again, year after year. So, we review over and over again that Hashem freed us from the Egyptian slavery and that in exchange we accepted the responsibility to be Hashem's servants. It is our hope that, with years of constantly repeating this concept, with mentioning the Exodus every week in kiddush, remembering it every day in our Tefillos, and every twelve hours in Krias Shema, it will finally become a part of our feelings!

3. "*M'lameid shehoyu m'tzuyanim sham*—this teaches that the Jews were distinctive in Egypt" [*Medrash Tanchumah* 114:4]. Even in Egypt we remained unique. We didn't change our distinct mode of dress, our language, or our Jewish names. We can utilize this opportunity to emphasize to our children that, although we were living in a decadent society and we were lowly slaves, we still maintained our personal modesty in dress. We should impress upon them that this trait, a dedication to tznius, modesty, has been with our people from the beginnings of our nationhood, and we should

encourage them not to fall prey to the temptation of cutting corners when it comes to hem lengths, sleeves, or slits in skirts, and so on.

In the same vein, we should emphasize to our children that our adherence to the Jewish language means much more than just being able to read or speak Hebrew. It means that, just as our ancestors diligently avoided the curse words and gutter language that was common amongst the lewd populace of Egypt, we must be equally vigilant in today's society.

4. "*Vayishma Hashem es koleinu*—Hashem heard our voices." We can use this verse as a springboard to talk to our children about how effective prayer can be. We can teach them that this is why we were saved in Egypt. We can instruct them that we are called Yehudim (Jews) because we are a people that give *hoda'ah*, thanks. One of our main characteristics is that we praise Hashem. We can share with them that Hashem created us in order that we should emulate His attributes. The posuk teaches us this concept when it says, "*Am zu yatzarti li t'hilasi y'sapeiru*—This nation I created for me, they will relate my praise!" [*Yeshaya* 41:21]. Indeed, the name of the holiday, Pesach, is a contraction of two words: "*Peh sach*—The mouth relates." This underscores the importance, on this festival in particular, of learning to speak often with Hashem in praise and supplication. Proper prayer is a great legacy to start introducing to our children, even at a young age!

5. "*Dam, tzfardei'a, kinnim…*—Blood, frogs, lice…" The recitation of the ten plagues is a wonderful point at which to impart to our children the life lesson of *middah k'neged middah*—that whatever we do in life is repaid to us in kind [*Shabbos* 105b]. Thus, the Egyptians, who drowned our babies in the Nile, filling it with Jewish blood, were punished by having the Nile turned into blood. And since the fish ate the

Jewish babies, the fish were asphyxiated in the blood. Similarly, just as the Egyptians didn't let us bathe and caused us to become infested with lice, so they were struck with swarms of lice.

Each plague was sent by Hashem as a perfectly fitting punishment for each of the Egyptian's heinous crimes against the Jews. We therefore tell our young charges that, if we are unkind or curt or impatient with others, Hashem will punish us by having others act to us the same way. On the other hand, if we are pleasant and patient, kind and affectionate, Hashem will ensure that we receive the same treatment. This lesson alone can make the whole seder worthwhile!

6. *Matzah.* We can use the matzah to teach them about the importance of zerizus, alacrity, in performing mitzvos. We can explain to them how the matzah has to be prepared with great haste so it doesn't become chometz. We should teach them about the dangers of procrastination, particularly in cases where it comes to spiritual matters!

This is just a small sampling of the opportunities for chinuch that we have at the seder table. Let's make a commitment to utilize the seder experience to plant important Torah concepts in the minds of our children! Let's make sure that we don't fritter away this glorious time fighting about the afikomen, or about when we should eat! And in the merit of working on passing the mesorah, our traditions, to our children and grandchildren, may we see much nachas and good health for our families and all of Klal Yisroel.

Sefirah: **Paradigm Shifts From Pirkei Avos**

If we have a problem with our car, it would be foolish to take a tip from our gardener on how to repair it. We should obviously read the owner's manual, written by the car manufacturer. Similarly, when it comes to aches and pains, we don't need advice from our barber. We need to ask a doctor, who is schooled in healing the human body.

So too, when we want to know the correct way to behave as a Jew, and how to refine our character, we turn to the Manufacturer of mankind, namely Hashem. What manual do we have as a resource for this information? The answer is the wondrous masechta called _Pirkei Avos_.

This anthology of ethical teachings, transmitted to us by our most inspiring teachers, presents us with a truly great opportunity to achieve personal excellence.

The name "Pirkei Avos" is a cause for question. Names such as *Sefer HaMiddos* (A Compendium of Character Traits) or *Hilchos Deios* (Laws of Proper Jewish Attitudes) spring to the mind as more appropriate titles. Yet the name *Pirkei Avos*, Chapters of our Fathers, reveals many secrets about this masechta.

The many parents who read this book are charged with the duties of educating their youth. After all, the posuk [*Mishlei* 1:8] tells us, "*Shema benee musar aveecha, v'al titosh Toras eemecha*—Listen, my son, to the lessons of your father, and don't turn from the teachings of your mother." Wow! That's putting a hefty responsibility upon us. Where is the guide-book to direct us in how to teach our children?

Voila! Here we have it—*Pirkei Avos*, a syllabus and full curriculum for parents on how to mold their children into well-rounded and refined Torah human beings. So we see that the name "Chapters of our Fathers" is a fitting title for this collection replete with lessons about humility, generosity, and self-control.

This title also teaches us how to correctly view those who teach us how to behave ethically. It is quite natural to dislike those who criticize and rebuke you. After all, nobody likes to be put down. Because of this tendency, a mashgiach (super-visor of ethical behavior in a yeshivah) might not be popular among certain students, and a Rav might not win many friends. Yet the name Pirkei Avos impresses upon us that the Sages, who teach us lessons of character and ethical behavior, should be loved by us just as we would love our own fathers. For, when we follow their advice and pay attention to their criticism, they actually give us life in the World to Come. Thus, they actually *are* our "fathers," for eternity. In this vein, the next time our knee-jerk reaction is to be upset that the

Rabbi is once again on a tirade about something, we should stop and think that he might actually be giving us the priceless gift of a wonderful eternity, if we only stop to listen to what he has to say.

It is interesting to note that we study this awesome collection in the spring time, precisely when the physical world is budding and awakening, and our own physical yearnings begin to stir as well. Specifically at such a time, we need direction to remain focused on our spiritual journey. This is also the time when we count the sefirah, and commemorate our climb of spiritual refinement from the time we left Mitzrayim until Shavuos, when we received the Torah. Sefirah recalls how we rose from the forty-ninth degree of tumah (impurity) to the pinnacle and zenith of Har Sinai. When we learn in *Pirkei Avos* that we must pursue Torah, divine service, and acts of kindness, we are attempting to climb the same ladder that our ancestors successfully ascended.

It is a shame that many do not open up Pirkei Avos with a sense of thirst and exhilaration. Perhaps, if we would keep it in a glass case, and charge ten dollars a minute for a peek inside, people would better appreciate its value. Its lessons on how to balance our lives and how to order our priorities are indeed priceless and eternal.

One reason why people tend to ignore its life-enhancing treasures is that they have superficially read its teachings over and over again. Therefore, unfortunately, too many people think of *Pirkei Avos* as "tired" or "old hat." To put it in other terms, we think we've "Been there, done that." This is a terrible shame for, as we grow wiser with experience, we can mine many new and profound lessons from its teachings.

Those who want to be intellectually challenged and spiritually improved by these ancient insights should consider finding a new commentary that they have not studied before. Drink from its words of wisdom with spiritual excitement! The Artscroll *Maharal on Pirkei Avos* and collections of Gerer teachings are but two examples that spring to mind immediately. Of course, the classic work of R' Irving Bunim, z"l, *Ethics From Sinai*, is a wonderful companion if you haven't as yet enjoyed it.

Pirkei Avos begins, "*Moshe kibeil Torah miSinai*—Moshe received the law directly from [G-d at] Sinai." Now, we would think that this statement, which tells us that the Oral Law is of Divine origin, should be at the very beginning of the Talmud, in Tractate *Brachos.* Why is it first taught to us so much later in the Talmud, in *Pirkei Avos*?

The answer is that when we see a whole section of advice on character traits such as humility and kindness, we may mistakenly think that these are the theories and opinions of our Sages learned through trial and error and personal observation. We may not realize that they are actually the Divine, absolute Truth given to us by G-d Himself. Thus, it is essential that specifically this tractate start by telling us that all of its contents originated from Sinai.

With this in mind, I'd like to suggest a method that I use for learning *Pirkei Avos* which I think can most successfully help us perfect ourselves. What I try to do is, as soon as the mishnah raises a subject, before reading the mishnah's advice, I try to think of what my opinion would be on that subject. Then, upon seeing the mishnah explain it differently, I strive to alter my opinion and thereby reorient my way of thinking towards the Torah way of looking at things. This is, in fact, the true meaning of becoming a ben Torah—working to transform yourself through the Torah that you learn.

Let's take an example. Chapter 2, mishnah 8 begins,

"*Marbeh nechosim...,*" referring to one who has many material possessions. Now, the mishnah will follow with a comment about how that condition impacts a person's life. Here I play my little "game," and speculate about how having many acquisitions would impact upon a person's life.

I would tend to assume that it would make a person happy, and contribute to the advancement of his goals and dreams. It would make him popular with his wife, family, and friends. All in all, it seems an immensely positive thing indeed. And now, I look back at the Mishnah and I'm in for a rude awakening. The Divine perspective on "more acquisitions," is "*Marbeh da'agah*—more worry and anxiety."

Try to use this method throughout *Pirkei Avos*. When Ben Zoma queries who is wise, contemplate what your response would be. Then absorb the critical truth that the wise man is one who learns from every person.

There is a concept which describes this method. It's called a "paradigm shift." A "paradigm" is a mindset which locks us into thinking in a particular way about something. We often fall into the habit of looking at things in a certain way, and it is as difficult for us to change this way of thinking as it is to change any habit. Pirkei Avos is the perfect "paradigm shifting" tool. It offers us a way to think "out of the box" and look at life in new ways—the time-tested ways of the Torah.

May we succeed in refining ourselves from this wonderful masechta.

Sefirah: *Learning Day and Night*

As we engage in the seasonal mitzvah of counting the sefirah, and observe the national period of mourning for the tragic deaths of the 24,000 disciples of R' Akiva, we should take time to reflect upon what these experiences are supposed to teach us.

Firstly, the Gemara [*Yevamos* 64a] informs us that R' Akiva's disciples died from *askara*, a type of lethal diphtheria or croup. The *Maharsha* informs us that this was a punishment for the sin of "*lashon hara*—evil gossip." This should jolt us with the realization that even rarefied "bnei yeshivah," lofty Torah scholars, can succumb to this deadly sin! Thus, at this time of year, we should be stimulated by our abstention from music and public entertainment to pick up the Chofetz Chaim's holy seforim on lashon hara, and become more aware of the many intricacies of the Torah's directive to guard our tongues. Without the proper perusal of these laws, it is all too possible that we might engage in this ugly sin, *chas v'shalom*, without realizing our transgressions.

Take, for example, the Chofetz Chaim's comments in klal 10:12, where he informs us that if someone fails to do you a favor (which is not exactly a terrible crime), and you reveal this to others, it is absolutely considered lashon hara! In the same vein, if you went to a town and you weren't greeted warmly, and you subsequently relate this to your townspeople, you are guilty of defaming a whole town. (This means that we must be extraordinarily careful about making casual remarks like, "The people in that shul aren't friendly.")

In klal 9:5, the Chofetz Chaim charges us not to hesitate to berate our young children if we hear them talking badly about people. He elaborates that the neglect of this sort of discpline is a primary reason for the proliferation of this sin in adults. Obviously, if children grow up saying whatever they want, it will be an enormously difficult habit for them to break as adults. It is therefore incumbent upon us as parents to cultivate in our children a strong aversion to speaking badly about others, just like we condition them from a very young age to be sure not to put forbidden food into their mouths!

Regarding the mitzvah of sefiras haomer, the *Chinuch* [mitzvah 306] explains that we are making a statement, on a national level, that the one occasion Jews count towards, just as others would count excitedly towards a vacation or a wedding day, is the day of Matan Torah—Shavuos. This is our public declaration that our number one national treasure and our source of identity is the Torah! However, as in all areas, Hashem doesn't want mere lip service from us. Thus, the true spirit of sefirah is to examine our daily schedules and see if we give enough time to our Torah.

The Gemara [*Sanhedrin* 7a] informs us, "*Ein tchilas dino shel adam ela al divrei Torah*—Man's final judgment will begin with evaluating the time he spent in Torah study." In Masechta *Shabbos* [31a], the Gemara elaborates that we will be asked by the heavenly tribunal, "*Kavata ittim la Torah?*—Did you set fixed times for Torah study?" The *Shulchan Oruch* [*Orach Chaim* 155:1] defines this responsibility as setting aside a specific time each day for learning, and ensuring that we do not violate this set time, even if it means losing substantial profit. The *Mishnah Brurah* [siman 155, seif katan 4] adds that if one must miss his appointed time, he should "pay it back" by learning double the next day!

The *Biur Halacha* informs us that in *Yoreh Deah* [246:1], we are further instructed that one should have a fixed period during both the daytime and the nighttime. He therefore recommends having a study period right after the morning prayers and again in the gap between afternoon and evening prayers. Of course this prescription will not fit for everyone, as some people must rush out immediately after davening in the morning to catch a bus. Those individuals might want to make their set time before shacharis, while other people who daven maariv right after mincha might establish their nightly time right after maariv.

Whatever our lifestyle, we should carve out two fixed times for Torah study in our daily life, even if they're initially only five minutes each. Women should encourage their husbands and sons in this and unmarried girls should seek a husband who learns regularly. We must all strive to answer the question that will determine our eternal fate (after 120 years of good life) with a resounding affirmative!

As to what we should learn, the *Mishnah Brurah* offers us the following guidance. He explains that one who only has a limited amount of time for Torah study should learn practical halachos (laws) in order to know how to live like a proper Jew. Additionally, we are guaranteed that one who studies halochos every day is assured a place in the afterlife!

As to other particulars of what to learn, the Chofetz Chaim assured us [*Orach Chaim*, siman 285, seif katan1] that a review of the weekly Torah portion not only develops our emunah, but also increases our longevity [*Masechtas Brachos* 8]. The preface to *Medrash Talpios* states that learning mishnayos helps protect one from the fires of Gehinnom. Finally, we should include a regimen of mussar study (Torah ethics and lessons of self-analysis and improvement). Firstly, this will assist us in acquiring the fear of Heaven which is our primary purpose in life. Secondly, as the baalai mussar tell us, once we include mussar in our learning, we are likely to find even more time to learn!

I recommend strongly that, when planning this most important schedule, a married man should sit down with his wife and solicit her input as to when he can make the time for set learning times. This will give her a great cheilek (portion) in the mitzvah and will insure that you don't choose a time that you will regularly have to miss because of other household responsibilities.

Finally, the *Mishnah Brurah* [siman 155, seif katan 4] cautions that we should not consider our "fixed" times as the only times we have available to study Torah. A Jew must study Torah at all available times! These fixed times are merely the ones that are sacred and not to be violated except in cases of extreme urgency.

In the merit of having a regular daily diet of Torah study

may we all merit the blessing of *"Orech yomim biymina, b'smo-la osher v'kavod*—Long life to the Torah's right and wealth and honor to her left" [*Mishlei* 3:17].

Sefirah: Our Customs Guide Us

The prevalent minhag (custom) is that the Rav makes the brachah of sefiras haomer first, followed by the rest of the congregation. One might wonder: Is it not a touch of gaiva, of haughtiness, for the Rav to take this honor for himself forty-nine days in a row?! Especially in today's day and age, when there's so much cynicism, wouldn't it be safer to allow the shliach tzibur to perform this task?

Perhaps one reason the Rav counts first is to drive home the concept of proper *kavod HaTorah* (honor for the Torah), specifically during the days of sefirah. After all, this period commemorates a time when 24,000 students of R' Akiva died because they did not give honor to one another. Thus, in our time, isn't it crucial that we take measures to stress honor for the Rav?

As we explained previously, the *Sefer HaChinuch* points out that the nature of people is to count the days towards something they deem as precious, and Klal Yisroel, on a national level, count in unison towards kabbolas HaTorah, the time at which we received our national Treasure. It follows that the Rav, whose livelihood is Torah and who, of all the members of his congregation usually spends the most time in Torah study, should step forward to lead our national counting. He is likely to do so with the deepest feeling and understanding. (R' Yaakov Kaminetsky, zt"l, once remarked that the Rav can pray for Torah knowledge in the brachah of *"Ata chonein l'adam da'as,"* the blessing for wisdom, as we all do, but since Torah is his livelihood he can also pray for knowledge in the brachah, *"Boreich aleinu,"* the blessing for parnasah, livelihood.) It is perhaps for this reason that in many congregations, during the Torah reading, the Rav is given the coveted aliyah of shlishi (the first aliyah possible for a Yisroel) because he can say most appreciatively the blessing of, *"Boruch ata Hashem, nosein haTorah."*

On a practical level, the task of counting sefirah is not routinely relegated to the shliach tzibur because he is often an *ovel* (a mourner within the first year after his loss), and it is not appropriate for an *ovel* to say the brachah for the entire congregation. Hence, the duty was given to the Rav to simplify matters.

Probably, the main reason that the brachah is said aloud by one person and then repeated by the congregation is so that everyone will have in mind the correct number for that particular day before starting their own brachah. This will keep people from making the brachah while unsure of the actual day and needing to listen to their friend's count. By ensuring that everyone already knows the number before making the brachah, we help everyone perform the mitzvah in the most ideal way. Since the person who says the brachah first bears the responsibility of ensuring that everyone counts the proper day, the job was given to the one who bears the spiritual responsibility of the kehillah, namely the Rav.

In addition, we know that one who misses a day cannot say the brachah on subsequent days. Thus, it is possible that the person who makes the brachah first should be motzee, or have in mind, those in the congregation who unfortunately did miss a day. However, it is important that the person who needs to appoint another person to count on his behalf should not feel embarrassed about revealing his oversight. Therefore the best person to be privy to this information is the Rav, who will surely commend the honesty and diligence of an admission of this nature and definitely not embarrass his congregant for his mistake. In this vein, it's also possible that the Rav was chosen to say the brachah each night in order to be sure not to embarrass a shliach tzibur who, though obliged to daven publicly because he is an ovel or has a yahrtzeit, forgot to count one day and as a result would be publicly humiliated when unable to count for the congregation.

These examples are typical of Judaism's extreme emphasis on not causing other people public embarrassment for, as it states in *Masechtas Sanhedrin* [107a], "*Hamalbin p'nei chaveiro b'rabim, ein lo cheilek l'Olam Habah*—Whoever shames others in public loses his share in the World to Come!"

So next time we hear the Rav count sefirah, let's not view it cynically. Instead, let's appreciate this multi-faceted *minhag avoseinu*, tradition of our fathers, and, in the merit of our counting towards Kabollas HaTorah, may we be zocheh to a multitude of Torah blessings.

Shavuos: **Becoming Ambassadors of Peace**

The Torah testifies that, as we stood at Har Sinai, "*Vayichan shom Yisroel neged hahar*—the Jews encamped there in front of the mountain" [*Shemos* 19:4]. The Eben Ezra immediately question the fact that the word "vayichan" is written in the singular form, not the plural. This is unusual because we know that the Jews numbered over 600,000, and that figure only includes men of age to serve in the army. That number doesn't include the women, children, and elderly, who also left Egypt. Rashi explains the singular form indicates that we were united "like one person, with one heart." Thus we learn that the dream of achdus—total unity and national oneness—was achieved at the foot of Har Sinai. Clearly, then, one of the primary messages of Shavuos is to strive to reach, once again, this pinnacle of accomplishment that we attained on this festival so long ago.

Don't make the mistake of thinking that this description of our unity is unrelated to the giving of the Torah. To the contrary, this is one of the major purposes of the Torah. As the Rambam teaches us at the end of *Hilchos Chanukah* [4:14], the whole Torah was given in order to make peace in the world, as it says *"Deracheha darchei noam, v'chol nesivoseha shalom*—Its ways are ways of pleasantness and all its paths are paths of peace" [*Mishlei* 3:17]. This is an amazing concept. The Rambam is teaching us that the common thread running through all of the 613 mitzvos is—peace. Thus, it is no wonder that, as it says in the Gemara, the sages did not let their disciples stand up for the scholarly Geniva. Although he was a brilliant sage, he was a controversial figure, not a man of peace.

We too must make sure we are in sync with the major thrust of Torah—namely, the pursuit and maintenance of peace and harmony.

To illustrate how the study of Torah fosters peace, let's take a look at the following amazing Gemara: We are taught in *Masechtas Shabbos* [33b] that R' Shimon Bar Yochai and his son Elazar had to seek refuge from the authorities for many years in a cave. A miracle occurred—a spring of water and a carob tree appeared there to sustain them. They stayed there, deep in Torah learning, for over a decade. When they finally exited, and looked around at people involved in regular workday activities, their gaze instantly burned to a crisp anyone that entered their line of sight. They couldn't fathom, on their holy level, how people could waste their time on non-spiritual pursuits. At that point, Hashem commanded them to return to their cave. R' Reuven Feinstein, shlit"a, queried: if it was their assiduous Torah study that had caused them such lofty and rarefied holiness, would not their return for more Torah study make them even more out of touch with the regular world? How would it help for them to go back into the cave?

R' Feinstein explains that Hashem told them to go back into the cave and learn the Torah of shalom, the Torah of peace. When they came out one year later, they had successfully accomplished this objective.

The word achdus, unity, is a much misused and maligned term. It is amazing to me how people hurl it at others as an accusation. "Why, *they* have no sense of achdus!" Or, with the banner of achdus unfurled as a defense for their own misbehavior or spiritual neglect, they fling an accusation of lack of achdus upon those who properly rebuke them. In truth, the Torah teaches us that at times it is not just proper, but incumbent upon us to chastise others and even to distance ourselves from people who are negligent in their religious observance.

What, then, is true achdus? I believe that achdus is primarily what we ourselves do. It is how we ourselves exhibit tolerance. It is how we reach out to others and—with great self-control—look away from those who belittle or insult us. Our own actions are the only way to promote real achdus. Others will then learn from our example, for this kind of behavior is truly infectious. It is in this way that we can really make strides towards friendship and unity. I'd like to reiterate —if you are among those who primarily tout achdus to others, it's time for a little soul searching.

The Gemara [*Shabbos* 88b] teaches us that tzadikim are, "*Ne'elavin v'einan olvin*—They accept insult but do not answer back. *Shomin cherpason v'einan m'shivin*—They hear words of disgrace but do not respond." While at first glance this sounds admirable, there is an obvious question. Shouldn't

a righteous person rebuke insensitivity? What about the obligation of tochacha, of chastising the wrongdoer? If he stands
meekly by, won't this just encourage insensitivity to others?

Rather, the Gemara explains, tzadikim hold back and are
silent when dealing with people who simply will not listen.
If someone is obviously too rigid to change or too arrogant
to be told anything, the appropriate behavior is to look away.

Knowing when to be silent is a great step in the direction
of achdus. It follows in the spirit of the famous Gemara
[*Chullin* 89a] that asks, "What is a person's profession in this
world? To train yourself to be like a mute." Another Gemara
[*Chullin* 89a] informs us, "The world survives because of the
one who knows how to shut his mouth during a quarrel."

Whether in the workplace or in the synagogue, whether
in the arena of marital harmony, parental relationships, or
raising children, the pursuit of peace will serve us well and
surely give us success in all our endeavors. May Hashem bless
us all with healthy, happy and wonderfully peaceful lives.

<u>Shavuos</u>: **Committing Ourselves to Torah**

Each year, when Shavuos is over, we are left with pleasant memories of sweet blintzes and scented flowers. But it is imperative for the thinking Jew to walk away from the Festival of Torah with more than just memories of cheesecake and other dairy delights.

The thrust of this Yom Tov is two-fold: A renewed commitment to Torah study and a revitalized attitude to Torah observance. Let's dwell upon Torah study first.

In *Pirkei Avos* [2:8], we are taught that we should not be haughty if we have learned a lot of Torah, for this is the reason we were created. Do we hear those words? This is why we were created! It's important to ponder this powerful statement. For, if we let days go by without opening a sefer, it means that during those days we are missing out on life's true meaning. In the same vein, we should bear in mind the Gemara in *Sanhedrin* that teaches us that, when we get to the next world, we will first be judged regarding our commitment to Torah learning. Once again—stop to consider! Our eternal status will be determined, to a large extent, by how much time and effort we expend on Torah study.

We are further taught that there are three types of people Hashem cries over every day. The first type are those who could have learned Torah, but didn't. What a potent message! Of all the human failings, ranging from anger to greed, jealousy to lust, G-d cries first over one who does not avail himself of the extraordinary gift of Torah study. When R' Akiva taught Papus that a Jew without Torah can be compared to a fish without water, R' Akiva was emphasizing to us that Torah is the life-breath of every Jew. And indeed, just like a fish is in severe agony from the moment it is plucked out of the water, so too our soul is in spiritual anguish when it is away from Torah study.

Besides the strong obligation upon us to study Torah, and the eternal rewards if we do study, we have many other incentives for being diligent about this mitzvah. Proper study of Torah rewards a person with life, as it says in *Mishlei* [3:16], "*Orech yomim biymina*," and with wealth and honor, as it further says, "*Bismola osher v'chavod*." It also brings a person good health, as it states [*Mishlei* 4:23], "*Ul'chol b'soro marpei*," and the blessing of peace, as it says [*Mishlei* 3:17], "*v'chol nesivoseha shalom*."

It is therefore important that, each year as we take leave of Shavuos, we take a new look at how much of a daily dosage of Torah we have in our lives. In *Shulchan Aruch* [*Yoreh Deah*, siman 245], which has the final say about how we should run our lives, we are taught that every Jewish male must study Torah every day and every night. This means that we should never allow twelve hours to elapse without some Torah learning.

In order to succeed at this, we must plan effectively. We might want to embark on the study of *Kitzur Shulchan Aruch*, whereby we could learn a few short sections every day. Perhaps we could carry around an English siddur to study in our spare moments, in order to better learn some of the prayers' meanings. Maybe we could make a project of finally studying those summer Torah portions we may have never yet learned.

Tehillim tells us, *"Limnos yameinu kain hoda v'navi lvav chochma*—Teach us how to count our days and this will bring us a heart of wisdom"* [90:12]. The simple meaning of this is that, if we learn to realize that life is quickly passing us by, and that our days on this world are in fact finite, we will arouse ourselves to begin a career of obtaining authentic wisdom.

It is related that R' Elya Lopian, zt"l, used to stop in the middle of a droshah, lift up and gaze at his beard, and muse aloud that, since his beard already had some gray hairs, it meant that half of his life had already passed. Many of us who are middle-aged would do well to take stock and ask ourselves as life is passing, "Are we as well accomplished in the main task of life, in the study of Torah, as we should be?"

The *Orchos Chaim L'harosh* makes a clever suggestion. He proposes that we should schedule a bit of time to study just before we eat. I believe that his reasoning is as follows: No matter how busy we are, we always still find time to eat. Thus, if we link our Torah study to our eating times, we will ensure that we have to learn regularly. This connection is not merely one of convenience. Actually, learning is just as essential as is eating! We require a diet of food and beverage for our bodies;

we require a diet of Torah for our souls. Indeed, R' Yehuda Zev Segal, zt"l, of Manchester, would habitually learn while eating.

So, in order to make each Shavuos last, let us see if, especially as we head into the long summer months, we can make a commitment to learning at least some Torah during every twelve-hour period of our lives.

Now, let's talk a moment about the second element we need to take from Shavuos: A commitment to elevated Torah observance. *Tosefos* in *Brachos* [11b] asks a powerful question, "Why is it that, every time we enter the sukkah after some time has passed, we make a new brachah? Yet, when it comes to Torah, we make one series of blessings in the morning—and that's it for the entire day. It seems strange. After all, if we don't open our Gemara again from early in the morning until the evening Daf, shouldn't we make a new brachah? Certainly many things have taken place between our morning blessings and our night-time study session!?

Tosefos answers that a good Jewish male is never distracted from Torah. At first this may sound like a lofty ideal, for we know that the average person goes to work and gets busy with clients, faxes, e-mails and the like, and his mind is unfortunately far from Abaya and Rava, Rashi and Tosefos. How can we possibly say that by the time the night rolls around there have not been hours of distractions?

What Tosefos means is, although in the morning a man might close his Gemara and not open it again until the evening, he never ceases from living a Torah lifestyle. Remember, the blessing is, *"La'asok b'divrei Torah*—To be involved in words of Torah."* This, in fact, is what he is doing the entire day. When he returns from shul and greets his wife sweetly, he fulfills *"V'seemach es eeshto*—and he should gladden his wife" [*Devarim* 24:5]. He performs the rabbinical commands of washing his hands before eating, he makes a blessing, and washes after eating. Then he bentches, thereby fulfilling the Biblical command of "*v'achalta v'savata uveirachta*—and you should eat and be satisfied, and bless Hashem. [*Devarim* 8:10]. If he reminds his children before they depart to school to be kind to their classmates, he thus fulfills, "*V'sheenantom l'vanecha*—Teach your children" [*Devarim* 6:7]. He then goes to work where, when he is careful to speak truthfully, he fulfills the mitzvah of "*Mid'var sheker tirchak*—Distance yourself from falsehood" [*Shemos* 27:7]. He practices business with integrity, and thus follows the directive of "*Nosasah v'nosatah b'emunah*—dealing faithfully in business" [*Shabbos* 31a]. If he goes home on the bus and stands up for the elderly, he fulfills "*Mipnei seiva takum*—Stand up before the aged" [*Vayikra* 19:34], and if he smiles at Jew and gentile alike, he makes a kiddush Hashem and sanctifies G-d's name, fulfilling the rarified mitzvah of "*V'nikdashti b'soch Bnei Yisroel*—I will be sanctified amongst the Jewish people" [*Vayikra* 22:32]. Such a person, when he opens the Gemara in the evening, has certainly not been distracted from Torah, for he has been occupied in Torah the whole day. That is why he does not need to make a new blessing.

This is the heightened sense of Torah commitment we should take away with us as we leave Shavuos: The state of mind of "*B'chol d'rachecha da'eihu*—Acknowledge Hashem in all your ways" [*Mishlei* 3:6]. May Hashem help us succeed both in consistent Torah study and in heightened Torah observance, and in that merit may Hashem bless us with good health, happiness and everything wonderful.

Tisha B'Av: Avoiding The Perils of Habit

In *Masechtas Nedarim* [81a], the Gemara cites a verse in *Yirmiyah* [9:11], "*Mi ha-ish hechacham v'yavein es zos...al ma avda haaretz*—Who is the man who is wise enough to understand the reason...why the land was lost?" The Gemara elaborates and says that this matter was asked of the Sages, Prophets, and even the Celestial Angels. However, they were stumped and unable to shed light on the disaster of the first Temple's destruction and Jerusalem's ruination, until Hashem Himself revealed the secrets. As Rav informs us, Hashem explained that the disaster occurred because the people at that time didn't make the blessings on the Torah properly.

First, let us understand the Prophet's question. Don't we know why the destruction occurred? Weren't we taught that the first Beis Hamikdash was destroyed because of the heinous crimes of idolatry, immorality, and bloodshed? Nevertheless, the question arises because we still should have had a saving grace of our Torah study. We are taught that Torah study is a shield from retribution. Since the generation of the churban, the destruction, was replete with Torah study, there should have been sufficient protection to prevent the many catastrophes of that era. It is this that bewildered the greatest sages, the prophets of vision, and even the most powerful Heavenly Angels.

Only Hashem, Who penetrates the depths of every person's heart, was able to discern that, although there was plenty of Torah, there was something wrong with their Torah, specifically with the blessings they made on the Torah. Rabbeinu Yona elucidates that a proper blessing is made when a person appreciates something and is excited to thank Hashem for it with a blessing. He goes on to say that although Klal Yisroel learned plenty of Torah, they did not appreciate the Torah as a pleasure. They viewed it more as a chore that had to be completed.

Let's ask ourselves how this relates to us. Are we learning because we have to, or because we want to? Is the Daf Yomi a burden to be shouldered or a luxury to be enjoyed? Is the weekly review of the Torah portion a yoke or a privilege? These are crucial questions we must ponder and work on as we take leave of Tisha B'Av.

R' Yehuda Zev Segal, zt"l, taught that when making the blessings on the Torah one should do so with excitement as if he just won a multi-million dollar lottery. As Dovid Hamelech said, "*Tov li toras picha mai'alfei zahav vachesef*— Better for me is the Torah of your mouth than thousands of gold and silver coins!" [*Tehillim* 119:72].

But there is more to be learned from Hashem's diagnosis.

Blessings are critical in helping us focus and channel our minds in the proper direction when we embark upon a mitzvah. For example, take the mitzvah of netilas yadayim, washing our hands before eating. Without a meaningful brachah, we can easily slip into the bad habit of viewing this washing as a mere exercise in proper hygiene. However, when we thoughtfully say the words, "*Asher kiddishanu b'mitzvosov vitsivanu*—Who has sanctified us with His mitzvos and commanded us...," it impresses upon us that this is also a ritual of holiness and an opportunity to fulfill the will of Hashem.

Thus, Hashem explained that the reason our Torah learning failed to protect us at the time of the churban was because it lacked the necessary amount of "*lishma*—learning for its own sake." What an important lesson! How easy is it to get into the routine of trying to finish a masechta and forget in the process that we are learning because it is the will of Hashem and the fulfillment of the mitzvah of "*V'dibarta bam*" [*Devarim* 6:7]. In order to protect our families with the shield of Torah, we must train ourselves to preface our Torah study with the proper thoughts—that we are engaged in this activity in order to fulfill the supreme command of Hashem, the study of His Torah.

The danger of living life habitually affects all areas of Judaism. It is the daily trial of the religious Jew. If we are not careful, we can easily go through the routines of religiosity— putting on tefillin, eating kosher food, keeping Shabbos—all without thinking about Hashem. It is therefore of immense importance that, when we say our brachos and perform mitzvos, we learn to train our minds to think about Hashem.

Before we leave of this all-important Gemara behind, I'd like to make one more comment. How the Gemara rings true for us, living in the aftermath of the Holocaust, when it says the destruction of Jerusalem puzzled and perplexed the Sages, Prophets, and Angels! It should be no surprise to us that we are unable to explain the atrocities of the Holocaust, when even Prophets and Angels were confounded by the disasters of yesteryear.

Finally, there is another lesson to be learned from Tisha B'Av, which R' Chaim Volozhin taught us. He points out a similarity between the opening words of *Megillas Eicha* [1:1], "*Eicha yoshva vadad*—Alas! The city that is alone and desolate," and the Torah directive to Klal Yisroel, "*Hein Am l'vodod yishkon*—Behold the Nation which dwells apart" [*Bamidbar* 23:9]. He explains the connection as follows: When the Jews fail to keep themselves distant and distinct from the neighboring nations, Hashem punishes us with the likes of "Eicha" (i.e, destruction and mourning). We've seen this to be true throughout the ages—assimilation and imitating the style of other nations brings about disaster! Such, the Midrash tells us, was the fate of the Jews in Egypt, who embraced the ways of the Egyptians and desisted from circumcision. Their effort to blend into society resulted in enslavement. So also was the fate of the Jews in Spain, who became too close to the ways of their host nation and then suffered the dreadful consequences of the Spanish inquisition and the expulsion.

One summer, I had the pleasure of being together with R' Lichtig, shlit"a, of Queens. In his youth, he attended the legendary Yeshivas Chachmei Lublin founded by the great R' Meir Shapiro, zt"l. R' Lichtig told me that R' Shapiro once traveled to America to raise funds for his yeshivah. Upon his return to Europe, they asked him to describe the American Jew. He responded with the following concise assessment: "They know quite well how to make kiddush but they are lacking in their understanding of havdalah." What he meant was that they knew how to do beautiful mitzvos but were missing the discipline to distance themselves from the ways of the gentiles. More than half a century later, this failing is still typical of many of us. We must be extremely wary of the influence of gentile culture upon our manner of dress, our method of speech, our behavior with our spouse, our treatment of our children, our attitudes towards our parents, and the respect we show our elderly and our sages. Let us remember this golden rule: When we keep ourselves distinct from the nations, Hashem blesses us with His divine protection. On the other hand, when we strip ourselves of the proper boundaries, Hashem forcibly ejects us in order to force us to maintain our Jewish identity. Hashem wishes to keep us apart. It can be voluntary, with a yarmulke, or forced—with a Jewish star.

In the merit of our attempting to better ourselves from the lessons of the Churban, may we be spared from any further Jewish suffering and see the rebuilding of the Temple and the Final Redemption speedily in our days.

In
Memoriam

The Legacy of
Rav Avigdor Miller, zt"l

The world has lost an unparalleled mentor with the passing of the tremendous tzadik, R' Avigdor Miller, zt"l. R' Miller's influence reached all denominations of Judaism—from Chassidic to Zionist, from Yeshivish to Sephardic, to many who had previously known nothing of Yiddishkeit whatsoever. His devoted disciples can be found all over the globe.

What was the secret of his amazing ability to penetrate the hearts of the masses and bring them closer to Hashem and His Torah? First of all, we are taught that, "*Devarim hayotzim min haleiv, nichnasim el haleiv*—Words that emanate from the heart enter people's hearts." R' Miller lived and practiced the lifestyle he taught, and thus his words were able to successfully influence us.

In these cynical times, when many of our speakers have

their own personal agenda, R' Miller stood out from the crowd. Those who heard him speak understood that he had no agenda other than bringing us closer to Hashem. He, who sat on a plain folding chair when delivering his lectures, who refused to allow his admirers to build him a beautiful new shul, who declined to even put a sign on the front of his synagogue, was certainly not motivated by the desire for honor and glory. Nor was he interested in money. As his son-in-law, R' Brog, shlit''a, said, perhaps one of the reasons he enjoyed such longevity (he lived ninety-two years) is because he never took a gift from anyone—he thus earned the reward promised in the verse, "*Sonei matanos yichyeh*—He who despises gifts will live" [*Mishlei* 15:27]. His lectures were not motivated by the hope of winning wealthy benefactors and adherents. His whole interest was only, "*Shet'hei sheim shamayim misaheiv*—that the Name of Hashem should be loved."

Like Avraham Avinu, who spread monotheism throughout the world, R' Miller taught vast myriads the meaning of yiras Hashem, fear of G-d. He would say to us that the root of "yirah" is "r'ei," to see, and that the primary challenge of life is to pierce the veil of darkness and perceive the presence of Hashem in every area of life.

We find this directive throughout the Torah. Moshe Rabbeinu taught it to us when he said, "*Ma Hashem Elokecha sho'eil mei-imoch, ki im l'yirah es Hashem Elokecha*—What does Hashem ask from you but that you should constantly see Him and be aware of Him?" [*Devarim* 10:12].

Shlomo Hamelech, the wisest of men, taught us in *Koheles* [12:13], "*Sof dovar, hakol nishma. Es HaElokim yirah, v'es mitzvosov shemor, ki zeh kol ha'adam*—After everything has been examined, be aware of G-d and keep His commandments, for this is the essence of man." *Tehillim* teaches us,

"*Reishis chochmah yiras Hashem*—The first wisdom that a Jew should acquire is awareness of Hashem" [111:10]. R' Miller worked tirelessly to infuse us with a deep appreciation of the importance of Yiras Hashem.

He showed us how to see the hand of Hashem in nature. Just look at the potato, he would tell us! Why, he would ask, is a potato a dirty earth-like color? Why isn't the potato a luscious color—maybe wintergreen, or bright, like an apple or an orange? He explained that the Creator, in His kindness, wanted to show us that you couldn't just take a bite out of a raw potato. Hashem made it an earthy color, like the ground, to show us that you have to process the potato before you eat it, through cooking or baking—just like the ground, which needs to be plowed and planted.

He would show us how to perceive Hashem in a seed. Every apple, he would say, comes with coupons inside! Buy one and get a tree for free! He would point out the vast difference between the wisdom of humans and Hashem's wisdom. With batteries, for instance, which are a human creation, if you put a battery in the flashlight the wrong way, it won't work. However, with a seed, which is Hashem's creation no matter which way you plant the seed, the roots always reach down and the flowers always grow up. The seed is really a mini-computer, forever pointing the plant in the right direction. Furthermore, he would tell us to look at the branches, and challenge us to find a tree that has branches stacked one on top of another. The branches are always staggered so that every leaf should receive adequate life-sustaining light from the sun to carry out its miraculous photosynthesis. Further, since they are spread out, they provide us with protective shade from the beating sun!

He would ask us to consider why the sky contains so

many galaxies, infinitely more than humans will ever be able to explore. Since the whole purpose of the creation is for the benefit of humans, why did Hashem make such a vast expanse, which is entirely beyond our reach? He would answer that the sole purpose of the far-flung cosmos is to give us a heightened awareness of the vastness of G-d Himself. When we look out at the universe, we gain some inkling of the awesome vastness of Hashem. As the posuk in *Yeshaya* [40:26] says, "*S'u morom eineichem u'reu mi bara eileh*—Lift your eyes up high and you will see (i.e., grasp) Who created all these things."

R' Kanarek, shilt"a, one of R' Miller's prestigious sons-in-law, commented how, when R' Miller would eat challah, he behaved as if he were eating munn. He would say, "What a miracle. From a small dry seed came this beautiful challah!" He would observe how remarkable it was that you could feed a cow a little grass and get nutritious and delicious milk in return!

We say in our prayers, "*Ma rabu ma'asecha Hashem, kulom b'chochmah asisa*—How great are Your deeds, Hashem! They are all invested with wisdom." Everything in the world has a plan and a purpose—and the thinking person can see the Creator in everything around him. This ability is the wisdom of yiras Hashem.

With countless examples, R' Miller would prod us to think about Hashem at every moment. This was indeed the essence of his being.

There is a popular saying, "Acharei mos, Kedoshim." (These are two consecutive parshiyos of the Torah, and are therefore often mentioned together.) Literally this means, "After death, they are holy." In a cynical way, people take this to mean that everyone becomes holy after they pass on. But, in a truer sense, there are people whose righteousness we discover only after their passing. Since they lived their lives with great humility, they were able to conceal much of their greatness. Thus, it is only now that we are beginning to find out many amazing qualities of the great gaon and tzadik, R' Avigdor Miller, zt"l.

Apparently, for sixty years he slept on a board covered with a sheet, instead of on a mattress. It turns out that he never ate cake, and that, whenever he ate his meals, between each bite of food, he would turn over his fork, in order to cause himself to pause and focus on eating *l'sheim Shamayim*, for the sake of Heaven. His Rebbetzin revealed, during the shiva period, that for the sixty-six years they were married, she doesn't remember R' Miller ever opening the refrigerator. How incredible! He had obviously conquered his yetzer hara to eat, and ate only in order to live and serve Hashem.

While these pieces of information are amazing in themselves, I believe there is a profound thread that runs through many of these awesome details of this tzadik's lifestyle. The essence of R' Miller was a constant awareness of being in the Presence of Hashem. He was the very embodiment and personification of, "*Shivisi Hashem l'negdi samid*—I set Hashem before me constantly" [*Tehillim* 16:8]. His sole desire was for closeness to Hashem. In this, he followed in the footsteps of Dovid Hamelech, who said, *Achas shoalti mei'eis Hashem, osah avakeish, shivti b'veis Hashem kol y'mei chaiyai, lachazos b'no-am Hashem*—One thing I asked of Hashem, this I will request, to dwell in Hashem's House all the days of my life and see the sweetness of Hashem" [*Tehillim* 27:4]. This does not mean that Dovid Hamelech wanted to abdicate his throne, or to cease being the commander-in-chief of the Jewish army, or to stop judging laws of family purity. Rather, it means that

Dovid yearned to feel the presence of Hashem in everything that he did.

R' Miller seems to have structured his life to remove any possible obstacles to achieving this goal. By not opening the refrigerator, he disciplined himself not to hunger for a nosh. By sleeping on a board, he subdued his natural craving for sleep. By not eating cake, he rid himself of the desire for delicacies.

This type of behavior sometimes caused people to misunderstand him. His grandson, R' Simcha Bunim Cohen, shlit"a, said at the funeral that some people thought R' Miller didn't want to speak with people. This was not so, he explained. Rather, R' Miller related that he couldn't do two things at once, and he didn't want to be distracted from thinking of Hashem. In this sense, R' Dushinsky, shlit"a, said that R' Miller was like a living *Chovos Halevovos*, which says that being among people distracts one from awareness of Hashem, and there is no greater aid to closeness to Hashem than solitude [*Shaar Cheshbon HaNefesh*, cheshbon 17]. R' Miller used to say that, in this, he couldn't equal R' Moshe Feinstein, zt"l, zy"a, who was able to go to four weddings a night and still be totally immersed in his study.

It has been the custom since the time of the Gemara (see *Masechtos Megilla* 27b, 28a, *Taanis* 20b and *Shabbos* 118b) to ask our sages who merited longevity: "*Bameh ha'arachta yomim?*—To what merit do you attribute your long life?" When they asked this question of R' Moshe Feinstein, zt"l, he answered, "In my entire life I have never caused pain to another person." When they asked R' Yaakov Kamenetsky, zt"l, the same question, he said that in his entire life he did not tell a lie and that he tried not to cause another pain. When they posed the question to R' Shach, shlit"a, he answered that he was always careful to bentch from a bentcher. It is important to note that while all these sages learned Torah day and night, and were thus deserving of long life because of their Torah study (as the verse says in *Mishlei* [3:16], "*Orech yomim beeminah*—Long life is at its [Torah's] right"), they were obviously offering us information about specialties that they worked on, ones which we could relate to and try to incorporate into our daily lives.

R' Brog, shlit"a, R' Miller's son-in-law, said that his saintly father-in-law never took anything from anyone. Thus, when the sephardim offered to replace his small shul with a magnificent edifice, he declined. R' Brog concludes that R' Miller lived with the Talmudic adage "*Sonei matanos yichye*— He who hates gifts will live" [*Mishlei* 15:27]. Perhaps this was one of the secrets to his longevity.

I would like to share with you a personal experience I had regarding this trait of R' Miller's. My father, of blessed memory, used to visit us from time to time when we were learning in Camp Yeshivah Staten Island up in Kerhonkson, New York. At that time, R' Moshe Feinstein used to stay with us for the summer. My father would go to Ossie's Fish Market on Thirteenth Avenue (in Brooklyn, New York) and ask Ossie (may he rest in peace) for the finest and best cuts of fish to bring to R' Moshe. One time, having learned from my father's example, I went to Ossie for the finest cuts of fish, and he gave me three sparkling, ruby-red pieces of salmon. I brought them to R' Miller's house where I knocked on the door. The Rebbetzin answered and she looked at me with a puzzled face, asking, "What's this?" I answered, "It's for the Rav and Rebbetzin. Some very fresh fish." She looked surprised and answered me, "Oh no. The Rav won't take anything." I persisted, telling the story that I was following in my father's footsteps but she was equally adamant saying, "Sorry, the Rav will not take anything." I had to turn on my heels and admit defeat, and I returned home with my salmon in tow.

While this is an amazing trait in our day and age (where everything is "What's in it for me?" and so many people operate with ulterior motives), I believe that this behavior is consistent with the other characteristics of R' Miller which we have discussed. R' Miller's goal was to remove any possible ulterior motivation from his activities. By not accepting anything from anyone, he forestalled the possibility that his activities would be motivated by trying to impress others, to win benefactors, or to achieve fame or fortune. Consistent with this is the fact that he shunned the limelight, never speaking at such showcases as the siyum daf yomi at Madison Square Garden, the Kenesiah Gedolah, or the keynote session of an Agudah convention. As we mentioned before, he didn't even have a sign on the front of his shul!

By not taking things from people, and not allowing himself to bask in public recognition, he prevented these ulterior motivations from adulterating his pure service of Hashem. We can only look in awe at his amazing self-discipline and self-negation in his striving for perfection, for the level of "*Ani Avd'cha*—I am Your servant, Hashem" [Tefillas Hallel].

R' Kanarek, shlit"a, commented in his eulogy in Eretz Yisroel that R' Miller lived a life of machshovah, contemplation. As he put it, he was "*k'seder getracht*," meaning that he was always in a state of meditation. He further elaborated that his father-in-law did nothing without first giving it thought. He quoted, from the sefer *Das Torah*, one definition of mussar: "*Hisbonenus achar hisbonenus*—Meditation, and more meditation."

Indeed, R' Matisyahu Solomon, shlit"a, mashgiach

ruchani of the famous Lakewood Yeshivah, commented in the eulogy he gave that, without exaggeration, R' Miller was the Avraham Avinu of our time. He elaborated by citing from the Rambam in *Hilchos Avodah Zarah* [1:3], that Avraham Avinu, in his formative years, meditated day and night until he arrived at an awareness of the Creator.

At the very beginning of R' Miller's magnum opus, *Rejoice O' Youth*, which was published in 1962, and which changed the lives of thousands of searching Jews, R' Miller illustrated the importance and urgency of using one's mind. He referred us to the famous mishnah in *Pirkei Avos* [4:13] in which R' Yochanan ben Zakkai sent out his five top disciples to discover the most desirable human character trait. When R' Elazar ben Arach answered, "leiv tov," a good heart, R' Yochanan ben Zakkai agreed with him, for it included the answers of his other four students. R' Miller explained that the definition of "leiv tov" is not merely "a kindly heart," for, if that would be the case, it wouldn't have included R' Shimon's choice, the trait of "*Ro'eh es hanolad*—Maturity to anticipate the future and plan accordingly." Rather, R' Miller used his encyclopedic knowledge of Tanach to prove that "leiv tov" means "a good mind," and proceeded to extol the virtues of one who learns to think and use his mind constantly.

He would say that when the famous posuk [*Michah* 6:8] tells us, "*Hatzneiah leches im Hashem Elokecha*—Walk privately with Hashem your G-d," it means that we should spend time with Hashem in the privacy of our minds.

It is in the arena of thought that he cautioned the world not to justify the accusation of Haman, who accused us of serving Hashem like sleepwalkers. He wanted us to perform mitzvos meaningfully. He taught us that husbands and wives who train themselves to properly appreciate the mitzvah of mezuzah would avoid much marital distress. A husband who had an irritating day at work and a wife who had a vexing day at home are often like colliding atoms at the end of the day, ready to explode. However, if the husband has trained himself upon entering his home to look at the mezuzah and think about its message, and his wife, when coming downstairs to answer the door has done the same, then they will be aware that Hashem is watching, and the tension will dissipate.

Both R' Shternbuch, shlit"a, and R' Miller's son, R' Shmuel Miller, shlit"a, commented on R' Miller's original way of thought. Who else would carry seeds in his pocket to remind himself of the greatness and genius of the Creator? Who else would keep his keys in his siddur for ninety days because he once forgot, "*V'sein tal u'matar livracha*" (the phrase we insert in Shemoneh Esrei during the winter months), and wanted to make sure it wouldn't happen again?

One of the highlights of R' Miller's tapes, and one of the features that made them so interesting to thousands of listeners, was when we heard his beautiful voice beckoning, "And now...questions on any subject?" Who else could say this, week after week, year after year, fielding thousands of questions on the vast array of Jewish life and Torah, and be able to answer all of them off the cuff, in a scholarly, clear, and satisfying way? One can only surmise that he was able to accomplish this amazing feat because, as we mentioned, he spent his entire life in uninterrupted meditation and study, and therefore had already considered carefully most of the questions that would come to our minds.

R' Miller attracted many devoted followers with his sparkling wit. The story is told that when he was the Mashgiach of Chaim Berlin he once noticed some students wasting their time with idle chatter. He went over to them and asked them, "Gentleman, what will it be? Scotch, or rye?" With that witticism, he jolted them to the reality that they were acting as if they were in a saloon.

He used to take a daily walk for his health. As he was walking one Rosh Hashanah morning, an African-American gentleman walking with his young daughter stopped R' Miller and asked him why so many religious Jews dress in black. R' Miller answered him, "Because we believe that black is dignified." The man then bent down to his daughter and said, "Always remember what this Rabbi said: 'Black is dignified.'" In one fell swoop, R' Miller both demonstrated his sharp mind and created a wonderful kiddush Hashem.

R' Shternbuch focused on the fact that R' Miller passed away on erev Shabbos (approximately two a.m. Thursday evening). He explained that the Gemara [*Kesubos* 103a] that says, "*Mi shemeis b'erev Shabbos, siman yafeh hi lo*—It is a good sign for someone to pass away on Friday," is to be understood not just literally, but figuratively, that it is a good sign if one lived his life "like erev Shabbos." Just as all Jews prepare for Shabbos on erev Shabbos, if one lived his life in constant preparation for the World to Come, he has led a fulfilled existence. This was indeed an apt description of R' Miller. He would plead with us that we should always focus on life's most important purpose—to prepare for the afterlife. He would say that years ago children would bring a dollar to school once a month to deposit with their own bankbook. This trained them in the importance of saving. So too, he would say, we must train ourselves in our youth to think everyday about what we are putting away for our real futures in the World to Come.

R' Shmuel Yakov Borenstein, shlit"a, the Rosh Yeshivah of Yeshivas Chevron, commented on R' Miller's amazing Torah diligence, that he was virtually unique in his generation in this aspect. He related that, even when attending a grandchild's wedding, R' Miller would dance with the chasan while holding his own overcoat. When people offered to put it down, he would comment that he needed the reminder that he had to leave shortly, in order to return to his learning.

Incredibly, he finished Shas (the entire Talmud) sixty-seven times. Please note that, learning at the rate of the Daf Yomi cycle (which covers one page a day), one would have to live over four hundred and fifty years to accomplish this amazing feat. In a similar vein, the Slabodka Rosh Yeshivah, R' Rosenberg, shlit"a, said that R' Miller studied with such diligence that it was almost impossible for anyone to meet with him even for the most pressing issues. In his heyday, it is said that he gave forty shiurim (classes) a week in thirty-five different masechtas. R' Shmuel Miller testified that, on top of that, his father never said any of his shiurim without preparing beforehand, even if he had studied the material many times before.

To appreciate R' Miller's amazing discipline, it is worth noting some of the apparent contradictions he embodied in his life. He was a master of the English language and he wielded it masterfully to attract generations of Jews to a more passionate lifestyle of Yiddishkeit. Indeed, the Slabodka Rosh Yeshivah commented that he wasn't only a "m'karev rechokim," bringing close to Torah many baalei teshuvah (newly religious Jews), he was also a "m'karev krovim," educating already religious Jews to serve Hashem in a much more meaningful way. Nevertheless, despite his mastery of the English language, he never spoke a word of English at home. As his son R' Shmuel Miller testified, he also asked his family members to only speak Yiddish in their homes. He believed that this was the only way that he could keep the influence of the hostile secular environment from invading his family. What discipline! Usually, if you are an expert at something, you enjoy using and demonstrating your expertise. Not R' Miller!

He was also a baal mussar and most of the world knew him from his mussar teachings. Yet most of his waking hours were spent studying Gemara, Rashi, Tosefos, *Ketzos Hachoshen, Avnei Milu'im,* and so on. He was the quintessential oheiv es habrios (lover of mankind), yet as we mentioned it was very hard to find time to talk with him. All of these behaviors demonstrate his tremendous self-discipline.

R' Meir Bergman, shlit"a, said in his eulogy (and this was corroborated by countless others), that R' Miller never spoke a word of lashon hara. He would comment that the Gemara tells us that the bells on the Kohen Gadol's robe atoned for the sin of lashon hara—"Let that which makes noise atone for the sin of slanderous noise." The Gemara in *Yuma* [44a] also says that the ketores, the incense brought in the Temple, also atones for the sin of lashon hara, as it says, "Let that which is brought in the secret innermost chamber of the Temple atone for lashon hara which is also done in secrecy." He explained that these two atonements were needed for two different types of lashon hara, the slander of the tongue and also the more delicate sin of thinking badly about people in our minds. R' Miller, who always tried to inspire us to keeps our minds pure, cautioned us to not even *think* badly of others. He would often say that the Torah teaches us "mind control," admonishing us not to hate others in our hearts and adjuring us not to covet that which is not ours.

It has been written that the great Gaon, R' Moshe Feinstein, zt"l, zy"a, commented about R' Miller that he was the "Ish Emes" (man of truth) of America, the very embodiment of Torah Truth. In this vein, R' Shmuel Miller related that his father used to say on the verse, *"Karov Hashem l'chol kor'ov, l'chol asher yikra-uhu be-emes*—Hashem is close to all who call to Him, to all who call to Him in Truth" [*Tehillim* 145:18] that we need to call to Hashem truthfully, believing what we say. A person who says, *"Boruch atah Hashem, shomei-ah tefilah*—Blessed are You, Hashem, Who listens to our prayers" [Shemoneh Esrei], must train himself to really feel that Hashem is indeed listening to him at that very moment.

He used to say that if we really mean, *"Ashrei yoshvei Veisecha*—Fortunate is he who sits in Your House" [*Tehillim* 84:5] (which today is the beis medrash, the study hall), we wouldn't look at the clocks longingly until a lecture is over, and we wouldn't dash out of the synagogue the minute we finish our prayers.

R' Kanarek mentioned that on the verse, *"Zecher rav tuvecha yabiu*—A remembrance of Your abundant goodness they will utter" [*Tehillim* 145:7], R' Miller would say that we are obligated to thank Hashem for the many kindnesses He did for us before we became old enough to know how to thank Him for them. Thus, we should thank Hashem for helping our mothers nourish us, for the comfortable cribs we slept in, and for the pacifiers that soothed us. As Dovid Hamelech said, *"Borchi nafshi es Hashem, v'al tishkechi kol gemulov*—My soul blesses Hashem, and I will not forget all that He bestowed upon me" [*Tehillim* 103:2].

He would warn us not to fall prey to the American attitude of "What have you done for me lately?" but rather to remember and be appreciative for all past favors. When couples would encounter marital difficulties, he would advise them to remember the good times and to use that energy to overcome adversity.

R' Solomon, in comparing R' Miller to Avraham Avinu, referred to how Avraham went out to show the people of Ur Kasdim the falseness of their idolatrous ways. In the very same way, R' Miller valiantly exposed to the world the falseness of other religions, and of scientific theories that denied the existence of a Creator. In speaking of the mishnah in *Pirkei Avos* [2:19], "*Da mah shetashiv la-apikoros*—Know what to answer the heretic," he would ask, "What would we be doing talking to a heretic? We're supposed to distance ourselves far away from such a sinner!" He would explain that the mishnah means that we should know how to answer the heretic within ourselves, the subconscious murmurings and nagging doubts in the back of our minds that call our beliefs into question.

He would point out the folly of other religions. Throughout the Middle Ages, he would remind us, the Christian Church launched numerous "blood libels"—false accusations against the Jews of their having murdered Christian children in order to mix their blood into matzah. He would question how anyone could give credence to Christianity, which named so many of its churches, its holiest places, after these martyred "saints," these children whose disappearance was the basis of such vicious and unfounded charges. How can one give credibility to the Koran, the "holy" book of Islam, which is filled with many childish errors, such as the ridiculous comment that every righteous person is destined, in the next world, to be rewarded with three hundred and ten young maidens. Moslem "scholars" mistook the word "olomos," meaning "worlds," in the famous statement at the end of Shas, for "almos," which means "young maidens!" In the same way, he exposed the fallacies of the scientists who claim the world is millions of years old and the many errors that scientists make in their study of fossils.

Thinking about the greatness of R' Avigdor Miller, zt"l, should stimulate us to emulate him as much as possible. We should all learn R' Miller's seforim on Chumash, ideology, and history. What better way is there for parents to inculcate in their children the fundamentals of Yiddishkeit than to steer them in the direction of R' Miller's tapes? Any married person should listen to his tapes on the "Ten Commandments of Marriage." His tapes on gratitude, the afterlife, ten steps to Greatness, and hundreds of others are all gems that will enhance your outlook on life. R' Miller once told us that if someone listened to one hundred of his tapes, that person could be considered an idealist. What an excellent goal to adopt for ourselves!

In closing, it is a fitting testimony to the life of this spiritual giant that among the last words of his earthly existence was the brachah of "Borei Nefashos." When I heard this from his family, I thought to myself how fitting it was that this man, whose life's essence was the concept of praise to Hashem, ended his life with a blessing that thanks Hashem. "*Al kol mah shebaroso l'hachai-os bahem*—For everything that You created to give them life…" In fact, when I went to be *menachem ovel*, R' Shmuel Miller told me that tzadikim used to say that "Borei Nefashos" is the blessing that we will say at techiyas hameisim, at the resurrection, when we will come back to life. Hashem will be "Borei Nefashos," He will recreate the soul, "*L'hachai-os bahem nefesh kol chai*—To give life to all souls." R' Miller used to say that we thank Hashem daily in the Shemoneh Esrei for being "mechaiyei hameisim," even though it hasn't yet happened, because when it does happen, we will no longer have bechirah, free will. So, we thank Him now in order to do so with our bechirah. Thus, R' Miller made the brachah, "Borei Nefashos," with passion, to thank Hashem for his eventual resurrection while he yet had the bechirah to do so.

Let's forge in our memory the teachings and lifestyle of this incredible man, and in that merit may he look over us and all of Klal Yisroel, interceding on our behalf for all our needs, and may the time of the techiyas hameisim come speedily in our very days.

Glossary

Glossary

Achdus—togetherness, brotherhood, Jewish unity.

Afikomen—the final matzah eaten at the seder.

Aliyah—being called up to make a blessing on a portion of the Torah reading.

Amen—affirmative response to another saying a blessing.

Arayos—immorality.

Aron Kodesh—the ark which holds the Torah.

Arurim—the curses Hashem promised for violating the Torah.

Aseres Y'mei Teshuvah—the Ten Days of Repentance, from Rosh Hashanah until Yom Kippur, inclusive.

Askara—lethal diphtheria or croup.

Assur—forbidden.

Avodah Zorah—idol worship.

Ayin Hara—lit., "evil eye;" envy.

Baalei Teshuvah—lit., "those who have returned"; newly religious Jews.

Balabustah—homemaker.

Balhabus—lit., "homeowner," a working man.

Bashert—predestined.

Bas Kol—a heavenly voice.

Bechirah—free will.

Bein Adam Lachaveiro—between man and his friend.

Beinoni—average person.

Beis Din—Jewish court or tribunal.

Beis Hamikdash—the Temple in Yerushalayim.

Bentch—say Grace After Meals.

Bentching Licht—blessing and lighting Friday night or Yom Tov candles.

Bikur Cholim—visiting the sick.

Birchas Hamazon—Grace After Meals; blessing said after eating bread (see "Bentch").

Bnei Yeshivah—yeshivah students.

Bnei Yisroel—lit., "the Children of Israel." The Jewish nation.

Bochrim—young, unmarried boys who learn in yeshivah.

Brachah—(pl., brachos) blessing.

Brachah L'vatalah—blessing said in vain.

Bris Milah—Jewish circumcision ceremony.

Challah—braided loaves of bread made for Shabbos and holiday meals.

Chas V'shalom—G-d forbid.

Chasan—groom.

Chasanah—wedding.

Chashmonaim—group of Jews who fought against the Greeks.

Chassid, Chassidic—a pious individual.

Chazan—synagogue cantor.

Chazaras Hashatz—the chazan's repetition of the Shemoneh Esrei.

Cheilek—portion.

Cheirem—excommunication.

Cheit Haeigel—sin of the Golden Calf.

Chesed—an act of kindness.

Chilul Hashem—desecration of G-d's Name.

Chinuch—education.

Chochmah—wisdom.

Chochom—a wise man.

Chol Hamoed—intermediate days of Pesach and Sukkos.

Choleh—a sick person.

Chometz—leavened food, of which even a minute amount is forbidden on Pesach.

Chupah—wedding canopy under which the couple stands during the marriage ceremony.

Churban—the destruction of the Temple.

D'oraysah—Jewish law coming directly from the Torah.

D'rabbonan—Torah law enacted by the Rabbis.

Daf Yomi—learning schedule in which Jews around the world study the same page of Talmud on a daily basis. The entire Talmud is completed every seven-and-a-half years.

Divrei Mussar—words of reproach.

Divrei Torah—words of Torah.

Dor Hamidbar—the generation of the desert.

Droshah—(pl., droshos) speech.

Eizer K'negdo—lit., "his helpmate against him;" wife.

Emunah—belief in Hashem; faith.

Eretz Yisroel—the land of Israel.

Gaiva—haughtiness.

Gashmius—materialism.

Gedolim—lit., "great people;" refers to extraordinary Torah sages.

Gehinnom—place where the soul is cleansed of its sins after death.

Gematria—calculation using the numeric values of Hebrew letters.

Gemilus Chassadim—acts of kindness.

Geshmake—tasty.

Gezeira—decree.

Gilui Arayos—(see Arayos).

Goyim—non-Jews.

Haggadah—the telling of the story of leaving Egypt, read at the Pesach seder.

Hakoras Hatov—appreciation; gratitude.

Halachos—laws.

Hanhogos Tovos—positive forms of behavior.

Har Sinai—Mount Sinai.

Hatzlachah Rabbah—(a wish for) much success.

Havdalah—blessing recited at the conclusion of Shabbos.

Hefsek—an interruption.

Hishtadlus—effort.

Hoda'ah—thanks.

Issur Melacha—prohibition of creative activity on Shabbos.

K'sones Passim—the coat of fine wool that Yaakov gave to his son Yosef.

Ka'as—anger.

Kabbolas HaTorah—receiving of the Torah, celebrated on the holiday of Shavuos.

Kaddish—a prayer said for the deceased.

Kal V'chomer—a fortiori, deriving a lesson from that which is lenient to that which is more severe.

Kallah—bride.

Kashrus—the body of Jewish laws regarding food, including specifications about meat, forbidden mixtures of milk and meat, etc.

Kavanah—concentration.

Kavod—honor.

Kavod HaTorah—honoring the Torah.

Kedushah—holiness.

Kehillah—congregation.

Kesubah—marriage contract.

Kibbud Av V'eim—the mitzvah of honoring a father and mother.

Kiddush—the blessing that sanctifies the Shabbos or Yom Tov, usually recited over wine.

Kimcha D'pischa—matzah (and other foods) for the needy on Pesach

Kisei HaKovod—the heavenly throne of Glory.

Klaf—parchment.

Klal Yisroel—the community of Israel.

Kohen Gadol—the High Priest.

Krias HaTorah—the reading of the Torah.

Krias Shema—recitation of the Shema.

L'shem Shamayim—for the sake of Heaven.

L'vayas Hameis—escorting the dead to the burial ground.

Lashon Hakodesh—lit., "the holy tongue;" Hebrew.

Lashon Hara—evil gossip.

Lechem Hapanim—the "showbread" in the Temple.

Leitzonus—scoffing; mockery.

Licht Bentchen—(see Bentching Licht).

Lo Aleinu—lit., "not upon us." An expression of the hope that misfortune not befall us.

Lulav—the branch of a palm tree, used in the celebration of Sukkos.

Ma'asim Tovim—good deeds.

Mabul—the great flood which destroyed the world in the time of Noach.

Machlokes—argument and conflict.

Makom Kavua—lit., "fixed place;" usually refers to where one usually prays or sits at the table.

Malach Hamavess—angel of death.

Masechta—a tractate of the Talmud.

Mashgiach—a rabbi in a yeshiva who oversees the spiritual growth of the students.

Matan Torah—giving of the Torah at Mount Sinai.

Matanos L'evyonim—gifts to the poor; one of the required mitzvos of Purim.

Matzah—(pl., matzos) unleavened bread, which we are required to eat on Pesach.

Me'aras Hamachpelah—the cave where the Patriarchs and Matriarchs are buried.

Mechabed—to honor; one who honors.

Medrash—a collection of derived lessons from the Torah.

Megillah—lit., "scroll," usually refers to the book of Esther.

Melachah—prohibition of work.

Menachem Ovel—(pl., menachem aveilim) to comfort mourners.

Menorah—Chanukah candelabra.

Mentsch—lit., "a man;" refers to someone with good character traits.

Mesorah—the oral transmission of Torah law.

Mezuzah—Scriptural sections placed on thr door-posts of a Jewish home.

Middah—(pl., middos) lit., "measurements," commonly used to refer to an individual's character traits.

Middah K'neged Middah—the method with which Hashem exercises justice, rewarding and punishing "measure for measure."

Middas Chassidus—extremely pious behavior.

Mishloach Manos—gifts of food given to friends and acquaintances in the observance of Purim.

Mishnah—the oral law as codified by R' Yehuda Hanasi.

Mitzrayim—Egypt.

Mitzvah—(pl., mitzvos) a Torah commandment.

Mizbe'ach—the altar in the Temple.

Morror—bitter herbs, eaten during the Pesach seder.

Moshiach—the Messiah, the one who will bring the final redemption.

Motzoei Shabbos—lit., "the leaving of Shabbos;" Saturday night.

Munn—manna, the spiritual food which G-d fed the Jewish people in the desert.

Mussaf—additional prayer service on Yom Tov and Rosh Chodesh that corresponds to the additional sacrifices brought on these occasions in Temple times.

Mussar—the study of improving one's character.

Mutar—permitted.

Nachas—to take pride in something or someone.

Nefesh Chaya—a living being.

Ner Tamid—lit., "eternal flame;" a light over the ark in a synagogue that is always left burning.

Neshama—soul.

Netilas Yadayim—ritual hand-washing, performed in the morning and before prayer, Torah study and eating bread.

Nisayon—test.

Nusach Sefard—the version of the prayers primarily used by Jews of Middle Eastern or Chassidic descent.

Olam Habah—the World to Come.

Olam Hazeh—this world, in distinction to the World to Come.

Ovel—a mourner within the first year of his loss.

P'shat—the simple explanation of a Torah text.

Parnasah—livelihood.

Parshah—(pl., parshiyos) section of the Torah.

Poseik—(pl., poskim) a Torah scholar with the authority to decide rulings of Jewish law.

Posuk—a verse in the Torah.

Rabbonim—rabbis.

Rabosai—lit., "my teachers;" a respectful way to address a crowd.

Rachaman—one who exhibits the attribute of mercy.

Rachamim—mercy.

Rachmana Litzlon—lit., "may Heaven save us," colloquially used to say "G-d forbid."

Rachmonus—mercy; pity.

Rashah—a wicked person.

Rechilus—slander and tale bearing.

Refuah Shelaimah—the wish that one should receive a complete recovery.

Ribbono Shel Olam—Master of the Universe.

Rishonim—Rabbinic sages and leaders from the tenth to fifteenth centuries.

Rosh Hashanah—the Jewish New Year holiday.

Rosh Yeshivah—head of a Talmudic academy.

Ruchnius—spirituality.

S'chach—vegetation used to form the roof of a sukkah.

Satan—accusing angel.

Seder—the traditional, festive meal eaten on Pesach during which the story of the Exodus is told and numerous acts are performed in commemoration.

Sedrah—weekly Torah portion read in the synagogue.

Sefirah, Sefiras Haomer—the annual period from the second day of Pesach until Shavuos, during which Jews are commanded to verbally count each day.

Seichel—intelligence; common sense.

Selichos—forgiveness prayers.

Seudah—festive meal.

Shabbos Hamalkah—the Shabbos Queen.

Shacharis—the morning prayer service.

Shalach Manos—see Mishloach Manos.

Shalom Bayis—marital harmony.

Shas—acronym for "shisha sidrei mishna" referring to the entire Talmud.

Shechinah—the Divine Presence.

Shemoneh Esrei—lit., "eighteen;" a term that designates a collection of (actually nineteen) prayers recited silently three times a day.

Shevet—(pl., shevatim) tribe.

Shiluach Hakan—the commandment of sending away a mother bird before taking her chicks or eggs.

Shiurim—Torah lessons.

Shiva—the seven days of intense mourning observed upon the death of an immediate family member.

Shliach Tzibur—the one who leads the congregation in prayer.

Shlit"a—acronym for "sheyichyeh l'yamim tovim aruchim—may he live good, long days;" blessing for longevity.

Shmata—rag.

Shmiras Halashon—lit., "guarding the tongue;" making certain not to speak badly of someone.

Shofar—ram's horn blown in synagogue as part of the High Holiday services.

Shomrei Shabbos—people who keep Shabbos.

Siddur—prayer book.

Sinas Habrios—hatred among people.

Siyata D'shmaya—Heavenly assistance.

Sotah—married woman suspected of having an extramarital affair.

Sukkah—temporary home built to dwell in during the holiday of Sukkos.

Sukkos—Holiday of Booths. Commemorating the booths the Jews dwelled in during the forty years they wandered in the desert.

Tadir—frequent.

Talmid Chochom—(pl., talmidei chachomim) Torah scholar.

Tam—the simple son.

Tana—Torah authority from the Mishnaic period.

Targum—translation. Usually refers to Targum Onkelos, an ancient Aramaic translation of the Torah.

Techiyas Hameisim—the resurrection of the dead.

Tefillah—prayer.

Tehillim—Book of Psalms.

Teshuvah—lit., "return," repentance.

Tochacha—chastising the wrongdoer; admonition.

Tzadik—(pl., tzadikim) a righteous person.

Tzaros—troubles; hardships; pain.

Tzedakah—charity.

Tzidkus—righteousness.

Tzitzis—ritual fringes worn on a four-cornered garment by Jewish males.

Tznius—modesty in dress and behavior.

Ushpizin—spiritual guests that visit us in the sukkah.

Vidui—confession; prayer said during the High Holy Days and before death.

Yahrzeit—anniversary of someone's death.

Yam Suf—Red Sea.

Yeshivah—religious school.

Yetzer Hara—the evil inclination.

Yetzias Mitzrayim—the exodus from Egypt.

Yiras Shamayim—fear of Heaven.

Yom Kippur—Day of Atonement.

Yomim Noraim—the Days of Awe.

Z'nus—immoral behavior.

Zechus Avos—merits of the fathers.

Zechuyos—merits.

Zerizus—alacrity in performing mitzvos.

Zocheh—worthy.

Zt"l—an abbreviation that stands for "zecher tzadik livracha," may the remembrance of this righteous person be a blessing.

Zy"a—an abbreviation that stands for "zechuso yagain aleinu," may his merit protect us.

Bibliography

Partial Bibliography
of Sources Quoted

Abarbanel—Commentary on Torah by R' Yitzchok ben Yehudah of Lisbon (1437-1508) treasurer to King Ferdinand of Spain.

Alter of Kelm—R' Simcha Zissel Ziev (1824-1898) renowned mussar personality and Rosh Yeshiva of the Talmud Torah of Kelm, Lithuania.

Auerbach, R' Shlomo Zalman—(1910-1995) Rosh Yeshiva of Yeshiva Kol Torah, halachic authority and a foremost leader of world Jewry.

Avnei Eliyahu—A commentary on the siddur by the Vilna Gaon and his son R' Avraham.

Avodah Zarah—A Talmudic tractate dealing with the subject of idolatry.

Baal HaTurim—Commentary on Torah by R' Yakov Ben Asher (1268-1340), renowned author of the *Tur*.

Bach—Commentary by R' Yoel Sirkis (1561-1640) on the *Arba Turim*.

Bava Kama—A Talmudic tractate dealing with the subject of damages in Jewish law.

Bava Metzia—A Talmudic tractate dealing with the subject of property ownership, wages and civil law.

Biur Halachah—Commentary on *Shulchan Aruch, Orach Chaim* by R' Yisroel Meir Kagan of Radin (1838-1933).

Blazer, R' Itzele—(1837-1907) Also known as R' Itzele M'Peterburg, a prominent mussar personality and author of *Kochvei Ohr*.

Bnei Yissaschor—Book of chassidic thought by R' Hirsch Elimelech of Dinova, Poland (1795-1851).

Brachos—A Talmudic tractate dealing with the laws of blessings and prayer.

Bunim, Irving—(c. 1920-1980) American Jewish leader instrumental in founding the Young Israel movement in America and author of *Ethics from Sinai*, a commentary on Pirkei Avos.

Chasam Sofer—R' Moshe Schreiber (1762-1839), Rabbi of Pressburg, was known by this name after he authored works of responsa and novellae with this title.

Chayei Adam—Condensed compendium of Jewish law written by R' Avraham ben Yechiel Michel of Danzig, Poland (1748-1820).

Chazon Ish—R' Avrohom Yeshaya Karelitz (1878-1953) of Bnei Brak was known by this name after he authored halachic works with this title.

Chidah—Acronym for R' Chaim Yosef Dovid Azulai (1724-1806), reknowned Kabbalist and author.

Chofetz Chaim—R' Yisroel Meir Kagan of Radin (1838-1933), was known by this name after he authored a work with this title on the subject of proper speech.

Chovos Halevovos—Work of Jewish ethics by R' Bachya ben Yosef Ibn Pekudah (1050-1120).

Chullin—A Talmudic tractate dealing with the subject of dietary laws.

Dubno Maggid—R' Yakov ben Wolf Kranz of Zhatil Poland (1740-1804). Prominent lecturer who traveled widely through Europe exhorting his audiences to improve and mend their ways.

Eiger, R' Akiva—(1761-1837) Rabbi of Posen and author of a commentary on the Talmud as well as numerous responsa.

Emden, R' Yaakov—(1697-1776) Respected scholar and author of a commentary on the siddur as well as halachic responsa.

Eybeschutz, R' Yonasan—(1690-1796) Rabbi of Altoona, Hamburg, and Wandsbek, and author of numerous works on Torah and halachah.

Feinstein, R' Moshe—(1895-1986) Rosh Yeshiva of Mesivta Tifereth Jerusalem in New York. Halachic authority and one of the foremost leaders of American Jewry.

Frand, R' Yissochar—Noted lecturer and Rabbi in Yeshivas Ner Yisroel in Baltimore, Maryland.

Ibn Ezra, R' Avraham—(1080-1164) A prolific Spanish author, scholar and poet. Best known for his extensive commentary on the Torah.

Iggeres HaGra—A inspirational letter written by the Vilna Gaon to his family.

Iggeres HaRamban—A inspirational letter written by the Ramban to his son.

Igros Moshe—Eight volume compilation of responsa by R' Moshe Feinstein.

Iyyun Tefilla—Commentary on the siddur by R' Aryeh Leib ben Shlomo Gordon of Jerusalem.

Kaminetsky, R' Yaakov—(1891-1986) Rosh Yeshiva of Torah Vodaas in Brooklyn, New York and recognized leader of American Jewry.

Kesuvos—A Talmudic tractate dealing with the subject of marriage contracts.

Kiddushin—A Talmudic tractate dealing with Jewish marriage.

Kitzur Shulchan Aruch—Condensed compendium of Jewish law written by R' Shlomo Ganzfried of Ungvar, Hungary (1804-1886).

Kol Bo—Halachic compendium by an anonymous author (c.1400).

Ksav Sofer—R' Avraham Shmuel Binyomin Schreiber (1815-1879), a leader of Hungarian Jewry was known by this name after he authored a collection of responsa and commentaries with this title.

Leff, R' Zev—Prominent lecturer and spiritual leader of Moshav Matisyahu, Israel.

Levin, R' Aryeh—(1885-1969) His piety made him known as the "Tzadik of Jerusalem."

Lopian, R' Elya—(1876-1970) Prominent mussar personality whose lectures were compiled in the work Lev Eliyahu.

Mabit—Acronym for R' Moshe ben Yosef Trani (1500-1580), leader of the city of Safed, and author of the ethical and philisophical work *Beis Elokim*.

Maharal of Prague—Acronym for R' Yehuda Loew ben Bezalel (1512-1609). Rabbi of Prague and prolific author noted for his profound works on halachah and Jewish thought.

Maharsha—Acronym for Moreinu HaRav Shmuel Aidels of Poland (1555-1631). Author of famous commentary on the Talmud.

Mateh Moshe—Halachic compendium by R' Moshe Mos of Premysl (1540-1606).

Matnas Kehunah—Commentary on *Medrash Rabbah* by R' Yissochar Ber Katz (c. 1580).

Me'am Loez—Monumental commentary on Tanach by R' Yaakov Culi (1689-1732). Originally printed in Ladino, it has been translated into Hebrew and English.

Medrash Tanchumah—A medrash on the Chumash based on the

teachings of R' Tanchuma bar Abba (c. late fourteenth century).

Meiri, R' Menachem ben Shlomo—(1249-1316) Author of *Bais Habechira*, an extensive commentary on Talmud.

Miller, R' Avigdor—See essay in this book.

Mishnah Brurah—Commentary on *Shulchan Aruch, Orach Chaim* by R' Yisroel Meir Kagan of Radin (1838-1933).

Mordechai—A halachic work on Talmud by R' Mordechai ben Hillel (1240-1298).

Nedarim—A Talmudic tractate dealing with the subject of vows and promises.

Nefesh Hachaim—Ethical and philisophical work authored by R' Chaim of Volozhin.

Negaim—A Mishnaic tractate dealing with the subject of leprosy.

Orchos Chaim L'harosh—Mussar work by R' Asher ben R' Yechiel (1250-1328).

Pachad Yitzchok—Ethical and philisophical work authored by R' Yitzchok Hutner (1907-1980), Rosh Yeshiva of Yeshiva Chaim Berlin in Brooklyn, NY.

Pam, R' Avraham—Rosh Yeshiva of Yeshiva Torah Vodaas in Brooklyn, NY.

Pe'ah—Mishnaic tractate dealing with the subject of leaving crops unharvested for the benefit of the poor.

Pele Yoetz—Mussar work written by R' Eliezer Papa.

Pesachim—A Talmudic tractate dealing with the holiday of Pesach.

Pirkei Avos—"Ethics of Our Fathers," a Talmudic tractate dealing with ethical and moral practices.

Pliskin, R' Zelig—noted author and counselor who resides in Jerusalem, Israel.

Pri Megadim—Commentary on *Shulchan Aruch* by R' Yosef Tumim (1727-1792).

Rabbeinu Yona—(1180-1263) Author of a commentary on the Talmud and Rif. Best known for his mussar work, *Shaarei Teshuva*.

Rama—Acronym for R' Moshe Isserles (1530-1572), Rabbi of Cracow and Torah leader of East European Jewry. Author of many works including *Sefer Hamapeh*—annotations on *Shulchan Aruch*.

Rambam—Acronym for R' Moshe ben Maimon (1135-1204), also known as Maimonides, of Spain and Egypt, one of the leading authorities in all areas of Jewish law and thought. He served as personal physician to Saladin, Sultan of Egypt and Syria.

Ramban—Acronym for R' Moshe ben Nachman (1194-1270), also known as Nachmanides of Spain. He was a leader of world Jewry and a prolific author of numerous works on Bible, Talmud, philosophy, Jewish law, kabbalah and medicine.

Rashi—Acronym for R' Shlomo Yitzchaki of Troyes, France (1040-1105). Rashi is considered the "father of commentators" and is famous for his commentaries on the Torah and the Talmud. About two hundred supercommentaries have been written on his commentary on Chumash, attesting to its greatness.

Rokeach—Code of Jewish law and ethical practices by R' Elazer of Garmiza (1164-1232). He authored many works including a commentary on the Torah.

Rosh Hashanah—A Talmudic tractate dealing with the holiday of Rosh Hashanah.

Salant, R' Shmuel—(d. 1909) Prominent leader and Rabbi of the Jerusalem community.

Sanhedrin—Talmudic tractate dealing with the subject of the Jewish court system.

Satmar Rebbe—R' Yoel Teitelbaum (1887-1979), Rebbe of the Satmar Chassidim.

Sefer Chasidim—Work of laws and customs of the Chasidei Ashkenaz, written by R' Yehudah Hachasid (1150-1217).

Sefer HaChinuch—Commentary on the 613 commandments by R' Avraham Halevi of Barcelona (1233-1300).

Sefer Hatodaah—Contemporary work on the Jewish lifecycle by R' Eliyahu Kitov (1912-1976).

Sefer Yereim—Commentary on the 613 commandments by R' Eliezer ben Shmuel of Metz (1115-1175).

Segal, R' Yehudah Zev—(1910-1993) Rosh Yeshiva of Manchester Yeshiva in England.

Sfas Emes—R' Yehudah Leib Alter (1847-1905), the third Rebbe of Ger, was known by this name after he authored a commentary on Torah and Talmud with this title.

Shapiro, R' Meir—(1887-1933) Rosh Yeshiva of Yeshivas Chachmei Lublin, Poland.

Shelah—Acronym for Shnei Luchos Habris, a work of Jewish laws, customs and ethics by R' Yeshaya Horowitz of Prague (1560-1630).

Shibolei Haleket—Halachic compedium by R' Tzidkiya ben Avraham Harofeh (c. 1242).

Shmulevitz, R' Chaim—(1902-1978) Rosh Yeshiva of Mirrer Yeshiva in Shanghai and Jerusalem. Author of *Sichos Mussar*.

Shulchan Aruch—Universally accepted compendium of Jewish law compiled by R' Yosef Karo (1488-1575).

SM"AH—Acronym for Sefer Meiras Eynamim, a commentary on Shulchan Aruch by R' Yehoshua Falk of Prague (1545-1614).

Specter, R' Yitzchak Elchonon—Rabbi of Kovno, Lithuania and leading halachic authority of his time (d. 1886).

Steipler Gaon—R' Yaakov Yisrael Kanievsky (1899-1985), of Bnei Brak.

Ta'amei Minhogim—Work by R' Avrohom Yitzchok Sperling expaining reasons for Jewish customs.

Taanis—Talmudic tractate dealing with the subject of fast days.

Tamid—Talmudic tractate dealing with the subject of the daily Temple offerings.

Tosfos—A collection of commentaries on Talmud produced by scholars of France and Germany between the years 1100 and 1300.

Tur—R' Yacov Ben R' Asher, author of the Arba Turim, a halachic work and a commentary on the Torah (1270-1343).

Uktzin—Mishnaic tractate dealing with the laws of spiritual impurity.

Vilna Gaon—R' Eliyahu ben Shlomo Zalman of Vilna (1720-1797). He was a leading authority in all fields of Torah study and authored more than seventy works on varying subjects in Judaism.

Ya'aros D'vash—Anthology of lectures by R' Yonasan Eibshitz (1690-1764), noted author and kabbalist and chief Rabbi of the triple community of Altona, Hamburg and Wandsbeck, in Germany.

Yalkut Shimoni—Talmudic and Medrashic Anthology compiled by R' Shimon Ashkenazi of Frankfurt Am Main.

Yevamos—Talmudic tractate dealing with marrying one's widow.

Yoreh Deah—Section of the Tur and Shulchan Aruch dealing with dietary laws.

Yuma—Talmudic tractate dealing with the holiday of Yom Kippur.

Zohar—Classic work of Kabbalah from the school of R' Shimon Bar Yochai (c. 120 C.E.).

לעילוי נשמת

יוסף בן חיים הכהן Weiss זצ״ל

and

לעילוי נשמת

בננו היקר חיים ז״ל בן אשר הכהן שליט״א

Dedicated by
Anchel and Pessie Weiss

In honor of

Rabbi Moshe Meir Wiess

Morris & Lilian Lieberman

Dedicated in loving memory of

Avrohom ben Nissim Gordon, ז״ל

by

Mr. Richard and Frima Gordon

*May the merit of those learning
from this sefer help those that
are in need of a shidduch find their
life's mate quickly and easily.
And all those that desire
children be blessed speedily
with healthy offspring.*

לזכרון עולם בהיכל ה׳

מוקדש לזכר ולעליוי נשמת האשה החשובה

יהודית סערקע בת ר׳ יצחק אייזיק גאלדבערג ע״ה

נפטרה י״ט שבט תשנ״ד

מאת בניה ונכדיה שיחי׳
ר׳ יצחק בן ציון ורחל גאלדה קורצער
אהרן, חיה שרה, קלמן אברהם, איטא מלכה,
שמואל מנחם, יהודית סערקע, משה נח

"She opens her mouth with wisdom
A lesson of kindness is on her tongue."

In loving memory of

Zlata bas Reb Zev
Lorraine Bennett, z"l

Dedicated by

Martin and Rebecca Bennett
and
Naomi Speiser

PASSIONATE JUDAISM

Read Rabbi Moshe Meir Weiss's first book, *Passionate Judaism*. You'll discover many ideas that will enhance your outlook, and be inspired toward a new and exciting way to live your life.

SUBSCRIBE TODAY!

For only $20.00/month recieve a Torah tape from Rabbi Moshe Meir Weiss every week!

To subscribe—write, call or email your name, address, and phone number to:

Rabbi Moshe Meir Weiss

P.O. Box 140726, Staten Island, N.Y. 10314

Tel: 718-983-7095 / Email: 73552.3477@compuserve.com

$20 for one month / $120 for 6 months / $240 for a whole year